THE LAST HOT BATTLE OF THE COLD WAR

THE LAST HOT BATTLE OF THE COLD WAR

*South Africa vs. Cuba
in the Angolan Civil War*

PETER POLACK

CASEMATE
Philadelphia & Oxford

Published in the United States of America and Great Britain in 2013 by
CASEMATE PUBLISHERS
908 Darby Road, Havertown, PA 19083
and
10 Hythe Bridge Street, Oxford, OX1 2EW

ISBN 978-1-61200-195-1
Digital Edition: ISBN 978-1-61200-196-8

Cataloging-in-publication data is available from the Library of Congress and
the British Library.

10 9 8 7 6 5 4 3 2 1

Printed and bound in the United States of America.

For a complete list of Casemate titles please contact:

CASEMATE PUBLISHERS (US)
Telephone (610) 853-9131, Fax (610) 853-9146
E-mail: casemate@casematepublishing.com

CASEMATE PUBLISHERS (UK)
Telephone (01865) 241249, Fax (01865) 794449
E-mail: casemate-uk@casematepublishing.co.uk

CONTENTS

Preface 7

Acknowledgments 9

Dedication 15

Introduction 17

1. Cuito Cuanavale—An Overview 21
2. The Cuban Forces 27
3. The South African Forces 41
4. The FAPLA Soviet Advisors 63
5. The Angolan FAPLA 65
6. The Angolan UNITA 73
7. General Ben Ben 81
8. The Beginning of the End 87
9. Commandant Robbie Hartslief 110
10. The Retreat 115
11. The Siege of Cuito Cuanavale 135
12. The Air War 152
13. Casualties of the Battle of Cuito Cuanavale 164
14. Prisoners of War 176
15. Ceasefire 184

Glosssary 189

Appendix A—The Cuban Forces 191

Appendix B—The South African Forces 194

Appendix C—U.S.S.R. Forces 200

Appendix D—FAPLA Forces 201

Appendix E—UNITA Forces 203

Notes 208

Bibliography 217

Index 219

To my peerless wife Monique who taught me love and living; my extraordinary daughters Vanessa and Olivia who have blessed me with blind adoration and loyalty; my brother George who stood shoulder to shoulder with me in the greatest storms: my gratitude, devotion and eternal admiration.

PREFACE

In 1992 I met two Cuban Angola veterans who were refugees in Jamaica and I was told the most amazing stories about a little known war in Angola that sparked my interest, but there were few publications available on the subject. I was finally able to visit Cuba in early 2009 where I was able to obtain a few books on Angola that put my limited Spanish to the test. This was when I first heard of Cuito Cuanavale and became hooked on the subject, much to the delight of my family for a man with no hobbies.

I have tried unceasingly to be objective in my account of this little known battle in an obscure war that appeared to herald great changes in southern Africa. The first draft of this book, purposely written from a wide selection of sources, went through countless revisions from other sources that came to the fore in an effort to come to my own view. I have been pleasantly surprised by the open support and encouragement from many persons of different backgrounds and nationalities. To those who are skeptical of someone from the Caribbean writing this account you are invited to explore the written material on the subject that draws one to the inevitable conclusion that an objective and accurate account should be attempted by someone who is not from any of the countries participating in this conflict. Errors of any kind are mine alone, and while I have done my best to ensure accuracy and independence of thought, any lapses are regrettable. In every available instance eyewitness accounts or narratives by soldiers in the field have been preferred over the distant recollections of senior officers, several of whom have written about this conflict.

What began as a solo effort was embraced by many and I acknowledge the end result as a completely collaborative effort by the many I have acknowledged. Finally, I have to mention the peril of research in the Cayman Islands where, reminiscent of apartheid South Africa and other totalitarian societies, certain publications are banned despite my pleas to Governor Stuart Jack and Attorney General Sam Bulgin.

ACKNOWLEDGMENTS

I wish to express my profound and humble thanks to all who participated in this effort primarily my brother George Giglioli who has been a constant source of encouragement along with his able assistant Mrs. Annette Espinoza and the patient Afrikaans translator Ms. Merinda Ferreira.

The teachers of Denstone College, England, past and present, who continue to inculcate a pursuit of excellence cautioned with generosity of spirit in their charges with special mention of P. T. I. Smith (History) and T. N. Tookey (English). I offer respectful gratitude to the great English and Drama teacher K. C. Ryder, an exemplary mentor and man among men, leading almost his entire mixed-bag English Language class of 1975 to "O" Level success at grade A, a rare feat.

To my mother Clarisse McNamee Polack, who persevered and sacrificed so much for her undeserving children.

Juan Tamayo, *El Nuevo Herald* staff writer for publication of the list of Cuban casualties.

Broadcaster Nelson Herbert Lopes of Voice of America Portuguese service for encouragement and assistance. To Pascal Fletcher, Reuters Bureau Chief, Southeastern United States and Caribbean, who was introduced to me by Tony Boadle, also of Reuters. Pascal immediately offered guidance and assistance. He visited Cuito Cuanavale on two occasions and once barely escaped with his life during a bombardment.

For Angola resources Colonel Manuel Correia de Barros, Vice-Presidente do Conselho Executivo (Deputy CEO), Centro de Estudos Estratégicos de Angola-Strategic Studies Center of Angola. Åsa Lund Moberg of

Nordic Africa Institute Library. The generous Fernando Costa who had the most remarkable African childhood. The courteous and kind journalist Ms. Eliana Giannella Simonetti who opened doors for me. Thanks to Luis Marques of forum4611 blog for the Cuito Tower photo. The affable and well connected journalist Alexandre Solombe, indefatigable humanitarian Tako Koning who has managed to combine geology and social assistance in some of the poorest areas of Angola, Kier Schuringa IISH-Southern Africa archive project, aid expert and author Leon Kikkuk, and Julian Hocken of Halo Trust Angola for connections while doing the dangerous work of clearing mines.

The brilliant historian and journalist Edward George, author of the best book ever written about the Angolan civil war, *The Cuban Intervention in Angola 1965-1991*, for his great kindness, advice and encouragement.

Cuban sources were rare but for the penetrating interview by the learned Professor Russ Stayanoff MA, Academia Interamericana de Panama, Panama City, Republic of Panama. Invaluable assistance from the Cuban MiG pilot Lieutenant Colonel Eduardo Gonzalez Sarria, author of *Angola: Relatos Desde Las Alturas* (*Tales from the Heights*), who was very generous with time and photographs. *A mi amigo Luis, gracias por todos.*

From South Africa, a great bounty of help and information that guided to the truth, even from the most cynical who, I believe, also learned. There were none more able and industrious than my persistent researcher, Mrs. Audrey Portman. The generous and patient Piet Nortje, 32 Infantry Battalion (Ret.), who authored the excellent book *32 Battalion*. Colonel Fred Oelschig-SADF Senior UNITA liaison officer Angola 1987, a clear minded and helpful officer who cleared away much of the fog of war.

> Mrs. Gabriele Mohale: Historical Papers, The Library, University of the Witwatersrand.
>
> Mike Cadman: Historical Papers, The Library, University of the Witwatersrand.
>
> Michael Boer: School of Mechanical, Industrial and Aeronautical Engineering, University of the Witwatersrand, Johannesburg, for immeasurable help in Afrikaans translation.
>
> Archivist G. W. Prinsloo of the SANDF Documentation Centre for the important work being done by that institution and permission to use photographs.
>
> Jennifer Reichel, cousin of Bombardier Clinton Hendricks, deceased.

Gerhard Gerber

Dr. Marna Cilliers-Hartslief

Rifleman Evan P. Lyon (Ret.) 8 and 4 South African Infantry

Mrs. Joan Marsh, Treasurer S A Military History Society

Waynne Pienaar

Corporal Brad W. Saunders (Ret.), SADF Intelligence NCO
    61st Mechanised

Chris Lofting for MiG 21 Fishbed photo

Jens Frischmuth: *Hangar Talk Online Aviation Magazine*

Anthony Turton

James Dekker: sa-soldier.com

Anthony Robinson

Tom Cooper: acig. com

Derek Walker: Allatsea

Dr. John Mendelsohn

Helge Denker: Photographer helgedenker.com

Lieutenant John Dovey, Durban Light Infantry

Vernon Vice, SAAF Intelligence Officer (Ret.), 320 Forward
    Air Force Command Post, AFB Rundu, Namibia.

Russell Jones, SADF SAMS (Ret.)

Warrant Officer Steven Halsted, SAAF

Keith Evans, webmaster 32battalion. org

Marielle Ford

First Lieutenant Petrus Snyman, 101st Battalion (Ret.)

Joshua the Parabat

Eddy Norris: Old Rhodesian Air Force Sods

Brigadier General Dick Lord, SAAF (Ret.)

Garth Calitz

Craig Fourie

Sean Morgan, formerly of SAAF Base Langebaanweg

Estelle Pretorius, secretary at the Voortrekker Monument

Gert Minnaar, Administrator 61 Mech Veterans Association

Lieutenant Ariel Hugo, 61 Mechanised Battalion

Commandant Jan Malan, 4 South African Infantry/62nd
    Mechanised Battalion

Colonel Paul Fouche (Ret.), Commander 20 Brigade

Colonel Gerhard Louw, Honoris Crux, Regiment President Steyn

Colonel Roland de Vries, Deputy Commander, 20 Brigade

Colonel Pierre Franken (Ret.), Forward Observer "Pappa Fox"

Terry Cawood, Coordinator South Africa War Graves Project

Christopher Crossley, Special Services Battalion conscript, SADF (Ret.)

Maarten Geerlings

Richard Wiles, 4 South African Infantry Battalion conscript, SADF, Ratel driver

Rifleman Arno Casius, 32 Infantry Battalion, P Battery, Ratel driver

Rifleman Brett George, 4 South African Infantry Battalion

Corporal Gavin Allwright, 1 Parachute Battalion

Gunner Tyrone Heyl, 4 South African Infantry Battalion (4 Artillery Brigade)

Mariette Laubscher, sister of Captain A. D. McCallum, KIA 13 September 1987

Captain Walter Volker, 2 Signal Regiment 1981–1989

My thanks to Colonel Sergey Kolomnin of the Russian Union of the Veterans of Angola for our brief exchange.

In the USA the exceptional old Africa hand, Alex Belida of the reporter-regrets blog. Colonel Michael F. Morris, USMC, Commanding Officer, Expeditionary Warfare Training Group, Atlantic, for use of his insightful 1998 monograph "Flying Columns in Small Wars: An OMFTS Model." I confess to using many extracts with permission from this clear and objective review.

Ms. Ximena 'Wiki' Albisu of Uruguay for excellent and prompt translation skills with best of luck for her pursuits in Mandarin. Ms. Marly Joao of Brazil for assistance with Portuguese translation and You Tube video. Mrs Georgie Linford for assistance with You Tube video.

The Caribbean renaissance man and healer Dr. Victor Lookloy who saved my life and many others.

Philippe, Chris and all the crew from the best restaurant in the Cayman Islands, The Edge, who sustained me on this arduous journey.

Respect due to Arney Scott, John Ebanks, Nigel Golaub, and Richard Buban.

To our soldier of soldiers, Alton Bunny Doman, R. I. P.

Last but not least, the last of the Mohicans and pride of the Jamaica Constabulary Force, Deputy Superintendent Andrew "Tiger" Nish

But the Consul's brow was sad,
    And the Consul's speech was low
And darkly looked he at the wall
    And darkly at the foe.
Their van will be upon us
    Before the bridge goes down
And if they once may win the bridge,
    What hope to save the town?

———

Then out spake brave Horatius
    The Captain of the gate
To every man upon this earth
    Death cometh soon or late.
And how can man die better
    Than facing fearful odds
For the ashes of his fathers
    And the temples of his Gods.

—XXVI and XXVII from *Horatius*
by Thomas Babington Macaulay, Lord Macaulay, 1842

Then Jesus said to his disciple Peter:
"For all who take the sword will perish by the sword."—*Matthew 26:52*

DEDICATION

In this life we have a few important moments when we decide which direction to follow ending in no effect, a positive result or disaster. In the mad, post-colonial rush to gather up scarce resources for the few and perpetuate the fiction of independence for the many there were countless casualties created by the imaginary gaps of tribal, political party, or regional loyalty pushed into the collective psyche by a few in their often earnest, but ruthless search for power or wealth.

In all of this, the young, the poor, the ignorant, the weak, and the reckless were gathered up as if so much flotsam and discarded in a sea of conflict from which very few would return; so, now their lifeless remains are scattered among the mechanical carcasses of war and the unexploded mines: unrecognized, unrewarded, but not forgotten.

This book is dedicated to the thousands of unknown young Africans of all colors who gave their lives in a meaningless outrage for whom family and friends silently mourn for an unrequited return.

INTRODUCTION

In the early 1970's the aging colonial power of Portugal faced long overdue movements for independence in its Southwest African colonies including Angola. The Portuguese armed forces waged counterinsurgency campaigns against the pro-independence forces with limited manpower and old equipment supplied across a great distance from the mother country. These unpopular and costly wars beset the capital of Lisbon with regular antiwar protests that in 1974 led to a coup and a new government: the Carnation Revolution. The new government decided to grant Angola independence in 1975.

The former Portuguese military forces in Angola sided with the People's Movement for the Liberation (MPLA) of Agostinho Neto, who died in 1979. There were two other factions, one of which was the Angolan National Liberation Front (FNLA) led by Holden Roberto; it was a movement essentially composed of Bakongo tribe members from the north that disbanded after independence in 1975. Many former members of the FNLA ended up as capable fighters in the famed South African 32 "Buffalo" Infantry Battalion. The second was the National Union for the Total Independence of Angola (UNITA) headed by Jonas Savimbi. UNITA membership was largely drawn from the Ovimbundu tribe from southern Angola.

It was the MPLA and UNITA parties that fought a protracted civil war for almost three decades until the death of Jonas Savimbi in 2002. The MPLA was massively supported by the Soviet Union and Cuba while UNITA was backed by many supporters including China, South Africa and the ever present United States of America. During this period there were many campaigns for control of parts of Angola culminating in late 1987 with the Battle of Cuito Cuanavale, which marked a turning point in the history of Angola and southern Africa. The final chapter would be left to the enduring plague of AIDS that was to be unleashed shortly thereafter.

Thus it came to be that on a beautiful but sparsely populated part of Central Angola between Summer 1987 and Spring 1988 the interests of the world's two superpowers, the United States and the Soviet Union, collided in a monstrous battle near a little known trading town called Cuito Cuanavale, which had sprung up during the period of Portuguese colonization. The hostilities substantially began in September, joining other famous battles of the same month such as the Battle of the Marne, Antietam, and the Battle of Britain.

The competing superpowers did not battle on their own territory, but used the convenient Angolan civil war that began in 1975 to advance their narrow foreign policy ambitions. They fought not with their own armed forces, but through their proxies Cuba and South Africa, who came to surprise the world in their tactical and logistical abilities using second tier or self-designed weapons that proved themselves on the battlefield.

There were many surprises and similarities between the warring factions that came out of that intense period. Years after a substantive peace reigned, the Angolan people were left with a triple legacy; the scourges of mines, AIDS, and poverty. Significantly, little information is publicly available about the Angolan military casualties; they were the soldiers who suffered the greatest losses, estimated in the thousands for the Cuito clash.

Although the South African Defence Force (SADF) acquitted themselves well, it was the Cuban army who proved themselves tactically superior to their Russian sponsors in the African bush war environment. The Cuban army was able to arrange an air and sea movement of massive forces over ten thousand kilometers, unlike anything in recent times excepting the Falklands or Malvinas War. This occurred despite the obstacle of limited or nonexistent forward international bases causing long journeys in old aircraft with overworked pilots. The American-backed cancellation of Cuban landing permission on the Cape Verde Islands, Barbados, and other places failed to stop the logistical juggernaut coming from behind the "mojito curtain." The idea that a pipsqueak country like Cuba, with its manifold domestic problems, could field an expeditionary force of sixty thousand troops to southern and eastern Africa, still staggers the imagination."[1]

Once the Cuban reinforcements were established in their positions in the soon to be destroyed Angolan town they resisted even the stiffest attacks.

The South African Defence Force was equal to the task using weapons that frequently outperformed outdated Soviet equipment, which had been developed over a long period of bush-war experience and arms embargo. They also operated some distance from home base being 400 kilometers from the Namibian border with a further 1,000 kilometers to the South African border. The SADF commanders had the edge in experience with familiar territory and independence in operation which worked well until the set-piece battle of Cuito Cuanavale ensued. Here the outcome depended on will: political will, will to take huge casualties, will to stand firm in the face of flanking attacks by emboldened Cuban troops.

In this way the Cuban and South African forces were more similar than dissimilar. Their respective political ideologies and aims were all for naught when the first shot was fired and it became a soldier's arena, often to the death. Accounts of this memorable battle are often masked by political or ideological slants if not rank inaccuracies and inconsistencies. This is why an attempt must be made to reconstruct an objective record with full available details, and most importantly, to honor all the fallen.

The Battle of Cuito Cuanavale took place in two parts: the misconceived, Soviet-advised attack across the Lomba River towards the UNITA stronghold town of Mavinga in southeastern Angola followed by the disastrous retreat to Cuito. Accurate narratives of this event, which are not complimentary of the FAPLA or their Soviet advisors, are best gleaned from sources other than Soviet or Angolan. Events at Cuito Cuanavale are best depicted by Cuban and to a lesser degree South African sources, although Soviet losses are best obtained from Soviet or FAPLA sources. This is not the case with estimates of SADF and Cuban casualties, which are wildly inaccurate with margins of error over 100 and even 200 percent, when measure against careful review of the pertinent records.

The political polarization and subsequent self-deception by the leaders of the armies involved in the conflict has made the accurate depiction of the Battle of Cuito Cuanavale a complex and difficult task.

CHAPTER 1

CUITO CUANAVALE—AN OVERVIEW

Originally this colony was known as Portuguese West Africa. Its name was changed to Angola in the early 1950's with the province of Bie being divided into what are still the two largest provinces of the country, Moxico and Cuando Cubango, which are hundreds of thousands of square kilometers in area. The province of Moxico was the UNITA heartland throughout the war and it was here that the UNITA leader Jonas Savimbi was killed in 2002 with the invaluable assistance of Geraldo Sachipengo Nunda, one of Savimbi's former generals. Nunda was a former UNITA brigadier who crossed over and is now head of the Angolan army.[2]

The old colonial capital of Cuando Cubango was also called Serpa Pinto, which is the name usually applied to the nearby air base that was the center of Cuban-assisted air operations during the Battle of Cuito Cuanavale. The name of the capital was changed to Menongue after independence and it is usually associated with the supply staging point for the battle that was to come. Cuito Cuanavale, or Kwito Kwanavale, was a small town in Cuando Cubango province in the heart of Angola, built on the confluence of the Cuito and Cuanavale rivers.

During the Portuguese colonial era, river crossings of the Cuito River were made by wooden ferry using a large log raft called a "jangada," with the vehicle perched precariously on this unstable platform. The ferry was anchored to each bank by a steel cable attached to tree stumps, and several men would then pull it across the crocodile infested body of water. It was only some time later that a bridge was constructed across the river to firmly connect Cuito Cuanavale.

The Portuguese colonialists referred to this area as *the land at the end of the earth,* probably because it was far from the developed and civilized parts of the country. It lay some 400 kilometers from the northern border of the now-independent state of Namibia, which was occupied by South Africa at the time of the Angolan or Bush war.

The Battle of Cuito Cuanavale took place east of the town, which had a crucial airfield for resupply of the defending Cuban and FAPLA units who were the ultimate target of the attacking SADF and UNITA forces. The actual battlefield was on both sides of the Tumpo River, 22 kilometers east of Cuito Cuanavale, and was part of what is sometimes called the Tumpo triangle of Angola. Many contemporary military analysts believed that the capture of Cuito Cuanavale would provide the gateway to Luanda, the capital of Angola, to the SADF and UNITA forces, and the potential for a complete UNITA victory.

Interestingly, UNITA was able to capture large swaths of Angola after the departure of the SADF and Cubans in 1989, proof positive of the ability of the Angolan soldier and the strength of UNITA's military leaders like General Ben Ben.

This battle has been variously described as Africa's largest land battle since World War II, the African Stalingrad, Angola Verdun, El Giron Africano (a play on the Cuban name for the aborted Bay of Pigs invasion), or more accurately the largest single conventional military engagement on the African continent since the Battle of El Alamein. This is a realistic comparison because both conflicts involved extensive logistical supply problems for the warring factions.[3]

The battle near the town of Cuito Cuanavale took place between November 1987 and April 1988, but had its genesis much earlier in the repeated failures by Soviet-led FAPLA forces to seize the UNITA headquarters to the west at Jamba. This was the consequence of a 1984 change in Soviet strategy to move from protection of cities, towns, and facilities to an active and aggressive counterinsurgency against UNITA. In this, they fell into the open arms of the American post-Vietnam policy of a cheaper option: supporting the UNITA guerillas. This particular engagement grew out of a misguided Soviet operational plan to attack the UNITA controlled stronghold town of Mavinga and then continue onward to Jamba. Mavinga had an important UNITA airstrip used by the South African Air Force (SAAF) and others to bring supplies and weapons to the UNITA army as well as a blood diamond trading post. The FAPLA viewed the closer town of Mavinga as a strategic portal to the UNITA headquarters at Jamba.

UNITA liaison officer SADF Col. Fred Oelschig recalled Mavinga:

> There were absolutely no fortifications and in my opinion, the only military value that the town had was the very good ground runway nearly two kilometers in length. The town consisted of only two roads; a short North/South road running from the river to the runway, past the house of the governor and a long East/West road running parallel to the runway where the school, post office and other lesser houses were situated. The town had been destroyed in previous battles between UNITA and FAPLA after 1975. The area was primarily an agricultural area where UNITA farmers produced maize in vast lands adjacent to the Mavinga river valley. The general Mavinga area of 100 square kilometers, however, was occupied by a number of UNITA bases: West of Mavinga at the confluence of the Cunzumbia and Lomba rivers was a large UNITA logistical base; East of Mavinga [approximately 30 km] was another large UNITA log base and a regional hospital; North of Mavinga, East of Cuito Cuanavale, at the source of the Cunzumbia River was a large UNITA training base. I was personally astounded as to why FAPLA (and their advisors) were so adamant about Mavinga—they made four attempts at taking the place, each time using the same routes and tactics [which only serves to prove the inadequacies of the Soviet military doctrine]. In my opinion, there were a number of other options available to them. If FAPLA had broken up their mobile forces into smaller combat teams and had advanced across a much broader front then I believe that they could have been more successful, but the Soviet military doctrine does not allow that degree of independent action for its commanders; therefore, it is always a nonstarter.

The Soviet plan was a manifestation of the commonplace military obsession with a knockout blow: the quest for a single, swift decisive strike that will bring victory, which more often than not proves misguided in conclusion and disastrous in implementation. "Shock and Awe" from America's war in Iraq comes to mind. The Soviet and American leadership sought knock out

MPLA propaganda on buildings in Mavinga.—*Richard Wiles*

blows, for example, the bombing campaign of North Vietnam and control of the Afghanistan countryside. These theories failed and became incrementalism.

The attack was originally planned in 1986 by Soviet chief military advisor Lt. Gen. Leonid Kuzmenko and later by his successor Lt. Gen. Pavel Gusev in 1987, advised by counterinsurgency expert Gen. Mikhail Petrov. The Soviet leadership decided to take over command of all Angolan and allied forces, mostly Cuban and a few East German, which led to the issue of a directive in February 1987 for the dry season offensive to be directed at Mavinga via the Lomba River in Eastern Angola.[4]

The Cuban high command, with greater experience in this type of war, undoubtedly had superior tactical knowledge in this instance when compared to the FAPLA Russian advisors and expressed doubts about the likelihood of success of such an attack. As Edward George pointed out in his book *The Cuban Intervention in Angola, 1965–1991*: "Once again, however, the Soviets failed to make contingency plans for a South African intervention, despite being warned in May 1987 by Ronnie Kasrils [one of MK's most senior commanders in Angola] that an SADF invasion from Namibia was imminent. [Umkhonto we Sizwe *or* MK was the armed wing of the African National Congress.]"[5]

This warning proved correct to the grave misfortune of the FAPLA forces and their senior Soviet advisors, who turned tail and were evacuated by helicopter when the going became hellish, a repeat of their cowardly actions in October 1985. The FAPLA were substantially left without the leadership that led them into the disaster for several months until relief by Cuban reinforcements west of the Tumpo River near Cuito. However, one source does suggest that some lower level advisors had to retreat with the FAPLA forces, paying the price for being left behind. There was limited evacuation capacity in the circumstances presented at the Lomba River, so it's not surprising that only the senior advisors made it out by helicopter.[6]

South Africa's initial objective was to secure the Jamba headquarters of the UNITA forces concentrated there as well as keep the area north of Rundu on the Namibian border clear of any SWAPO (South West Africa People's Organization) activities by occupying that area. SWAPO was the Namibian liberation movement that were militarily active in resisting South African control of their country by guerilla tactics and whose struggle led to Namibian independence in 1990. Significantly, Norway, the home of the Nobel Peace Prize, began to give direct aid to SWAPO starting in 1974.

Other FAPLA concerns were initially voiced about the supply distance in unfriendly UNITA territory, the high financial cost to the FAPLA with their limited resources, as well as insufficient air cover which made the operation precarious. Despite all this, and with stern Soviet insistence, the FAPLA offensive began from Cuito east towards Mavinga with the FAPLA 21st, 25th, 47th, 59th, and 16th Brigades.[7]

It was to be a bloody and unfortunate mistake rooted in post-Stalinist military apathy that FAPLA General and Minister of Defense Pedro Maria Tonha, also known by his nom de guerre Pedalé, would regret until he died prematurely in London in July 1995.[8]

CHAPTER 2

THE CUBAN FORCES

At Freedom Park, outside South Africa's capital city of Pretoria, is the Sikhumbuto Wall monument that includes the 2,106 names of Cuban soldiers who fell in Angola between 1975 and 1988. This is about 160 Cuban casualties per year in Angola, an extremely low casualty rate for this type of war, if you accept this figure. This was a tribute to the parsimonious and priority use of troops by the Cuban leadership. The Cubans used their substantial number of troops in a very careful manner. No wild rush attacks on UNITA positions or chasing units across the countryside. Although they were advisors, often large numbers of Cubans were used for defensive actions or security operations for important assets like oil installations.[9]

Among the Cuban troops sent to Angola was former Col. Pedro Tortolo Comas, the failed commander of Cuban forces in Grenada now sent to Angola as a private along with most of his Grenada command. Tortolo allegedly hid in the Soviet embassy during the United States invasion of Grenada.

On 26 October 1983, the second day of American invasion, Commandante Castro made the following announcement on the Havana Television Service:

> I feel that organizing our personnel's immediate evacuation at a time when U. S. forces were approaching would be highly demoralizing and dishonorable for our country in the eyes of world public opinion. The people know of the message exchanged between the commander in chief and Colonel Tortolo, the man in charge of Cuban personnel. This man, who had barely been in the country twenty-

four hours on a working visit, with deeds and words has written in our modern history page worthy of Antonio Maceo. Fatherland or death, we shall win.[10]

Cuba suffered a massive embarrassment and propaganda blow when Cuban Air Force (DAAFAR) Brig. Gen. Rafael del Pino defected to the United States with his family in May 1987. Del Pino severely criticized the incompetence of Cuban commanders in Angola, apparently in silent agreement with Cuba's commander in chief as events were to unfold. Worse was the misleading of relatives as to circumstances of the noncombat deaths of family members being described as heroic. He exposed how many Cuban soldiers were being buried in Angola, which may have led to the later refrigerated repatriation of Cuban remains described below and the confusion on actual Cuban casualty numbers. The later, Cuban-led turnaround at Cuito did not support del Pino's theory of a debacle and Angolan Vietnam but there was great truth in his view of Cuban officer discontent.[11]

All Cubans between the ages of seventeen and twenty-eight, men and women alike, are required to perform two years of military service with provisions to work in other areas other relating to the national security of the country in place of uniformed service. Internationalist combat units are usually all volunteer but refusal to fight abroad would have employment, academic, and other consequences for young Cuban soldiers who did not wish to volunteer for overseas duty.

Many SADF conscripts found themselves deployed in a foreign country, Angola or Namibia, without any choice in the matter. The Cuban forces that arrived in Angola, however, were portrayed as volunteers supporting the popular decision in Cuba to protect Angola. The compelling report below did not support this notion.

An interview of a Cuban combat veteran of Angola was done in Panama City, Republic of Panama, by Professor Russ Stayanoff and was published in *Small Wars Journal* in May 2008 titled "Third World Experience in Counterinsurgency—Cuba's Operation Carlotta 1975":

Ernesto C. is a tall, handsome, slightly graying man in his early fifties. He has lived for several years in Panama City, Panama, where he is a kitchen manager for a family owned Cuban restaurant. His soft-spoken manner and forced smile betrays a man whose life experiences are neither gratuitously given nor easily recounted. In 1975, at the age of sixteen, Ernesto was living with his mother in the Province of Havana, having just graduated from high school. Life was poor but predictable and he was looking forward to entering the University of Havana with his classmates. By law, university ambitions of all young Cubans were put on hold until the two-year compulsory military service obligation was satisfied. Within months of his graduation, Ernesto reported for his military training.

According to Ernesto, Cuban military entrance requirements at the time of his induction were quite lax, " . . . one only had to pass a medical exam. If you weren't deaf, blind or missing a leg you were in. It was obligatory, so there were no special considerations. "Ernesto joined other sixteen and seventeen year old males called up from Havana Province and began 45 days of basic combat training known as "*la previa*." Cuban conscripts were trained at the older isolated revolutionary-era military camps near the town of San Antonio de los Baños. Like all new soldiers, Ernesto encountered arduous training days that began early and ended late. Introduced to close order drill, physical training and weapons and marksmanship skills using the AK 47, the training company was also under the supervision of the very visible political officer. This officer conducted sporadic classes on Marxist-Leninist theory which were scored just as critically as marksmanship.

Ernesto and his colleagues were introduced to the RPG 7 and the older RPD5 machine gun. The RPG-7 is a shoulder-fired, muzzle-loaded, anti-tank and anti-personnel grenade launcher which launches a variety of fin-stabilized, oversized grenades from a 40mm tube. The RPD light machine gun was one of the first weapons designed to fire the new Russian 7.62 x 39mm intermediate cartridge, which became the standard round of the Soviet small arms arsenal. The weapon, developed in 1944, became the standard squad automatic weapon of Soviet army until the 1960s, when the Warsaw Pact generally replaced it with the RPK light machine gun. The RPD was extensively exported to pro-Soviet countries and regimes around the world.

"Training in "*la previa*" continued for Ernesto and his companions at San Antonio de los Baños. The training, similar to the U.S. Army COHORT system, prepared the recruits to be tactically indoctrinated and then technically skilled and subsequently integrated into a communications battalion assigned to a mechanized infantry regiment. Ernesto's company was tasked with the upkeep of the R-105 family of Soviet made backpack radio sets. These radios were by far the most common of all the Russian radios found throughout the world. The radio was relatively primitive by contemporary military standards and, unlike most Soviet equipment, was not easy to use. These radios were of the glass tube type design; the only transistors were in the radio's internal power supply. Introduced in the early 1950s, it was revamped in the 1970s, with more modern materials. Like most Soviet equipment of the Cold War period, the radio set was an updated copy of captured WW II German sets.

Near completion of training, Ernesto's group was unexpectedly assembled and informed they had been selected for a "special military course. "Things began to change shortly thereafter. Ernesto remembers "weird things going on . . . stricter custody, more security, and the military maneuvers began to get more complicated and more exhausting. We were taken to the medics for all sorts of tests and vaccines. We understood nothing of what was happening." It was during this period that Ernesto was issued his first international passport, showing him attired in civilian clothes. The civilian suit was issued to him solely for the purpose of the passport photo, then removed and given to the next soldier his size. Phony civilian occupations were listed on the passport. Ernesto and his companions, just months out of high school, abruptly became architects, engineers and science professionals. "The whole process took about a month and we had absolutely no contact with the outside world. That was forbidden. However they treated us better, with more respect. They even gave us ice cream."

The atmosphere at San Antonio de los Baños had quickly turned from conscript training to tactical. The new troops were in for some surprises, when one day " . . . beautiful air-conditioned buses appeared out of nowhere and we were taken to a large building. There, in front of us, were none other than Fidel and Raul Castro. They told us the story of Angola and its military situation. They told us that some 200 Cuban "special advisors" supporting the MPLA were now surrounded by FNLA troops who had come from Zaire . . . the imperialists were invading Angola, so the president of the MPLA had asked Cuba, based on the principles of Marxism-Leninism and proletarian internationalism, to give him military support. We were told the country would be proud of us because we were going to accomplish one of the three major principles of Marxism-Leninism, which was proletariat internationalism."

For the past three decades it has been debated whether *Operation Carlotta* was a Soviet designed operation or, as Castro maintains, an independent Cuban initiated response to a plea from Agostino Neto, the president of the

MPLA. Castro has long held that the Kremlin was never consulted prior to the operation, a contention which considering the players and proxies of the Cold War, is improbable at best. According to Ernesto, Fidel addressed the issue during this briefing, telling his soldiers that the Soviet Union was supplying modern and efficient weapons but "...because of their Warsaw Treaty obligations they could not bring their troops to Africa ... it was our duty to support and liberate Angola from the imperialist enemies."

Within three hours of meeting with Fidel, the entire brigade was taken to an assembly point called "El Chico" close to Havana. Here, the troops were issued weapons and civilian clothing. "They gave us civilian clothing and we packed our military clothes away. We looked very strange because the civilian clothes were tailored the same, so we were all dressed almost exactly alike." Three brigades were then marched to the port of Mariel where three Russian built cargo vessels, "30 Aniversario," the "Playa Giron" and the "Primer Congreso" awaited.

Ernesto's company was put aboard the rusting "30 Aniversario." There was no time for goodbyes. Three thousand Cuban troops, without fan-fare, embarked on each of the three ships, which sailed at daybreak on the morning of November 6, 1975. Ernesto remembers, "Most of us were adolescents, innocent and really had no idea what would happen to us. However, we really didn't have the time or the space to think about it."

The voyage from Mariel to the Congolese coast took 23 days. The 3,000 troops were never allowed above deck for fear of detection by American aerial intelligence. The troops were quartered in the cargo holds that had been used for shipping raw sugar. According to Ernesto, "...it was an unbelievable mess down there. Caring for natural necessities was difficult." There was not much to do below decks during these sailing days. Ernesto remembers the voyage full of sea-sickness, vomiting and unsuccessful attempts to adjust to stiflingly hot, cramped and nauseating conditions aboard the ex-sugar freighter.

The vessels arrived off the Congolese coast on November 29, 1975, and the troops began the welcome debarkation from the ships at Pointe Noir around midnight. Ernesto's company was then assigned to a mechanized infantry company equipped with the Soviet BMP-1 vehicle.

Within hours of arrival, the Cuban brigades were en route through Congo-Brazzaville. The convoy traveled throughout the day arriving at the Angolan border late the next evening. "It was there we got off and changed into our military clothing. We broke out ammunition and loaded our weapons and continued down the road into Angola." Their destination was the abandoned Portuguese military post at Landala about 30 km northeast of the capital city of Luanda.

Ernesto's brigade, composed of raw recruits and commanded by inexperienced officers, entered into the combat zone. "That first night I remember we had no idea where we were sleeping. We didn't even set up a proper camp. ...The next day we were surprised to see that we had slept in a sort of a plain surrounded by high mountains. The enemy could have killed us with a few rocks, as we had absolutely no protection." Basic combat intelligence was slim. Maps issued from Cuban military headquarters in Luanda became suspect. Most showed non-existent rivers that disappeared during the Angolan dry season. Cuban commanders planned routes down long-vanished Portuguese colonial roads passing over bridges and through villages which no longer existed.

Attacks on the Landala outpost by FNLA and its allies, became frequent. Ernesto's company was tasked with establishing a defensive perimeter around the post. This required an almost daily reconnaissance patrol of outlying villages. Ernesto observed, "We saw the great needs of the people. They were very poor and without education. We tried to help them. We gave them our food and much needed medical attention by allowing them to come into our fortified camps. Ironically, the people we helped were the same ones who would help the enemy to attack us. They knew our troop strength, our movements and because they lived close to the camp they became valuable informers to the enemy, they were easily bribed."

Most of the resistance encountered by the Cubans at Landala was from another armed group backed by the FNLA called the Front for the Liberation of the Enclave of Cabinda (FLEC). The FLEC had actively fought Portuguese colonial authorities, subsequently formed a provisional government and on August 1, 1975, declared Cabinda independent. After Angolan independence in November, Cabinda was invaded by the MPLA with Cuban support. Eventually, the MPLA overthrew the provisional FLEC government and incorporated Cabinda into Angola. In December, Ernesto's brigade was moved into arid Linche province, near the Zairean border, in order to reinforce MPLA forces under siege by the FLEC. "We left Landala around midnight," he recalls, "using the roads on the northern route toward Zaire. At dawn, around 5am, we heard the sound of drums. Drums! Just like in the films. We thought the drums were coming from a nearby village, and that the tribe was happy at our appearance and was playing them as a welcome."

The drums signaled FLEC fighters of the Cuban's approach. At the bottom of a canyon, known as *Bukusau*, Ernesto's column was ambushed. Enfilading fire from machine guns and RPG's hidden in the canyon's walls wreaked havoc on vehicles and men. Grenades rained down from hidden positions. Ernesto remembers, ". . . they threw a tremendous number of grenades at us, there was no cover. Of our soldiers, 47 died and more than 60 were seriously wounded. The ambush lasted 35 minutes, but we sustained a very large amount of casualties. I was personally wounded on that terrible day." Ernesto watched from behind an overturned truck as his company commander and a few others tried to seek cover. ". . . He hid beneath a truck loaded with gasoline. That was a mistake. The truck was hit with a rocket. They became ashes almost immediately."

Ernesto sustained shrapnel wounds. He and other wounded Cubans were sent to Americo Boavida Hospital in Luanda where Cuban doctors treated him. While recovering in the hospital, soldiers read "*Olive Green on an International Mission*," the weekly newspaper for the Cuban military in Angola. Its pages were filled with stories stressing "socialist self-sacrifice." One issue, translated by a *Carlotta* survivor, contained the story of a Cuban tank driver who explained why he had left his job in a metalworking shop to answer the call of duty in Angola: "In my house, to be an internationalist is something great," he was quoted as saying. "I was in too much pain in the hospital to read anything," replies a *Carlotta* veteran. "If I would have seen that article I would not have needed toilet paper." Even the *Operation Carlotta* military commander in Cabinda province, General Ramon Espinosa Martin, was severely wounded in Angola in 1976 and spent a year recuperating.

By August 1976, more than 100 of Ernesto's comrades from Havana Province were either dead or missing. Now recovered from his wounds, he and the other *Carlotta* survivors looked forward to the day when they would be going home. Patrolling and MPLA support missions occupied most of their time. They were bombed and strafed by South African Air Force fighter-bombers, and by "unmarked aircraft," most likely of mercenary origin from Zaire. Crack South African commandos ambushed the Cubans by night. Ernesto echoes what might have been said by an American soldier during another counter-insurgency of the 1960–1970's, "The longer we were there, the more I saw good comrades fall. There was no talk of ever leaving Angola. We began to feel somewhat depressed. Medical attention was always good. But our equipment began to break down, our clothes were not being replaced and our food supply was sometimes unpredictable" One day

Ernesto's unit was sent to ostensibly provide security to another port called Lobito, near Benguela. Benguela is Angola's deep water port and sea terminus for the Benguela Railway, the fabled diamond route into the Congo's Katanga Province. During the war, the bay had been used by Soviet freighters offloading military cargoes for the MPLA. "...They assembled us, took away our weapons and loaded us on-board ships bound for Cuba. It was a shock. Within a day, with the dust of Angola still in our hair, we were again at sea, going home, it was that simple."

When the ships approached the Cuban coast near the city of Cienfuegos, "...Several boats came toward our ships. They were full of barbers, doctors and dentists sent to fix us, because we were a mess. It was during our clean-up that they gave us a check for 100 Cuban pesos, the equivalent of more or less six dollars. We were all happy because it had been a while since we had seen Cuban money and we were never paid while serving in Angola. "The pay amounted to seven pesos for privates (71 cents per month) and fourteen pesos for sergeants ($1.43 per month). A revolutionary-internationalist, if he returned home alive, received less than $10.00 for the entire operation.

Ernesto's brigade returned to Mariel on September 5, 1976. They were met at the port by a convoy of busses and taken to the Carlos Marx Theater in Miramar. In dramatic fashion the lights came on, the curtain opened and Fidel appeared. He congratulated the men and, "...Talked about everything that happened...how we had survived in Angola with the strategies that he personally had devised."

From there they were taken to a place called *Cristino Naranjo*. This was an elite social club for the Ministry of the Interior. Once inside the guarded compound the veterans found themselves staring at tables laden with huge amounts of steaming food. "It was incredible the way we ate and drank. Strict security surrounded us and nobody else could get in. I lived very close to this place, and so, when we were finally dismissed, I simply walked home. I received so many hugs and kisses from my family...they were never sure where I was...the government told relatives we were in the Soviet Union. This was common for soldiers during this time. But my grandmother didn't believe it. She listened to the international news broadcasts and knew that we were in Angola. My mother had always refused to believe her."

Castro's reputation was at first enhanced by the purported independence of the Angolan intervention. Yet, as Cuban dependence on massive Soviet military, financial and logistical assistance became known, his claim that *Operation Carlotta* was a Cuban initiated operation undertaken without the

Kremlins' pre-approval was debunked. The indisputable fact remains that without Soviet military hardware, supplies, aircraft, transport ships, and vast sums of hard currency pumped into the Cuban economy, there would have been few, if any, Cuban troops in Angola. Yet, despite these facts, when Soviet support is factored, one cannot overlook the Cuban military successes in the mid-1980s. The experiences and the hard lessons learned of *Operation Carlotta*, paved the way.

Ernesto now lives within the sizable Cuban expatriate community in the Republic of Panama. Life after the army included, marriage, defection and resettlement. Like most expatriates he stays updated on Cuban domestic politics, and considers the fate of the island without Fidel. There can be no doubt that significant change will occur in Cuba in the near future. How those changes reflect the history of Cuba during its "internationalist proletariat" era that began with Che Gueverra and ended rather ignominiously in Africa remains to be seen. How will the Cuban people view "*Operation Carlotta?*" A circumspect Ernesto describes his feelings on the matter:

> At the time we were heroes. We absolutely believed that what we had done was productive and necessary for Angola . . . we have come to realize that it was truly a useless mission. So many comrades died without achieving any real objective. So many families were affected. The whole business was based on the absurd concept of the international-proletariat, where the poor of Cuba needed to help other poor people in different countries on their way to revolution and social development. I personally was affected in many ways. My nerves were affected. I was badly wounded and nearly lost my life. I never received compensation for my wounds. I was simply one of the internationalist-proletariats.

The Angolan government reportedly paid for food, clothes and medicine for Cuban troops in Angola as well as a cash payment to the Cuban government of U.S. $40 per day per soldier increasing to $1,000 to $5,000 per day for officers, depending on seniority. From this the Cuban troops were later paid a monthly salary of $7 and 150 Angola Kwanzas while officers received $24 and 3,000 Kwanzas. Cuban defector and Air Force General Rafael del Pino stated in a 1986 interview that the Angolan government paid 600 Kwanzas for noncommissioned officers, 900 to officers, and 1,200 to top officers.[12]

After the usual two-year tour of duty, Cuban soldiers would be allowed to shop for scarce appliances to carry home by ship or plane. A great irony of this conflict was that that much of the funding for the war came from the sale of Angolan oil to the American Gulf Oil Company.

In this bizarre situation UNITA troops financed by the United States attacked assets of a U.S. corporation in Angola protected by Cuban soldiers paid by the Angola government from oil revenue from the selfsame American corporation. The dollar was mightier than conscience or common sense.

This payment subject was addressed in passing by President Castro during his speech on 26 June1978 to mark the twenty-fifth anniversary of the assault on Moncada Barracks in Havana:

> Cuba's internationalist policies, the unbounded generosity of our country whose children fought in Angola against the South African racists to prevent them from stealing from the Angolans the independence they won after fifteen years of heroic struggle and our solidarity in the battle of the Ethiopian revolution against foreign aggression promoted by the United States, the NATO powers and Arab reaction are characterized by the Chinese leaders with the same, and even worse, vile and rude terms that the spokesmen of imperialism use, although the latter use more subtle and less wildly false terms. Internationalism is the most precious essence of Marxism-Leninism and of its ideals of solidarity and fraternity among the people. The Cuban revolution would not even exist without internationalism. In being internationalists we are paying our debt to mankind.[13]

President Eduardo Dos Santos reported to the Second Congress of the MPLA party in December 1985 that Cuba had ceased receiving payments from Angola a year prior: "There is no material reward for the internationalism it practices in Angola in such an exemplary way in the military field."[14]

In February 1984, before the Battle of Cuito Cuanavale, Soviet General Konstantin met Fidel Castro in Havana. In one version of that meeting Konstantin believed that the Cubans were not eager to fight and it was necessary to compel them to be more active in the interest of the cause. It would appear that the Cubans were not unwilling to fight, but disagreed with Soviet battlefield strategy, correctly as it would later appear at Cuito Cuanavale.

Commander in Chief Castro explained the reason for such an attitude to the Soviet general: "In your country the losses may be unnoticeable, but in our small country the human losses become known and have a great effect, therefore we are really trying to avoid losses in Angola."[15]

In 2006 at the Cuban war memorial dedication at Freedom Park, South Africa, General Leopoldo "Polo" Cintra Frias remarked that he preferred not to be compared to Soviet World War II hero Marshall Zhukov because Zhukov expended an enormous number of casualties in his campaigns. He went on to say that one must bear in mind when giving orders that people on both sides may be killed. It is reported that he received the most applause of any speaker at the dedication. This was virtually the same position to the South African leadership and their forces in Angola.[16]

In the early phase of the Angola conflict there was a three member committee of Soviet, Angolan FAPLA, and Cuban representatives that made decisions, however veto power was held by the Soviets. This could not hold true for Cuito Cuanavale and the fluid skirmishes during that period that led to a radical change to Cuban military frontline leadership for the defense of the town.

The command and strategic control of the defense stayed in Havana at all relevant times, and by the eventual outcome proved that Cuban Commander in Chief Fidel Castro was a capable military leader, even by remote. Castro had advised the Angolan leader Dos Santos to adopt a two-part strategy of reinforcing Cuito and then pressure South African bases near Namibia with joint Cuban and FAPLA patrols. This was accepted by Dos Santos who would not regret his decision as events unfolded. The Sierra Maestre, the Cuban Revolution, the defeat of exiles at Giron (Bay of Pigs) were not flukes and the Angola battle over 1987–1988 confirmed his place in history. Perhaps if the Commandante had been in charge of Grenada instead of the unworthy Colonel Tortolo, that 1983 battle would not have been lost.[17]

It was this intense drive to control strategy from Cuba that drove his relationship with former Hero of the Revolution Gen. Ochoa Sanchez to unbearable friction, which led to his replacement by Gen. Cintra Frias on the southern Angola front. Polo was one of six FAR generals who came from the small town of Yara in the foothills of the Sierra Maestre mountains of eastern Cuba and had their roots in 1958 revolution. He was later joined in Angola by another Yara companero, Gen. Miguel Lorente.[18]

An example of the Cuban chain of command at Cuito:

Fidel Castro	Commander in Chief
Raul Castro	Defense Minister
General Arnaldo Ochoa Sanchez	Commander Angola
Commander Leopoldo Cintra Frias	Commander Angola Southern Front
Colonel Venancio Avila Guerrero	Commander Cuito Cuanavale
Lieutenant Colonel Hector Aguilar	T-55 Tank Brigade Commander
Lieutenant Geomar Fernández	Antitank Platoon leader
Bernardo "Shogun" Heredia Perez	Antitank RPG specialist

In practice the Commander in Chief dealt directly with Commander Frias who would implement the strategic decisions, often sent in minute detail, by instructing Cuito commander Venancio Guerrero to follow instructions to the letter. There would be no improvisation at the actual front line that might suit the purposes of the moment, but could amount to a defective move overall. It was a sound although difficult policy for that time and place. Meanwhile, Ochoa monitored events like a third wheel from the air base at Menongue.[19]

Commandante Fidel reportedly would go to the Angola Command office at the Armed Forces Ministry in the afternoon and stay until dawn. Cuban Brigadier Juan Escalona, the man in charge of Angola Command office, stated that Fidel directed the Angola operation minute by minute, sending many cables often under his code name Alejandro.[20]

At the thirtieth anniversary of Cuban armed forces intervention in Angola Castro finally revealed that fifty-five thousand of his troops were in country at the time of the battle and that forty thousand of them were concentrated around the city. They also had six hundred tanks, artillery with support vehicles and equipment, as well as a squadron of MiGs operating out of Menongue, north of the site of the battle. This was much more than earlier published estimates.

The Cuban air arm operated in Angola under the FAPA banner, Forca Aérea Popular de Angola or Angolan People's Air Force, as the 25th Air Combat Fighter Regiment led by Brig. Gen. Rubén Martínez Puente, who was the chief of the Cuban DAAFAR or Antiaircraft Defense and Revolutionary Air Force in Angola with Brig. Gen. Francisco Cruz Bourzac. Bourzac did not survive the war due to a friendly fire incident. The Cuban pilots, most of whom flew MiG-23ML jets were some of the best from the combat pilot corps and included:

Colonel Carlos Lamas Rodríguez	Commander DAAFAR Cuito
Colonel Juan Oscar Hernandez	Deputy Commander
Colonel Humberto Trujillo Hernandez	Squadron Leader
Colonel Luis Alonso Reina	
Lieutenant Colonel Manuel Rojas Garcia	
Lieutenant Colonel Armando "El Guajiro" González	
Major Alberto Ley Rivas	
Captain Ramon Quesada Aguilar	
Capitan Lorenzo Morales Ramos	
Captain Carlos "El Gordo" Rodriguez Perez	
Captain Juan "Capri" Perez Rodriguez	
Captain Orlando Carbo	
Lieutenant Juan Carlos Chavez Godoy	
First Lieutenant Juan Francisco Alfonso Doval	
Lieutenant Ernesto L. Chavez Marrero	
Lieutenant Eduardo Gonzalez Sarria	
First Lieutenant Eladio Avila	
Warrant Officer Barbaro Raul Quiala Castaneda[21]	

Despite the various propaganda accounts, several of these pilots were killed or captured as revealed below in this account.

The workhorse of the Cuban FAPA air wing was the Soviet MiG-23 fighter-bomber armed with Soviet AA-8 Aphid air to air missiles. The MiGs dominated the air during the battle, but there were insufficient dogfights to make any true assessment of the pilots from both sides. What is certain was that the only decisive air-to-air combat engagement between Cuban and South African pilots during the Battle of Cuito Cuanavale was won by the Cuban FAPA on 27 September 1987.

Much later in the conflict, during July 1988, MiG-23BN fighter-bombers with an improved fuel capability and range were sent from Cuba to Angola onboard the Cuban ship *Las Coloradas*. They saw no action, but were capable of raiding the SAAF base at Grootfontein in Namibia from Menongue and were likely a factor in the eventual peace settlement talks. These long-range aircraft were sent from Cuba after the Soviets refused to supply a batch of auxiliary fuel tanks for the MiGs already in Angola.[22]

The operations of the Cuban FAPA limited but did not prevent the operation of SADF artillery and troop movements, with much effort being expended in concealment and avoidance for fear of MiG strikes. Other than the armored deadlock on the perimeter of Cuito Cuanavale this Cuban aerial domination was one of the most significant considerations in the eventual withdrawal to the south by the South African forces in 1988, along with the weak political will of the South African politicians.

CHAPTER **3**

THE SOUTH AFRICAN FORCES

The three branches of army, air force, and navy composed the South African Defence Force but the only distinction necessary for this campaign was between the South African ground and air forces. Their chain of command at the time of Cuito was a formal Western military structure with an overall commander in chief to design strategy for implementation of political policy while giving commanders in the field appropriate flexibility for operational plans. This was to prove a decided advantage in the fluid skirmishes around the Lomba River as the military wing of the MPLA, the FAPLA, pushed eastward towards Mavinga which required localized command and control, a concept outside established Soviet military command thinking. The control and involvement of South African politicians through SADF senior leadership grew exponentially as the South African forces came closer to Cuito Cuanavale for direct implementation of a policy of limited troop numbers and cautious tactics. The result of this later micromanagement speaks for itself.

Nevertheless, it was an excellent example of specific political goals implemented by limited military power, which South Africa largely achieved by employing a small but potent strike force supported by indigenous troops.

The French had originally perfected this operational method under Marshal Bugeaud in Algeria around 1840. Brigade-size task forces of infantry, artillery, cavalry, and engineers chased guerrillas throughout the deserts and mountains of Algeria. Accompanying supply trains transitioned from wagons to mules and camels to improve mobility. The SADF force selected was a modern version of the colonial war era flying column used by

English troops in the Boer Wars of the early twentieth century and subsequently adapted by the Irish Republican Army (IRA) in their struggle for independence from Great Britain. The SADF Angola task force was, in essence, a mobile battle group designed to operate effectively at the end of a long supply line.

Colonel Roland De Vries, 20 Brigade's deputy commander during the battle published a text on this South African doctrine in which he stressed the primacy of mobility and suggested the utility of combining conventional mobile warfare with the techniques of guerrilla action. He also noted the requirement to act in both tactical modes, conventional mobile and guerilla, proficiently at night. All three doctrinal elements (mobility, guerrilla tactics, and night operations) figured prominently in the Battle of Cuito Cuanavale.

Night maneuvers although difficult, were also more effective in disrupting the opposing force. Most SADF night movements during the battle were defensive in nature as artillery batteries moved at night to prevent attack by FAPA aircraft and daylight movements were often delayed while vehicles sought cover. Casualty evacuations were routinely made at night to protect the SAAF Puma helicopters from MiG attacks. Dense bush that complicated coordination and trapped vehicles as well as abundant and unknown FAPLA fighting positions all militated against a night offensive.

Previous SADF experience in Angola incursions had encountered the growing military capability of the FAPLA forces over time creating a need for significant antiarmor capability in future external operations. This was filled by Ratels, G5 howitzers and in extreme cases, Olifant tanks. Nevertheless these attacks were frequently able to achieve territorial gains of approximately 100 kilometers a day including skirmishes, remarkable at that time and place.

SADF commitment to the battle was some three to five thousand troops on the ground including support personnel within the supply line and the SAAF contingent at Rundu, Namibia. These South African troops were initially put in place as armored support for the UNITA troops on the field of battle but ended up taking the lead up to the siege of Cuito. There would be no waves of SADF troops striding across open grasslands or river deltas as if in some bizarre reenactment of Soviet infantrymen facing off against German armor on the Russian steppes. That particular role was filled by FAPLA foot soldiers driven by merciless mid-level officers who in turn faced the stony orders of Soviet advisors.

The established chain of command extended from combat groups to field tactical headquarters, forward headquarters at Rundu, SADF headquarters in Pretoria, and to the national command. A conflict that involved Cuban and the Soviet elements required close monitoring by senior military and political leaders. This required the presence of senior military leaders at forward bases, which resulted in a limited buffer between tactical commanders and well-meaning superiors seeking to micromanage. In addition, UNITA chief Savimbi, code name Stryker (Nail) or Mario, demanded the attention of senior SADF liaison officers and on occasion it took the intervention of the head of the SADF to obtain cooperation from Savimbi.[23]

A bird's eye view of SADF command chain was:

General Jannie Geldenhuys	Army Chief
Lieutenant Colonel Hutchinson	Operations Directorate
Colonel Renier Coetzee	Division Headquarters Mavinga
Colonel Deon Ferreira	20 Brigade Battle Group Commander
Commandant Robbie Hartslief	Combat Group Bravo
Commandant Johan Du Randt	20 Brigade Artillery Fire Leader
Captain A. D. McCallum	Ratel Company Commander
Second Lieutenant J. R. Alves	Ratel Troop commander
Corporal M. M. De Klerk	Ratel crew member

The last five of these men are all dead, one by his own hand in 2006 and the rest during the battle.

The SADF force, under the overall command of General Geldenhuys, were originally led into the Lomba River action in Angola by Col. Jock Harris. SADF leadership became nervous when matters escalated beyond their expectations and promptly replaced him with the aggressive Col. Deon Ferreira in the first week of September 1987. Ferreira was commander from 5 September until 1 December 1987 when he was replaced by Col. Paul Fouche, and he in turn by Col. George "Pat" McLachlan, who was commander from 7 February 1988 to 8 March 1988. Colonel Paul Fouche then returned to replace McLachlan and commanded 20 Brigade until it was disbanded on 8 May 1988. Most of the SADF troops in the field up to this point were conscripts who were near their termination date for two years service.[24]

The changes of commanders were partly due to exchange of National Service units with the Citizen Force units. The 61st Mechanised Battalion was replaced by the 4 South African Infantry Battalion, which was finally replaced by the Citizen Force brigades. The 32 Infantry and 61st Mechanised battalions as well as the UNITA liaison teams were the only constant SADF units of Cuito. The 4 South African Infantry was a National Service battalion that formed the basis for the 62nd Mechanised Battalion Group, which was the first unit deployed with Olifant tanks under command of Commandant Leon Marais in 1987. The 61st and 62nd Battalions operated jointly in early 1988 to enable the deployment of two mechanized units.

Nevertheless, four commanders in seven months could explain the eventual stalemate at Cuito, the result of a policy of spreading the exposure and experience among the officer corps for a limited conflict, or knee-jerk response to simple errors of judgment. Ferreira was brought in to stop the FAPLA advance and when this was accomplished the leadership presumably thought mission accomplished and started to effect changes in leadership and soldiers in the field. This was a grave error as the deadlock and eventual retreat from Cuito were to prove.[25]

This high-command shortsightedness was not exclusive to the South Africans. Later on there was a similar action on the Cuban side when the Angola and Southern Front commander General Ochoa was replaced by General Cintra Frias who became the de facto overall commander.

When Colonel Harris was transferred to Mavinga as senior staff officer, Ferreira organized the 4 Infantry, the 32 Infantry (Buffalo), the 61st Mechanised Infantry, and the 101 Light Infantry battalions into a newly created 20 Brigade, which was composed of three combat groups with artillery. The SADF armored vehicles consisted of Ratels, Buffels, and Casspirs, but no Olifant tanks, which had yet to be drawn into the conflict. Leading 20 Brigade's primary maneuver elements were:

Combat Group Alpha: Commandant Kobus "Bok" Smit with a Ratel company, infantry Buffel company, 81mm mortar group and an antiaircraft troop of 20mm Ystervark vehicles.

Combat Group Bravo: Commandant Robbie Hartslief leading an infantry Buffel company and platoon, two Casspir infantry companies, an antitank squadron and a support company.

Combat Group Charlie: Maj. Dawid Lotter and a mechanized infantry company, antitank platoon as well as an 81mm mortar group.

The 20th Artillery Regiment was part of the battle group in a support role as needed and included:

P Battery: 127mm Valkiri multiple rocket launchers (originally called the Vorster Orrel or "Vorster's Organ" after the former South African leader but later as the Valkiri), a 20mm antiaircraft troop and UNITA antiaircraft Stinger missile teams.

Q Battery: G5 155mm Leopard howitzers and UNITA antiaircraft Stinger missile teams.

S Battery: 120mm mortars.

SADF 127mm Multiple Rocket Launcher of P Battery, 32 Battalion, in Angola, January 1988.—*Arno Casius*

These artillery units had infantry protection as they operated, usually some distance from the actual front line but they would on occasion end up quite close due to the erratic movements required by a bush war.[26]

Brigade commander Col. Deon Ferreira was previously famous for leading a charge on FAPLA forces in 1980 after an intense firefight at Savate, Angola, where several soldiers nearby were struck down by small arms fire including his intelligence officer. He later went on to become a lieutenant general and chief of staff for joint operations with the creation of the South African National Defence Force in 1994.

The SADF would often produce written orders in great detail, very similar to how the Cubans in Angola operated. South African planners used aerial reconnaissance photographs, reconnaissance patrol reports, intelligence from UNITA patrols, and observations relayed by forward artillery observers.

The plans were rehearsed beforehand and combat groups would spend two days or more in assembly areas conducting routine deployment drills prior to kicking off an operation.

The SADF combat commanders operated far forward reflecting both the operational style of the leaders and the physical conditions of the area. Radio communication and physical line of sight were often problematic due to the thick African bush. Visibility could be less than ten meters when contact was made requiring commanders to move forward to gain a better feel for troop movement during a skirmish. In this "leading from the front" South Africans were completely different from FAPLA leaders who operated under Soviet doctrine, but similar to Cuban commanders.

The brigade operational headquarters was normally ten or more kilometers behind the front lines, being positioned to communicate with frontline units and tactical headquarters. Observation teams were often led by senior officers behind FAPLA lines throughout the battle and the SADF was lucky to have only lost a captain as their highest ranking casualty, excepting aerial combat.[27]

Three SADF UNITA liaison teams led by Col. Fred Oelschig, the senior SADF liaison officer, were deployed alongside UNITA headquarters to update unit movements within the area of operations as well as provide advice on conventional operations and to monitor FAPLA movements. Each team consisted of staff officers, translators, intelligence specialists, and a squad of elite pathfinder soldiers dedicated to the security of the team. The liaison teams would usually move around in Casspir armored personnel carriers and other support vehicles; they were a highly mobile force mandated to conduct limited operations against FAPLA with sufficient supplies to operate independently for up to two months at a time.

The SADF 32 Buffalo Infantry Battalion had operated substantively and successfully in secret during the initial phases of South Africa's border bush war. This unit was created with many former fighters from Holden Roberto's FNLA, whose force had suffered a crashing defeat in late 1975 at the Battle of Dead Road at Quifangondo near Luanda, the capital of Angola, on the cusp of independence. In 1975 South African paratroop commander Col. Jan Breytenbach and his officers went into Namibia with orders to create a hybrid counterinsurgency force from a base near Rundu, Namibia, to operate in South Angola near the Namibian border. This successful and capable force was a tribute to their commander's ability and expertise.

These troops were given proper equipment and operated as an elite operational force year round, often with UNITA troops until 1989. It speaks volumes that this was the most decorated unit of the SADF since World War II and was nicknamed "The Terrible Ones." Operational commands in the field were often made in Portuguese as most of the troops understood this language. Many SADF officers learned those basic commands as they worked extensively with the Buffalo soldiers and UNITA troops.

The Buffalo Battalion was disbanded in 1993, and the former Angolan soldiers were given South African citizenship, and many relocated to the desert town of Pomfret, South Africa, near an old asbestos mine. This Buffalo Battalion that performed many acts of courage and military genius was indeed the tip of the South African spear.

The core SADF battle group, 20 Brigade, was about a thousand men divided more or less equally between Combat Groups Alpha, Bravo, and Charlie. The brigade, was cobbled together with the 32 Infantry Battalion as its center without prior training together as a complete unit. It was a risky move that paid off substantially due to the unique and world class abilities of the SADF combat commanders such as Robbie Hartslief.

The South Africans had an advantage in relatively sophisticated electronic signal interception, translation, and decoding, which is commonplace today, but was revolutionary in 1987. Brigade commander Colonel Ferreira was able to harness this precious information to his strategic movements in a timely manner, which his multinational, leadership-challenged opposition was unable to do at that time. However, the highly fluid nature of the battle meant that centralized interception, translation, and processing of intelligence would never replace combat strength and skill.

Senior Air Force officers from Chile were seconded to the SADF as electronic surveillance operators. These Spanish-speaking aviation experts along with SADF Portuguese translators were able to monitor Cuban MiG and FAPLA radio traffic to provide the SADF with quality intelligence and warnings of impending action. This was supported by initial SAAF aviation logistics superiority compared to their foes, which decreased the closer they approached Cuito Cuanavale and Cuban air superiority.

Additionally, South Africa utilized a small Seeker drone aircraft that could provide a couple hours of aerial reconnaissance up to two hundred kilometers from its base. In a significant military development ahead of its time, but commonly used today, real-time video was fed to SADF controllers. The FAPLA air defense network was able to locate and track the Seekers, but they proved difficult to shoot down. It is estimated that FAPLA fired seventeen SAMs at the first drones before finally striking one. Two Seekers were shot down, the last by a SA-8 missile, but they provided great assistance in locating suitable targets for artillery without loss of precious SAAF aircraft. This antidrone activity also drained FAPLA of valuable SAM missiles.

Mobile electronic collection Casspirs monitored FAPLA tactical com-

A side view of two Soviet SA-8 Gecko short-range, all-weather weapon systems.
—defenseimagery.mil

munications sufficiently close to the front that they were subject to occasional MiG attacks such as on 21 February 1988 that killed two signalmen. This important capability obtained FAPLA casualty statistics, indications of morale, and movement plans. Signals intelligence also enabled gunners to adjust their artillery fire by listening to FAPLA shell reports to headquarters. More sophisticated electronic eavesdropping was done from Namibia and collected operational-level traffic between Luanda and the front.

Despite this, SADF field commanders often lacked accurate information on the exact location and plans of FAPLA forces as most human intelligence came from UNITA, which possessed sources throughout the area. Some deceptive information resulted from the recurring problem of UNITA manipulation of the SADF by disseminating information that might lead to military actions that only suited UNITA purposes.

Not to be outdone, the Cubans had an Afrikaans interpreter in Ronald Herboldt, a South African from Cape Town who had joined the Cuban Rev-

Colonel Deon Ferreira during a planning session in Angola believed to be counterattack plans, Lomba River October 1987.—*SANDF Documentation Centre*

olution when his ship docked there in 1959. He subsequently volunteered to fight in Angola and was a useful Afrikaans translator intelligence asset who also served on the Joint Military Monitoring Commission that oversaw South Africa withdrawal from Angola. Later in his life, one film portrayed him as between a rock and a hard place, unrecognized by his Cuban masters and returning home to impoverished anonymity. There were also less "public" intelligence assets such as ANC sympathizers in the SADF acknowledged by former ANC military wing (Umkhonto We Sizwe) official Ronnie Kasrils as likely sources of information leading to South African intervention in Angola. The perils of a divided South Africa at war.[28]

While Ronald Herboldt was an important intelligence asset for the Cubans battlefield communications (signals intelligence) have to be interpreted in real time, which is impossible for a single individual to accomplish. Also, battlefield communications are not just made by in-the-clear radio transmissions. One means the South African commanders used to communicate with front-line units was encrypted telex messages. While the East German component of the FAPLA had the capacity to intercept these messages, they could not always break the encryption. The telex messages were generally considered to be safe by the South African military.

Front-line communications were by voice, and the SADF technology at that time used the high-frequency scatter band that splits voice messages into millions of pieces over a range of difference frequencies called "frequency hoppers." As there was no time for encryption, these radio communications could be intercepted, but the use of VHF meant a limited transmission radius, so any interception unit would have to be relatively close to the transmitter. In the mobile warfare scenario at the Lomba River, this would have been a daunting challenge to any interception by FAPLA eavesdroppers.

Small data entry terminal (DET) devices, in combination with the frequency hopping capability of the radios to which they were attached, were extensively used for routine encryption of all messages between command headquarters. The DET was a handheld device that allowed keyed entry of messages which were subsequently sent via a manpack or vehicle-mounted radio. At the command-and-control level in the rear there was actually very little voice traffic, and no operations information was passed by voice; the only voice transmissions were at lower, tactical levels of the units.

The South Africans were able to intercept many FAPLA transmissions until they closed in on Cuito when FAPLA commanders began to use landlines, which limited the SADF intelligence gathering capability. A further development at this time was the radio silence adopted by MiG pilots in the course of their sorties to prevent any monitoring of their transmissions. This was a procedure later adopted by the 20 Brigade forces during MiG attacks as it was felt that the Cuban attacks could home in on their radio transmissions.

Reconnaissance units used coded text to protect their positions from compromise as they were deployed in visual contact with the FAPLA, usually as artillery and airstrike observers. Voice communications where local enemy interception was possible were risky and best avoided. During the SADF campaign leading up to Cuito their reconnaissance units had the FAPA airfields at Longa and Menongue under constant observation. Troops in the field were usually able to receive several minutes warning when the MiGs departed for a bombing run. Later on there was suspicion that FAPLA recon units had achieved a similar capability, but it was more likely due to their superior radar coverage.

In September 1987 effective tactical jamming of the FAPLA tank VHF radio network by the SADF at the Lomba River made a significant contribution to their confusion and ultimately, the destruction of many FAPLA tanks. Electronic countermeasures were performed by specialized Ratels that formed part of the 61st Mechanised Battalion.[29]

Soviet, Cuban and, FAPLA commanders had access to accurate satellite image maps whereas the SADF were thought to have been confined to aerial photos and older maps, but their field officers could access a satellite naviga-tion system. In one 1986 report, UNITA soldiers observed surveillance of the area near Cuito Cuanavale by a Soviet Antonov 33 reconnaissance plane at about 15,000 feet, outside range of their weapons, which could produce excellent images to be used for MiG attacks later.[30]

There was a limited amount of South African Air Force involvement in the battle due to restricted availability of Mirages as well as effective FAPLA

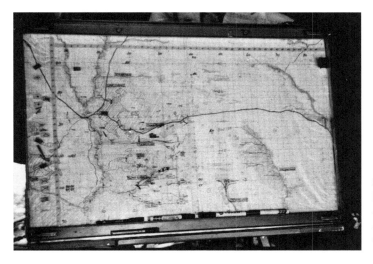

SADF Briefing Map Angola. —SANDF Documentation Centre

Soviet antiaircraft weaponry and radar. The SAAF Chief was General Den-nis Earp , no relation to Wyatt, who commanded Mirage F1AZ No. 1 and No. 3 squadrons during the battle. The squadrons were based in northern Namibia at Grootfontein and Rundu respectively. Squadron pilots included:

NO. 1 SQUADRON:
 Commandant Johan Rankin, Commander
 Major Frans Coetzee
 Major Ed Every
 Major J. P. Gouws
 Major Norman Minne
 Major Paulus Truter
 Captain Rikus de Beer
 Captain Digby Holdsworth
 Captain Dawid Kleynhans

Captain Trompie Nel
Captain Chris Skinner
Captain Willie van Coppenhagen
Captain Reg van Eeden

NO. 3 SQUADRON:
Commandant Carlo Gagiano, Commander
Commandant Dries Wehmeyer
Captain Les Bennett
Captain Mark Crooks
Captain Jaco de Beer
Captain Pierre du Plessis
Captain Seun van Heerden
Captain Pierre Joubert
Captain Johan Lubbe
Captain Rudi Mes
Captain Arthur Piercey
Captain Mark Raymond
Captain John Sinclair
Captain Frank Tonkin
Captain Clive Turner
Captain Anton van Rensburg
Captain Andre Schoeman
Captain Carel Wessels[31]

Other aircraft and pilots were Captain Andre Stapa who flew the light attack Impala Mk 2 and Lieutenant Richard Glynn who flew a light plane observation aircraft, the Atlas AM3C Bosbok Pilot, usually accompanied by an SADF forward artillery observer.

Frans Coetzee, a SAAF Mirage F1AZ fighter pilot from No. 1 Squadron achieved some notoriety later on when he was arrested in January 2003 for alleged involvement in a multimillion dollar cocaine smuggling scheme while being employed as a pilot instructor for British Aerospace in Australia. Coetzee, a former goldmine worker, was drafted to the infantry in 1975 and then transferred for pilot training with the SAAF. He was a respected pilot who flew many missions into Angola during the Battle of Cuito Cuanavale and retired from the SAAF in 1998 as a lieutenant colonel and flight instructor.[32]

The South African Air Force found that Western aircraft munitions were inappropriate for Angola and often exploded with little shrapnel damage in the sandy soil. The SAAF then developed its own fragmentation bombs with small steel balls that burst above the heads of ground troops and equipment, like a shower from hell. These were the 250 kilogram Mark 82 munition, some with high-drag tail fins for low altitude release that were changed with larger steel balls for maximum damage to vehicles. This type of airburst munition was cutting-edge at that time, but is in common use today.

On open ground a single SAAF strike could cause numerous casualties and equipment damage. G5 howitzer crews would use groundburst shells on a FAPLA bunker complex to collapse it followed by airburst ammunition to finish off any soldiers who escaped.

Segmented bombs with delayed fuses were also utilized to allow for immediate and later detonation in any dense FAPLA controlled area. In a precursor to laser-painted targets for bomb delivery the SADF had the capability for surreptitious insertion of a radio marker to guide bombs to FAPLA targets, although it could be a dangerous exercise in such close proximity to troops.[33]

———

The sanctions against South Africa lead to their development of weapons that did not see popular usage until conflicts nearly a decade or two later. Examples of these were the mobile G5 155mm howitzer with an accurate range up to 40 kilometers (Although according to Brig. Gen. Dick Lord, after international sanctions were put in place against South Africa, artillery captured from the Angolan FAPLA became the most reliable source of arms procurement.); armored all-wheel-drive vehicles with antimine capability like the Buffel and Casspir that operated well in the dusty bush conditions of the African bush over long distances; and small unmanned aircraft and smart bombs such as the one that destroyed the Cuito Cuanavale bridge in 1988.

It was the G5 and its motorized version the G6 that were one of the main equipment architects of battlefield success for the SADF. The G5 was produced by Lyttelton Engineering Works near Pretoria with steel manufactured at the Union Steel Corporation mill also in South Africa from a design by Canadian Gerald Bull. The barrel consisted of a muzzle brake and a hinged breech block with piston ram mechanism that positioned the shell uniformly at whatever elevation followed by hand loaded explosive charges. It was this human intervention aspect of the sequence that led to the occasional accident.

A useful and time saving feature was that it was not necessary to lower

The G5 155mm howitzer, and it's motorized version, the G6, were developed and produced in South Africa by Denel Land Systems. The G5 design was based on the Canadian GC-45 155mm gun, which was highly modified to suit southern African conditions. This 2005 photo shows an ex-*Iraqi G-5 on display at the U.S. Army Field Artillery Museum, Ft. Sill, Oklahoma.—Sturmvogel 66 (Wikimedia)*

the barrel between shots to ram the shell. After a shell has been fired and the barrel assembly has returned to its normal position, the breech would open automatically. The ram and load system consisted of a swing tray affixed to the rear cradle of the recoil system and moved in elevation with the gun.

When the G5 was to be fired, the carriage was lifted by a hydraulic firing platform with a wishbone and piston configuration that resisted fouling by debris and could be raised when the gun was being moved. The G5 utilized standard vehicle tires which was convenient when spares need to be cannibalized from other vehicles. On the G6 version the operator seat was mounted at the front to afford good visibility during movement. When being towed by the gun tractor, the barrel of the cannon was held by a barrel clamp, and although a crew of five was normally used to bring the gun into action, two men were able to do so, but less efficiently.

The fire control system included display units which show the firing data for the howitzer, with communication between the fire control center and the gun by radio or land line. The fire control system also included a muzzle velocity analyzer and a meteorological ground station. This unit, which was transported on a trailer, tracked, received, and processed information from the launching of the shell to its impact. This data was turned into meteorological information which was then supplied to artillery units. A meteorological balloon was also sent up, which was often mistaken as an aircraft and caused wasted SAM missiles being fired by the FAPLA or their Soviet advisors.

The gun-tow tractor was made from a converted Withings recovery vehicle chassis and would normally accommodate the crew of eight, although only five operated the gun when in action. Fifteen projectile pallets, each weighing nearly two hundred kilograms would be carried by the gun tractor, and a hydraulic crane situated at the rear of the vehicle provided the muscle for handling. Iraq obtained about a hundred G5's in 1985, and during the Iran-Iraq War (1980–1988) Iraqi artillery units fired several hundred rounds per gun per day, which often led to a shortage of shells.[34]

A strong arm of the SADF was the Ratel infantry fighting vehicle which performed reasonably well at the Lomba River and had several turreted versions with 20mm cannons and 90mm cannons, as well as an antitank guided-missile model. The Ratel 90mm replaced the Eland MK 6 which was itself an upgraded version of the French Panhard armored car. The 90mm cannon was a quick firing, low pressure recoil gun with a range of two thousand meters with high explosive (HE) and twelve hundred meters with high explosive antitank (HEAT) rounds. Other armament included a coaxial 7.62mm machine gun mounted on the side of the turret that was fired electrically by the gunner. A second machine gun was mounted on the turret for use by the crew commander against enemy infantry and other soft targets. A third cupola machine gun at the rear of the vehicle would normally be manned by one of the infantry passengers. It was also equipped with 81mm mortars and four rifle ports on each side. This vehicle usually carried a crew of three with a turret crew of gunner and crew commander who also acted as an ammunition loader. The driver sat at the front in the main compartment with a six-man

Denel G6-45 155mm howitzer at Ysterplaat Airshow, Cape Town, in December 2006.—*DanieVDM Wikimedia)*

infantry squad, but in this particular conflict several UNITA soldiers sometimes rode on the outside. The Ratel was not completely infallible with thin armor, poor mobility in muddy terrain, and tires that would fall victim to sharp pieces of tree branches, but it was very reliable and easy to maintain. In the event a rear or middle wheel was blown off the Ratel had the ability to hang one axle and still travel at a reduced speed.

These fighting vehicles were sufficiently robust to push through the African bush while providing a ready vantage point to locate FAPLA troops.[35]

SADF Ratel in Angola.—*SANDF Documentation Centre*

Eventually there were three SADF operations leading up to and the end of the Battle of Cuito Cuanavale being operations Modular, Hooper, and Packer in that order. During this time many of the SADF soldiers in Angola were National Service conscripts required by South African law to do a two-year tour of duty.

All white South African males were required to register for military service at age sixteen by completing a form and sending it to the registration office of the SADF in Pretoria. A registration certificate would be returned with an SADF number the first two numbers of which indicated year of registration and the last two letters whether the person was a volunteer or conscript. This number was frequently written inside boots, web belts or under pocket flaps. All immigrants who had lived in South Africa for more than five years and who were between the ages of fifteen and twenty-five were naturalized by a 1984 act of parliament and therefore all male immigrants were eligible to be called up for national service.

About a year before call-up for training the conscript would receive a notification of allotment for national service stating the place to go and the dates of service, usually two years. A further notice with a rail pass, if necessary, was sent a month before training was to start. Conscripts on the train were frequently accompanied by a guard from the citizen force called campers. The service period included training and dispatch to an operational area depending on factors such as the conscript himself, the need for troops, and the time units had already been in the field.

Recruits were all medically classified after inspection on arrival. An identification system of letters and numbers were utilized to denote physical and mental fitness. G1K1 was a physically and mentally fit soldier with the letter G for physical health and K, the mental state. The number indicated the level so a G1K4 was physically perfect but had serious mental issues. An asthma sufferer would be a G3K1 and would be given a non-physically demanding job such as desk clerk.[36]

Training took place in three phases over six to seven months:

1. Basics: drill instruction, physical training, rifle training, survival training and field craft for movement in the day or night as well as camouflage.
2. Specialization: gunnery, driving, or support infantry.
3. Troop handling: consisted of training together in troops of four Ratels with a support infantry section of eight men. Crew commanders were selected at the start of this phase from the soldiers who took the gunnery course.

A final evaluation of each soldier was undertaken in a mock combat situation to establish his readiness after which operational deployment would take place. Operational duty was five to six months for National Service combatants but could also include a second tour of duty. The SADF had to fight with conscripts who regularly rotated into the active-duty force because South Africa simply did not have a sufficiently large standing professional force at the time to otherwise fulfill its committments. With the end of apartheid this has been resolved by the creation of the modern South African National Defence Force (SANDF) and the end of conscription.[37]

Some national service conscripts such as university students or the well-connected were excused military or combat service by an exemption board. With only a few exceptions, rarely were sons of the rich and powerful sent to fight the sons of the poor and powerless in the Angolan bush.

Those who objected to conscription as conscientious objectors faced prison sentences. On 12 November 1987 Dr. Ivan Toms was charged under a 1983 law prescribing the imprisonment of conscientious objectors. Dr. Toms had been ordered to report to an SADF camp that day. He was sentenced to twenty-one months in prison in 1988 for defying the order and ultimately served nine months in Pollsmoor Prison. Toms had already served as a lieutenant in the SADF and completed two years of military service after which he founded the first permanent clinic in the shanty town of Crossroads near Cape Town. Prior to his civil disobedience, in 1985, Crossroads had been bulldozed and his clinic closed. At the time of his unexpected death in 2008 he was Director of Health for Cape Town. By 1988 the number of objectors and others who avoided conscription had increased from the hundreds to the thousands.

Training in Ratels at the time of the battle usually took place at the Lohatla Army Battle School located in the in the northern Cape and started with each platoon going out to a designated area to learn how to integrate infantry skills with the operation of the Ratel. Recruits were trained in the correct way to set up an overnight base or laager area with four vehicles facing outward aligned with a point of the compass and the troops dispersed in between the vehicles to create a defensive circle. The unit would attempt to simultaneously switch off engines, theoretically preventing the opposition from knowing exact vehicle numbers.

SADF soldiers usually rode in their armored vehicles until contact was imminent when they debussed to conduct conventional operations. FAPLA antiarmor units posed a serious threat as vehicles in transit or troops late in departing would ultimately discover in Angola. The vehicles also contributed to troop independence of movement with storage for food, water and ammunition to support the squad in the field for an extended period.

Training also included ambushes with claymore mines, mine mattresses to traverse a mine field and in minefield-extraction drills with and without injured personnel. A mine mattress was a meter wide piece of foam with a hard plastic stepping platform on one side and a center area painted yellow to stand on. It worked on the principle of distributing weight over the area of the mine mattress thereby preventing sufficient pressure to activate the mine.

The majority of training time was spent conducting fire maneuvers with each section broken down into fire teams.

Ratel integration was practiced to enable rapid exit followed by fire and maneuver in coordinated movement forward with the vehicle. Sitting in the back of the Ratel was often hot and uncomfortable in the full SADF combat gear of helmet, combat battle jacket, and rifle. Live-fire exercises included tracer rounds as part of the ammunition with the machine gun using four rounds of the normal ball ammunition followed by one tracer round. Tracer rounds have red phosphorous in the rear of the bullet to track the bullet, especially at night, but the impact can be used as a target indicator. Some soldiers used to load tracers as the last rounds in their magazine to warn them to change their magazine. Red tracers are the standard for NATO forces while green was used by the Soviets.

SADF officers were told to control their units directly to ensure minimum casualties and adherence to combat drills as well as standard operating procedures. Drill comprehension was essential to avoid unnecessary risks without hampering the initiative of the units. In the Angolan bush the SADF high command anticipated significant casualties while the South African political hierarchy insisted on achieving the greatest result possible with the least risk of casualties through employment of cautious tactics.

This was the basis of the standard SADF attack chain of air attacks followed by G5 and multiple-rocket-launched (MRL) artillery before the final assault by infantry protected in armored vehicles, often with UNITA soldiers riding on the outside. Close to Cuito the SADF always tried to wait for inclement weather to provide a protective screen for their assaults to prevent Cuban MiG attacks as they flew under strict ground-based radar control.

On some occasions the casualty-averse South Africans would delay or abandon planned attacks when faced with injuries or fatalities. Whole units would be brought to a standstill as commanders sought to evacuate the wounded and dead, often taking personal charge. The military and ultimately cultural differences between the opposing forces couldn't be greater in this method of operation.[38]

Many SADF conscripts who did end up in Angola received a two-year exemption from further national service; these exemptions, however were not always honored by the authorities. This was confirmed by a booklet with a special number denoting combat service after leaving the Angolan theater of operations. For the South Africans' Cuban counterparts, who usually served a full two years in combat, and the Angolans on both sides whose military service only ended through death, defection, or victory, there was no relief. It was not unknown for convicted South African criminals to be let out of prison to do military service and thereby reduce their sentences.[39]

Members of the SADF were issued a military pass book which they were required to carry on their person at all times when on leave. This book specified the authorized periods of absence from the particular SADF unit in sufficient detail to include form of attire that was allowed. In this the South African military mirrored the apartheid government's requirement that black South Africans also had to have a pass book outside their areas of residence: oppressed and oppressor conjoined by a robotic bureaucracy.

SADF field units usually communicated solely in Afrikaans, and official documents issued at the time of the battle would have both English and Afrikaans versions in the same document. It was quite natural, somewhat akin to the former southern-rural predominance of men in the American armed forces, that Afrikaaners from farm and hunting backgrounds provided the backbone of the South African military forces. English-speaking SADF troops were a definite minority and occasionally subject to discrimination.

Recruit Russell Jones had this confirmed to him on arrival for training:

> Once everyone had arrived we were called together as a company and introduced to our Company Sergeant Major (CSM) who was Staff Sergeant Basson, he was an ex-parabat who wore his para wings and jump boots, jump boots are higher than normal issue boots. He asked who amongst us were English speakers; whereupon a fair number of hands were raised. He then told us "The army is 50-50; 50 English and 50 Afrikaans, we have had fifty years English, *dis nou vyftig jaar Afrikaans, julle sal Afrikaans praat*" (it is now fifty years Afrikaans, you will speak Afrikaans). As I had not been in the country for the two years prior to this my Afrikaans, which wasn't excellent in the first place, was extremely rusty. By the end of basics I was fluent in Afrikaans and at times during my national service I would even speak Afrikaans in my sleep.[40]

Here is where another similarity shared by the opposing forces presents itself: just as there was a pervasive belief that black Cubans were more likely to be sent to the Angola front, so it was with English ancestry and speaking South Africans. While there are no published statistics to confirm or refute this belief, there is ample anecdotal evidence.[41]

The SADF followed Protestant Christian practice with prayers before meals and at meetings. Chaplains wearing purple berets often accompanied troops on operations as they do in other armies such as the American and British. The chaplains provided comfort to many troops, both believers and others. There was no official religious devotion among the Soviet, Cuban, or FAPLA troops, but there is pervasive speculation about the men's inner thoughts and cries of *Dios!* or *Dues!* on the Angolan battlefield.[42]

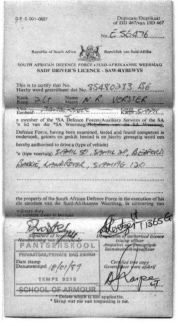

SADF driver's license.—*Roelof Voster/ Historical Papers Library, University of the Witwatersrand*

The basic pay for a SADF soldier was 193 rand per month making them the highest paid in combatant in Angola. They also received 4.80 Rand per day as danger money (combat pay) when in combat areas and an increase of 100 Rand if they were promoted to lance-corporal. Many SADF soldiers fantasized about the money they would have saved up after a combat tour.[43]

Despite poison warning by officers, it was common practice among SADF troops to loot food supplies, usually tinned seafood, from dead Cuban or FAPLA troops. Certainly the SADF lost the battle of quality, but not

SADF Olifant crew member preparing rations, Operation Modular, Angola 1987.—*Roland De Vries*

SADF soldier bush bath in Angola.—*SANDF Documentation Centre*

quantity of rations issued to their men. The standard SADF ration consisted of heat tablets, matches, coffee, tea, sugar, porridge, powdered drink, can of meat, can of vegetables, candy bars, a roll of sweets, cheese, and biscuits. Sometimes the troops received condensed milk which was hugely popular among all sides for its sweet taste and energy boost.

Troops in the field received mail from home which sometimes included parcels with extra goods, which certainly boosted morale. All letters from the troops to home, if allowed, would be censored by the immediate commanders for any combat-action and other operational information as well as issues of morale or living conditions.

After a period of time in the Angola operational area SADF troops began to be plagued by stomach ailments, jaundice, malaria and hepatitis which did not help morale and their limited numbers. Malaria tablets were standard issue and compulsory for all ranks. The most frequent illness was diarrhea, called "gippo guts" by the troops, which was caused by the unsanitary conditions of bush life. Evacuations of sick soldiers began in the tens of numbers and some died from their illnesses. Again, this was a mirrored by the Cuban soldiers who were also in an unfamiliar environment. It is possible that illness took more casualties than bullets or shrapnel during the battle.

South African troops returning from action in Angola were usually flown out from Mavinga to Rundu and then to Camp 22 for rest, good food, and psychological fitness tests in preparation for the return home.[44]

CHAPTER **4**

THE FAPLA SOVIET ADVISORS

There were about six thousand FAPLA Soviet advisors in Angola covering tactical and technical areas at the time of the Lomba River action in 1987–88. There were instructor pilots, air crews, and ZAS communication specialists.

Among them was Igor Zhdarkin who was attached to the FAPLA 21st Brigade as a a translator and specialist advisor. He confirmed that many Soviet military personnel were on front-line duty, operating equipment and directing combat action. This became clear at the first major clash between opposing forces at the Lomba River which caused the urgent helicopter evacuation of senior Soviet officers from the battlefield when the tide turned. This was not completely surprising as there were by some estimates between fifty and a hundred Soviets soldiers (officers and enlisted men) in each FAPLA Brigade often operating at front-line levels and assisting in combat operations. Despite reports to the contrary, however, there has been no confirmation that Soviet snipers were involved in Angola during this time period or at all; indeed no Soviet SVD sniper rifles were ever thought to be available.[45]

The Soviet forces in Angola were supervised by General Mikhail Petrov who would send directives to the Soviet overall commander in Angola, Lt. Gen.Leonid Kuzmenko, who about to be replaced at the time of Cuito by Lt. Gen.Pavel Gusev. General Gusev would then issue operational orders to the numerous Portuguese-fluent Soviets attached to FAPLA units such as the 21st Brigade. A few of the Soviet officers in Angola were:

Colonel Vyacheslav Alexandrovich Mityaev	
Colonel Gorb	Interpreter
Lieutenant Colonel A. A. Mikhailovich	Chief Advisor
Lieutenant Colonel S. Y. Pavlovich	Chief Artillery Advisor
Lieutenant Colonel Igor Anatolevich Zhdarkin	
Major D. C. Rashidovich	
Captain V. Vyacheslav	SA-8 AA Missile Specialist
Lieutenant Oleg Snitko	Interpreter
Second Lieutenant Z. I. Anatolyevich	Interpreter
Sergeant-Major F. A. Mikhailovich	Technical Specialist

Although there is some anecdotal evidence that Soviet pilots flew MiGs during the Battle of Cuito Cuanavale it is commonly believed that this was unlikely, although possible in the earlier period of the Angolan civil war. It is more likely that the Soviet pilots maintained a technical and training presence in the rearguard safety of Luanda.[46]

CHAPTER **5**

THE ANGOLAN FAPLA

The FAPLA army was led by the Minister of Defence Pedro Maria Tonha also known by his nom de guerre of Pedalé.

In addition there were:

General Antonio Dos Santos Franca (N'Dalu)	Vice-Minister of Defence and Chief of General Staff
General Alberto Correia Neto	Vice-Minister of Defence and Commander FAPA/DAA (Forca Aerea Popular De Angola/Defesa Aerea y Anti Aerea) Angolan Air Force and Antiaircraft.
Rear Admiral António José Condessa de Carvalho (Toka)	Vice-Minister of Defence and Commander MGPA (Marinhade Guerra Popular De Angola) People's Navy of Angola.
Paiva Domingos da Silva	Directorate Commander Directorate of People's Defence and Territorial Troops or ODP (Organização de Defesa Popular)[47]

Some of the FAPLA senior officers were:

General Roberto Leal Monteiro (Ngongo)	Deputy Chief of General Staff
General Geraldo Sachipengo (Nunda)[48]	
General Pedro Lima (Foguetão or Rocket)	Chief of Operations Division, Commander Lomba Front
General Matias Lima Coelho (Nzumbi)	
Colonel Mateus Miguel Angelo (Vietnam), General Vietnam	
Lieutenant Colonel Mario Placido Cirilo de Sa (Ita)	Intelligence Chief
Lieutenant Colonel Agostinho Nelumba (Sanjar), General Sanjar	Chief Advanced HQ, Cuito Cuanavale
Lieutenant Colonel Antas	Commander Logistics Supply from Menongue to Cuito Cuanavale
Lieutenant Colonel Armando da Cruz Neto	Commander 4th Military region, Huambo
Colonel Manuel Correia de Barros	Commander MGPA Kuando Kubango, Chief of FAPLA Central Headquarters, Operations Direction Center
Colonel Domingos Hungo	
Lieutenant Colonel Joao Baptista de Matos	Major Regional Commandant 1987
Colonel Da Silva Neto	
Colonel Alexandre Lemos de Lucas (Bota Militar)	

Major Joao Domingos Baptista Cordeiro (Ngueto)	Commander Cuito Cuanavale
Lieutenant General Ngueto[49]	
Brigade Commander N'Geleka	
Commander Silva	47th Brigade
Commander George Chikoti[50]	
Colonel Mele Francisco Camacho	
Major Armindo Moreira	
Major Batista	
Major Tobias	47th Brigade Commander
Major Mateus Timoteo	
Major Roberto Fernando de Matos	

General Roberto Leal Monteiro (Ngongo) served as Angolan ambassador to the Russian Federation 2000–2006 and and became the country's minister of internal affairs in 2006, but his combat record at the front in 1987–88 during the Battle of Cuito Cuanavale is unknown. In this he was similar to many in the present Angolan leadership who shared the spoils of war while not having had to face the inferno of Cuito.

Defence Minister Pedale would not live to see his successor General Ndalu enjoy the fruits of the unified state with his appointment to the board of De Beers Angola but succumbed to a protracted illness in London in 1995. Retired General Joao de Matos (FAPLA commander at Cuito) also enjoyed retirement with his diamond mining enterprise, Genius Mineira, in the former UNITA controlled territory of Cuando Cubango province. Portuguese legal authorities recently refused an attempt to stop publication of a book by Rafael Marques that highlighted the alleged corrupt involvement of Ndalu and seven other generals in the diamond trade.[51]

FAA Lt. Gen. Joao Domingos Baptista Cordeiro (Ngueto) also did not live to see a prosperous and peaceful Angola. Like many officers who distinguished themselves on all sides, he is prematurely no longer with us, having died in a helicopter crash shortly after the lasting 2002 peace accord with his former UNITA adversary Lt. Col. Felisberto Mortalha on board. Ngueto had featured prominently in many skirmishes near Cuito and proven himself to be a capable, but realistic commander. The Hind military helicopter he and Mortalha were riding in, along with with several soldiers and journalists crashed in bad weather east of Luanda near the northern Angolan city of Ndalatando while on the way to a UNITA demobilization ceremony at Mussabo. At the time of his death, Ngueto was the the military commander of the Kwanza-Bengo front.[52]

The way the FAPLA command structure at Cuito Cuanavale operated was that Minister Pedale would send instructions to Colonel Mateus Angelo (Vietnam), who had abruptly returned from training in Russia to participate in Cuito. Vietnam would then pass on orders to the relevant commander on the ground, such as Major Joao Domingos Baptista Cordeiro (Ngueto).[53]

The FAPLA had an estimated ninety thousand soldiers organized into more than seventy brigades throughout Angola's ten military regions. These forces were strategically placed in the oil-producing Cabinda Province, the area around the capital of Luanda, and the southern provinces where the majority of UNITA and SADF attacks occurred. Cuito Cuanavale was part of the 6th Military Region.

By 1987 the Soviet Union poured more than one billion dollars worth of military supplies to the FAPLA annually along with several thousand North Korean, East German, Russian, and Vietnamese advisors with various skills who assisted the FAPLA in a veritable Babellian counterinsurgency coalition against UNITA and their South African supporters. Included among this massive train of equipment and supplies were hundreds of T-55 tanks, assorted armored fighting vehicles, field artillery, multiple rocket launchers, mortars, antiaircraft systems, and antitank weapons. Some FAPLA units were equipped with Strela man portable (MANPAD) missiles and ZRK mobile SA-8 missile systems, a sophisticated Soviet air defence system designed to protect ground forces from air attack that proved highly effective against SAAF helicopters as well as discouraging Mirage attacks. The Soviet SA-8 missiles also turned out to be an effective but unfortunate assassin of SADF weather balloons and drones.

The FAPLA forces were organized in brigades of two motorized infantry battalions, three regular infantry battalions, and two marine landing and assault units. The 21st, 16th, 47th and 59th FAPLA Brigades operated in tactical groups comprised T-55 tanks, BTR armored personnel carriers, PB amphibious armored personnel carriers, BM-21 truck-mounted 122mm

Destroyed FAPLA Soviet-made T-55 tank.—*SANDF Documentation Centre*

multiple rocket launchers, and BMP or "Troyka" infantry combat vehicles with 73mm cannon. These were the units that saw the most action leading up to the Battle of Cuito Cuanavale, but they rarely operated at more than 50 percent strength due to shortages of material and manpower, as well as combat casualties.

Common Soviet tactical theory had a squad of T-55 tanks with infantry to deal with any antitank defenses lead an attack, followed by BMP, BTR, and BP armored personnel carriers for fire support. Perfect for fighting on the steppes of Russia, but difficult for the African bush. For example, the FAPLA lost fifteen vehicles when nine BMP's were destroyed and six BMP's were captured by the SADF and UNITA in October–November 1987 at the Lomba River. This archaic European World War II strategy was imposed on Angola, a desperate third-world country with limited resources and a nascent officer corps.

Contrary to popular belief, not all FAPA aircraft had Soviet or Cuban pilots with the exception of the Cuban-only MiGs during the Battle of Cuito Cuanavale. Angolan pilots were sent on year-long courses to the Soviet Union to train in Hind helicopters and these graduates were just beginning to come on line at the time of the battle. These included the Hind Mi-24 attack helicopter gunship, also known as the Devil's Chariot. One SADF soldier near Cuito described the Hind helicopter as a flying tank that had sufficient fire power to take out an entire unit. It was something that terrified the South Africans for they had no solution to this threat if they were caught while moving over open terrain.

Twelve Mi-24 helicopters were operated by the FAPA 4th Helicopter Squadron, a part of 22nd Helicopter Transport-Attack Regiment. The Hind's cabin could carry eight combat troops or four loaded stretchers. Wing systems allowed for mounting rocket pods, gun pods and antitank missile systems. Wingstubs compliment the armament by allowing the ability to arm the helicopter with air-to-air missiles for self-defense. An undernose turret system filled out the roster of firepower available to the pilot and gunner. This weapons platform was dangerous to ground troops caught in the open as happened during the the assault on Cuito.

FAPA Angolan pilot Vontade with Hind Mi-24 attack helicopter, 1988.
—Tom Cooper collection

The man with the most dangerous job in the FAPLA was Lieutenant Colonel Antas, commander of the logistics supply from Menongue to Cuito Cuanavale. This involved organizing and often leading road caravans that were often struck by aircraft and artillery bombardment, and had to watch out for landmines, as well. He was lucky to have come through the war unscathed. The Marinhade Guerra Popular De Angola (MGPA) or People's Navy of Angola could have made extensive use of the many navigable rivers of Angola to move material and troops free of aerial attacks or landmines. It would have been difficult for the SADF or UNITA to attack MGPA riverine boat traffic. An MGPA base could also have been conveniently established close to Cuito Cuanavale. Unfortunately for the FAPLA soldiers, little use was made of Angola's navy in a riverine role. The navy's rule was ultimately logistical and not offensive during the battle.

There is substantial evidence that elements under the control of FAPLA had engaged in forcible recruitment of minors at the time of the Battle of Cuito Cuanavale. The Angolan government has had conscription since 1993 for all males between the ages of twenty and forty-five. The conscripts are are required to serve for two years, including training time, and the government has rounded up young males who have not voluntarily reported for registration and drafting. There is a school of thought that the forced integration of young men from different tribes and dialects would help foster a stronger national identity under the coutry's common language of Portuguese.[54]

Although defections were almost unknown among the Cubans or SADF, they occurred with some frequency between the upper echelons of the FAPLA and UNITA, somewhat like what prevails in Afghanistan today.

The FAPLA artillery was substantially less effective than that of the SADF because FAPLA did not make extensive use of forward artillery observers infiltrated close to enemy positions as did the SADF. Both FAPLA field artillery and the high flying bombers of the FAPA units were known for their consistently inaccurate bombardments. This often led to apathy by the opposing forces, who were only occasionally caught off guard. The SADF soldiers never encountered any FAPLA forward observers, which was seen as a basic error in the conflict. Further, the arcs of artillery fire of the FAPLA units were closely tracked to create a deployment map which became a useful tool for SADF counterbattery fire. One desperate tactic employed by FAPLA units when under artillery bombardment by SADF's long-ranging G5 howitzers was to set off random explosions to try to confuse the artillery forward observers as to the actual location of their fire.

Cuban officers were in agreement on the high proficiency of the G5 fire and one declared, "If you fired a salvo to them, in less than two minutes the answer would land for sure in your place."[55]

One simple tactic attempted by FAPLA troops to prevent UNITA infiltration in the deep bush was dogs. Unfortunately they were no match for the stand-off forward observers and the withering SADF artillery that followed.

The overall quality of FAPLA forces may be discerned from a 1984 ANC Umkhonto we Sizwe report:

> FAPLA troops used in this campaign were poorly trained (on average, they had received only two weeks' training). Captain Sabastiao, the Brigade Commander is speedily singled out for his inefficiency in planning operations. There were also criticisms against some members of our administration. During one operation, our comrades, together with FAPLA comrades, spent three days marching on the other side of the River Kwanza in enemy territory without sufficient food. Most of the time no reconnaissance was carried out. No direct contact with the enemy forces was made. Every time they came to a base it was found to be deserted. On the other hand, they fell into ambushes. Comrades began to believe that FAPLA was heavily infiltrated and that the Brigade Commander Captain Sabastiao was quite incompetent and a "sell out."[56]

CHAPTER 6

THE ANGOLAN UNITA

One of the better UNITA military leaders was Division General Arlindo Chenda Pena, known as General Ben Ben after the Algerian revolutionary leader Ahmed Ben Bella. He was a nephew of Savimbi who had received extensive military training in Europe and Morocco before rapid advancement to general and front commander. He was the deputy UNITA chief of staff operating from headquarters on the Lomba River and assisted in his liaison with the SADF by Major Mickey and Captain Walther, so known in reference to his German sidearm.[57]

Among other UNITA officers at the time were:

Jonas Savimbi	Commander in Chief
Brigadier Demosthenes Amos Chilingutila	Chief of Staff
General Antonio Sebastiao Dembo	Northern Front Chief
Brigadier Samuel Martinho Epalanga	Chief Liaison Officer SADF
Brigadier Geraldo Sachipengo Nunda	Northern Front Commander 1984
General Abreu Muhengu Ukwachitembo (Kamorteiro)	
General Esteves Pena (Kamy)	
General Pedro Apolo Yakuvela	
General Eugenio Manuvakola	

General Abel Chivukuvuku
General Altino Sapalalo (Bock)
General Samuel Chiwale
General Jacinto Bandua
General AbÌlio Camalata Numa
    (Kamalata)
General Alcides Sakala Simoes
General Vaso Chimuco
General Lutoki Wiyo
General Ukama Regresso
General Antero Vieira
General Julio Armindo (Tarzan)[58]

It would appear that the number of UNITA generals was somewhat numerous for the size of the rebel army and the conflict. Rather than careful promotion over time with regard to experience and training it was as if, periodically, the cartoon character Elmer Fudd loaded up his shotgun with promotions to general and fired at any group of UNITA supporters milling around upper management.

UNITA General Eugenio Manuvakola parted company with the old and defected in 1997 with his family including brother Colonel Betinho Manuvakola after a period of imprisonment at the whim of Savimbi. He became President of the offshoot UNITA Renovada in 2002.

Two defections foreshadowed the 2002 downfall of UNITA as a military force: General Jacinto Bandua, the important commander of UNITA strategic procurement, who defected in 1999, and Private Manuel Tito, who was part of an execution squad for several generals in April 1999. Tito had fled in anticipation of also being executed.

It must have been particularly odious for a famous UNITA general like Chiwale to have UNITA's final 2008 campaign event followed by a public statement by his son, who justified his defection from UNITA alleging that his father's party was completely disorganized in Luanda and had no clear program. The apple fell far from the tree. He was not alone in this as towards the end of the war some children of Savimbi and others spoke out against UNITA.[59]

The military wing of UNITA was Forcas Armadas de Libertacao de Angola (FALA), or Armed Forces for the Liberation of Angola. A U.N. Report dated 7 January 1997 gives a figure of 18,901 UNITA soldiers who had been selected to join the Angolan army comprised of 1,587 officers, 1,430 sergeants, and 15,884 privates. The likely number of UNITA soldiers in 1987–88 would be about 30,000–40,000 of which 5,000–10,000 participated in the Battle of Cuito Cuanavale.

This would have been a smaller force than the entire Cuban contingent in Angola. However,it should be noted that later the Joint Military Commission reported in July 2002 that eighty-five thousand UNITA troops showed up for demobilization. In 1987, in a model of equal opportunity, FALA also created a unit of fifty women soldiers led by female officers who joined a military force that for the most part was unpaid, and voluntary in theory only as coercive measures were often adopted for recruitment.

At the time of the initial clash at the Lomba river, the UNITA chief of staff was Brig. Demosthenes Amos Chilingutila, but General Ben Ben was the commander of this front and had his headquarters at the Lomba River. UNITA's 3rd, 4th, and 5th Regular battalions were also in attendance with two irregular militia battalions. In August 1987 they were forced to move their headquarters along with the SADF liaison base when the FAPLA approached and threatened to outflank them. UNITA was referred to by the code name "Coronation" during the battle by the SADF.[60]

UNITA also had its own radio station: Voz Resistencia do Galo Negro (VORGAN), the Voice of the Resistance of the Black Cockerel. It was believed to consist of four former American-miltary mobile broadcast containers. The majority of content was centered around simple songs and morality skits designed to raise consciousness of the UNITA struggle. In this they were very similar to the Cubans and FAPLA organs of propaganda.

The UNITA facilities at Jamba included fourteen training camps with six month cycles that produced about eight thousand soldiers annually. The main camp was well equipped with a generator, hospital, troop barracks, and equipment maintenance areas. The trainees were given intensive physical, tactical, and weaponry training, mostly for the AK-47 assault rifle and PKM machine guns.

According to SADF senior liaison officer Col. Fred Oelschig, UNITA troop strengths could be assessed in the following manner:

Regular Battalion: By 1989 UNITA had nine regular battalions consisting of three infantry companies with five platoons each. A support company consisted of an 81mm Mortar Platoon with 8 weapons, an antitank platoon with 8 RPG 7 and a heavy Machine gun platoon with 23mm MG. Total strength of each Regular Battalion was with support elements was about 800 men with two regular battalions being trained per year.

Semi-Regular Battalion : UNITA had as much as 20 semi-regular battalions. Each battalion consisted of three companies with three platoons each, 60mm mortars, RPG 7 and light machine guns. Each was about 250 men strong and 4 were trained each year.

Artillery Battalion: Trained with 120mm mortars, 122mm howitzers, 107mm multiple rocket launchers and any other captured FAPLA artillery. There were 8–9 mortar units, 5–6 MRL sections, and a number of others with captured weapons.

Special Units: There were a number of other special forces units who were trained to perform reconaissance, special engineers for demolitions, and special antiaircraft groups who were trained to shoot down FAPA aircraft.[61]

Each unit was trained with its leader element and special courses were conducted for them. The UNITA training commander at the time was Lt. Col. Americo Gato who subsequently went on to join the unified FAA as chief of their military academy.

In general, from 1984 to 1988 UNITA trained about eight thousand soldiers per year with a large push in 1986 when about ten thousand were trained. A large number of militia were also trained and many rural villages had a well organized militia structure. Their value was appreciated by the SADF convoys driving from Rundu to Mavinga which did not need to be escorted as the UNITA militia along the way supplied the local security.

UNITA forces at Cuito cannot be accounted for with any accuracy, but possibly numbered six regular and ten semi-regular battalions along with various special units.

As to equipment, in a 2000 interview with the Canadian Ambassador Fowler UNITA General Jacinto Ricardo Bandua reported:

I held the post of chief of logistics for strategic equipment. UNITA bought a lot of material and many devices—tanks, mortars, mortar grenades, cannon, launching pads for missiles, ammunition and UNITA also bought a lot of tank accessories. These accessories made it possible for UNITA to rehabilitate the tanks it had captured over the sixteen years of war. Let me say here that over the sixteen years of struggle during those occasions when the South African force in the south of Angola near Dicinkulene area most of the Soviet equipment captured as it was not part of their doctrine was offered to UNITA. Antiaircraft guns, long-reach guns, all this equipment, throughout the peacetime was being rehabilitated by UNITA. If you add this to the material being imported, merely increased the potential or the mechanised assets for the force that UNITA was organising. In other words, with what UNITA bought, with what it had hidden, and with what it rehabilitated, the number was big.[62]

UNITA also had three regional hospitals at Mavinga, Jamba, and Mucusso staffed with SADF doctors for casualties. These hospitals were never totally full and on a ratio of one death to ten injured, UNITA casualties were kept remarkably low. Seriously injured soldiers were sent to 1 Military Hospital in Pretoria where there was a ward exclusively for UNITA patients. It doe not appear that FAPLA troops had access to such excellent medical care.[63]

In the remote southeastern corner of Angola next to the Kwando River and East of Jamba was a UNITA safe area called Boa Esperanza. This was where UNITA had schools for the children of the leadership as well as old age homes and orphanages. It was a peaceful area of maize fields, forests, and herds of game animals. Sufficiently far from the front lines, it was a useful place to keep UNITA leadership families unobserved *and* under the direct control of Savimbi.

Retired SADF senior UNITA liaison officer Col. Fred Oelschig had this to say about UNITA:

After the withdrawal of the SADF from Angola in 1976, the South African Government made a strategic decision to provide military support to UNITA. This decision lead to the establishment of a large buffer zone north of the Kavango river which effectively cut down the ability of SWAPO to operate in the Caprivi and Eastern Kavango. UNITA would regularly rout FAPLA forces from their headquarters at Jamba in south east Angola, well outside the operational ability of the MPLA government. UNITA was able to expand their area of direct influence to include Kwando Cubango province by 1985. This area they proclaimed as Free Angola where their supporters had freedom of movement with absolutely no military threat from FAPLA. Within this area, they had schools, clinics, industries and farms. There was a postal service, a trade union, airports, a student bursary system and sent their brightest students to University in Portugal and elections. The UNITA legal system catered for every form of criminal offence from stealing, poaching to murder. They had orphanages, old age homes, ten different church denominations represented by missionaries and pastors and they had three large, well-equipped regional hospitals. UNITA also had a well structured militia in the rural areas armed with weapons dating back to the Portuguese era and radio communication. Their task was to safeguard the rural areas from the infiltration of FAPLA agents and forces. The militia was so effective that the SADF never supplied escorts for their vehicles that travelled from Rundu to Mavinga. No convoy system was implemented which limited the manpower cost of supply. In short, UNITA ran a very comprehensive and effective society within the boundaries of Free Angola. UNITA enjoyed diplomatic representation in Washington, Lisbon and in Germany and were able to freely address the UN. They enjoyed recognition from the UK, USA, UN, Portugal, France, Germany, RSA, Congo, Ivory Coast and many other African Countries."[64]

UNITA had five fronts, usually commanded by an officer with the rank of brigadier or general, which were subdivided into twenty-two regions commanded by full colonels and then further broken down into sectors and zones under lower ranking officers. The main UNITA logistical center was at Licua in Cuando Cubango province, but there was a major special forces base at Panda in Bie province.

The UNITA military organization was based on a four-tier structure:

- Local defence forces with about six battalions of poorly armed militia.
- Mobile guerilla groups with a few months training of up to 150 soldiers tasked with harrassing FAPLA fixed and mobile assets.
- Over forty semi-regular battalions of several hundred with a few months training used for defence of fixed strategic locations.
- Regular Battalions of nearly 1,000 soldiers with longer training and some with specialised training by the SADF equipped with heavy weapons for offensive actions.[65]

Early UNITA leaders such as Gen. Samuel Chiwale received training in China, masked as recruits of SWAPO, at the Military Academy in Nanjing. In a 17 April 1996 interview with UNITA Secretary General Miguel N´Zau Puna by Tor Sellstrom in Luanda of the Nordic Africa Institute for Nordic Documentation on the Liberation Struggle in Southern Africa Project, Secretary-General Puna had this to say:

TOR SELLSTROM: Did SWAPO go through areas under UNITA control to enter Namibia?

MIGUEL N'ZAU PUNA: Yes. That was the only way that they could get into Namibia.

TOR SELLSTROM: Was there a tactical alliance between UNITA and SWAPO?

MIGUEL N'ZAU PUNA: There was a strategic and tactical alliance. Many soldiers from UNITA fought with SWAPO. We also made some incursions into Namibian territory under UNITA's General Commander Samuel Chiwale, who is now a general. There was Francisco Kulunga, who fought a lot on the other side to help our friends in SWAPO. We also had Commander Lucas Canjimi. He is from Kavango, on the border with Namibia. His nephews are here and his uncles on the other side. It is the same family.[66]

It may come as a great surprise to South African parents of conscripts who were killed in action that while their country was supporting UNITA, this organization was supportive of SWAPO, which was at war with South Africa in its quest for Namibian independence.

UNITA also had special forces or penetration groups that were small, highly specialized, and well-trained groups whose main function was to infiltrate deep into FAPLA rear areas. They were tasked with disrupting FAPLA logistical routes especially storage and strategic facilities as well as deep reconnaissance, ambushes and mine laying. In addition there were the BATE (Brigada de Accao de Tecnica de Explosivos—Action brigade for Explosive Techniques) groups that specialized in sabotage actions and were well trained in the use of explosives. These groups carried out actions against strategic targets such as oil-producing facilities and other infrastructure.

Not surprisingly, such an important operational group as BATE was commanded by a close Savimbi henchman: Brig. George Njolela Diamantino (Big Joe). His close and unrelenting loyalty led him to join his leader in death in February 2002. In all likelihood, it was his only avenue, having tied himself so closely to the Savimbi mast. There was a telling recollection of Big Joe recently during the Angola family reunion television show *Nacao Coragem* by a girl called Branca who had been kidnapped by UNITA soldiers from a convent:

> UNITA came at midnight. The nuns came around the dormitories telling us to come out, but I went back to find my younger sister, and that's when they found me. They chose five boys and ten girls, and I was the youngest of the girls. We were taken to their base. Others 'got married'—they were forced into that. I had to cook and wash and dance for celebrations. I was not abused, but I had a guardian who looked after me. A general. I was attached to his family and looked after his children. He was called Big Joe. After the death of Savimbi, everyone was dispersed. The general died. He was killed. Some of his family and his wife died at the same time. His children escaped, and Branca says she misses them but "I don't know where they are now. I hate UNITA, but Big Joe was a good man. He took care of many others." But in Luanda, where Branca now lives with her family, many remember him as pitiless and brutal. Of the ten girls captured at the same time as Branca, only three survived. Some died in the war, others of hunger and others of sicknes. The five boys all survived.[67]

CHAPTER **7**

GENERAL BEN BEN

Popular UNITA Gen. Arlindo Pena was nicknamed "Ben Ben" after the Algerian revolutionary leader, Ahmed Ben Bella, a favorite of his and a role model for any aspiring man of change like Ben Ben. The general, like most Angolan fighters, had a *nom de guerre* or war name. It was meant to be a security measure to provide some camouflage from prying eyes, but more often than not it allowed the commission of all manner of heinous acts without fear of reprisal, arrest, or identification. In the fullness of time the United Nations sanctions would disabuse senior UNITA officials of that notion.

On 17 November 1955 General Ben Ben was born Arlindo Chenda Isaac Pena in Caricoque, which is in the Bie Province of Angola, the same province where UNITA leader Jonas Savimbi was born. His parents were Isaac Pires Pena and Judite Malheiro Pena, a sister of Savimbi, His was a typically large African family with many brothers and sisters for young Arlindo. The Pena family was thus closely related to Savimbi and, making them closer still, they also were all members of the Ovimbundu tribe, which make up nearly 40 percent of the Angolan population.

He received primary education at the Chilesso Mission school near Andulo, the alma mater of his later, mentor Jonas Savimbi, going on to pursue secondary studies at the National High School of Bie before rounding out the end of his education at the Industrial and Commercial School. Clearly academia was not in his future and only rudimentary technical skills were necessary in the Angolan world of politics, power, and war in which he would become known.

In 1968, when Arlindo was thirteen, he joined his uncle's and the tribal elders' political party: União Nacional para a Independência Total de Angola (UNITA) or National Union for the Total Independence of Angola. His duties involved being a courier and political activist for UNITA in the surrounding towns and villages in what was at the time a Portuguese colony, with the attendant colonial security services watching for political disaffection among the populace.

Through Savimbi connections established by his own left-wing military training in China and elsewhere, Arlindo received military training in Europe and Morocco where he qualified as an artillery instructor. He achieved early fame in October 1985 when he made a two-week forced march over a long distance from Malanje to assist UNITA forces that were under severe attack at Lucusse by FAPLA and Cuban troops. At the time he was only thirty years old but it was here and by this action that he made his mark with the UNITA commander in chief. By thirty-four he was the UNITA chief of staff and heir apparent to Savimbi in an officer corps typically appointed based on tribal and family ties to the leader. Exceptionally, Arlindo Pena proved himself to be a commander of ability and courage.

The successful UNITA defense of Lucusse and counterattack thwarted this attempt to take Mavinga in 1985. Perhaps this became the bone in the collective throats of the Soviets and FAPLA that they sought to remove through the misconceived 1987 renewal of the operation to take Mavinga, which in the event came nowhere close to reaching its objective. Nevertheless, although the area around Mavinga was thought by some to have been extensively mined by Savimbi as a precaution, an SADF liaison officer with UNITA confirmed that the only areas mined in the vicinity of Mavinga were in the north along the old Portugese road from Cuito and to the east around the Tumpo river area.[68]

Young General Ben Ben, not quite a Hannibal but certainly better than the FAPLA's General Ndalu, led from the front and enjoyed the admiration and respect of his men. In the years that followed he led UNITA forces to a string of victories that saw large parts of the country under UNITA control for the first time. This would not have been possible without the support and largesse of the American and South African governments, which financed UNITA and supplied the landmines that litter the unusable countryside today.

General Ben Ben was the UNITA deputy chief of staff at the time of the Battle of Cuito Cuanavale, stationed near the Lomba River, but he soon moved to oversee the Longa front north of Cuito to increase pressure on

FAPLA forces. His temporary placement there soon began to bear the fruit of multiple ambushes with many casualties and great equipment loss along the Menongue–Cuito road. Later on he joined up with Commandant Robbie Hartslief south of the Mianei River. Neither of these two able young commanders were to survive the experience of the war.[69]

In a 1986 report of a visit to UNITA-controlled territory near Cuito Cuanavale Portuguese journalist Antonio Duarte described General Ben Ben as one of the most talked about officers in the area. Duarte observed General Ben Ben exercising his artillery expertise on a FAPLA 25th Brigade camp that was thought to house Soviet advisors.[70]

A 1984 assessment by Major Robert R. Burke (USMC) illustrates the talents of General Ben Ben as a military commander:

In February 1983, UNITA captured Cangonga on the Benguela Railroad. The manner in which it was taken not only shows the detail in planning made but also the sophistication of the force involved. Battalion 017, commanded by Colonel Ben-Ben Arlindo Pena, 28 years of age, had constructed a relief model the size of a badminton court of the town and its approaches to use for the battle briefing. Colored roads, arches, bark, twigs, and moss were used in the model town to symbolize the buildings and fortifications of Cangonga. Battalion 017 conducted endless rehearsals. The battalion consisted of 520 regular troops armed with 75mm cannons, 81mm mortars, RPG-7 antitank missiles, AK-47 rifles, a 45-strong platoon of "Special Forces," a 50-strong logistics team, 25 demolitions specialists, some 300 guerrillas, and a long chain of young men and women carrying ammunition on their heads. Finally, at 0300 on 11 February, a single rifle shot signaled that all units of Battalion 017 were in position. At 0500 the attack began. The MPLA's arsenal exploded and the entire town was soon ablaze. The MPLA garrison was stunned! Most of the 300 defenders fled. UNITA killed or captured the remainder. The importance of Cangonga's capture was two-fold. First, it allowed a secure supply line to be pushed to regular forces and guerrillas who had already infiltrated 200 miles north of the Benguela Railroad. This would help UNITA fulfill one of its major objectives of creating a corridor of "liberated" territory right up the center of the country to where a salient of Zaire juts into north central Angola. This would cut off the territory held by the MPLA in the east from its areas in the west. The significance of Cangonga's capture, however, lay in its propaganda value. UNITA wanted to show Western journalists as well as its own people that its forces were highly skilled and motivated, and fully capable of striking the MPLA in the very heart of Angola with a surgical precision devoid of help from external sources, especially South Africa.[71]

Pena's status was further enhanced in the 1992 Luanda shootout referred to by some as the Halloween Massacre when results of a bipartisan-approved election were rejected by UNITA and a three day urban battle ensued. The events were so fast paced that Ben Ben and his brother Elias Salupeto Pena, a UNITA official, had to fight their way out of the FAPLA controlled city past numerous street blockades.

This drama began to unfold in the embassy district of Luanda, also called Miramar like its counterpart in Havana, where senior UNITA officials and soldiers controlled a small section of the district. From this base they began to invade nearby embassies to kidnap safe-conduct hostages to assist their departure from Luanda. Many of these soldiers were part of the four-hundred-man UNITA military contingent in the capital that served as a security force for the organization's leaders and facilities. Some of them were probably responsible, along with local with sympathizers, for the sabotage explosion of an arms dump near the Luanda airport that ignited the fight.

Across the city at the Hotel Turismo in central Luanda, the temporary home of some senior UNITA officials, a number of police officers were being held hostage after a car bomb had exploded outside the hotel. Later, there was a drive-by shooting at UNITA soldiers who were outside the hotel; they responded by firing on police vehicles and nearby buildings. UNITA Gen. Renato Mateus, who remained committed to the election, arrived and assumed command of the UNITA forces in the city, possibly saving hundreds of lives from further violence.

In the meantime several hostages had been taken from foreign embassies, including British businessman David Chambers and his wife Eleonore who were forcibly removed from the official residence of the Swedish Ambassador by UNITA soldiers. Chambers later gave details of what subsequently occurred in the 1994 Human Rights Watch Report stating that they left the city in a convoy of three vehicles with Elias Salupeto Pena and Jeremias Chitunda. (Jeremias Chitunda was a vice president of UNITA who had come to Luanda to discuss a second round of elections.) leading in a Mercedes

Benz. The British hostages followed in a Toyota Camry with four UNITA soldiers. The convoy raced through the city for several kilometers at speeds of approaching 100 mph, running a gauntlet of FAPLA blockades and bullets. After a brief rush through the streets of Luanda during which their vehicles were riddled with shots, the Camry flipped several times before ending up on its roof. Everyone in the convoy was killed, numbering some sixteen persons, including Pena and Chitunda, except, miraculously, Chambers and his wife.

The bodies of Jeremias Chitunda and Elias Pena were later seen at a police station by a reporter. Jeremias had been shot through the jaw and throat while Elias had apparently died from head injuries. Chambers made no mention of the separate Ben Ben escape with Gen. Abel Chivukuvuku, who was later injured and arrested by Luanda police. Chivukuvuku remained in custody until 1997 and was elected chief of UNITA parliamentarians in Luanda one year later.[72]

Ben Ben, the ultimate survivor was also wounded but is thought to have bullied, bribed, and barged his way to friendly forces at Caxito, fifty kilometers north of Luanda, then controlled by UNITA Gen. Abìlio Kamalata (Numa). Ben Ben was later shown on television shouting into his radio: "The chief says burn everything. By everything he means everything. Women, children, everything."

Circumstances and, one hopes, conscience prevented this order from being carried out. In September 1993 the U.N. imposed sanctions on the sale of weapons or fuel to UNITA. General Ben Ben was then reported on Portuguese television saying that the sanctions were completely ineffective as UNITA had enough weapons and ammunition for ten years.[73]

Despite all this Ben Ben went from UNITA chief of staff in 1989 to become a member of the high command of the unified national Angolan army, the Forcas Armadas de Angola (FAA), in 1996 as deputy chief of staff. Ben Ben's attempts to join a government of unity involved several hiccups including a perceived assassination attempt when a bodyguard was shot in the foot in October 1995. After this he left Luanda but returned to the peace process that following November. It was, at the end, a hollow position that failed to utilize his valuable talents leaving him without direction or fulfillment.

In July 1997 the Ben Ben made a clear sign of support for the Luanda-based government, and estrangement from his former mentor Savimbi, when he gave a speech marking the integration of eleven thousand former UNITA soldiers into the FAA, the new Angolan national army. Unfortunately, many more soldiers, over fifteen thousand, fled the demobilization camps to rejoin UNITA.

In September 1998 Ben Ben was part of a group of former UNITA generals including Chilingutila, Wiyo, Henda, Pongolola, Sunguete, Regresso, and Ngele who issued a joint statement calling for UNITA to cease hostilities. Perhaps this further overt break with the past contributed to his ultimate and not-long-in-coming demise.[74]

When he died he left an extended family behind including two other brothers, one of whom was called General Well Well. A younger brother, Felisberto Isaac Pena was captured in combat on 20 October 2000 in Umpulo on the outskirts of the city of Cabinda in the province of Bie, but given amnesty by the government a couple months later.

In peacetime, General Ben Ben pursued drinking with a similar passion to his combat service while ignoring his health, including complaints of malaria that preceded his death at forty-three on 19 October 1998 from complications of septicemia at a Johannesburg clinic. Prior to this, several reports of erratic behavior could later be ascribed to neurological effects of cerebral malaria.

Margaret Anstee, a former U.N. special representative to Angola, recalled General Ben Ben as having a swashbuckling, piratical air about him and that he was charismatic. Angolan writer Sousa Jamba memorialized the General as an amiable, approachable character, a soldier's soldier who lacked the pretensions of many of his rank. There is no recollection of his rare opportunities to indulge his love of sport; forgotten by history is his prowess as a midfield defender in football games at the occasional UNITA congress meetings, a warrior's cherished moment of normalcy.

Even in death there was to be no peace with a dispute breaking out between his wife and the Luanda government who wished to bestow an official funeral and perhaps gain some political capital. The family's wishes, which included his parents who Ben Ben predeceased, sought a simple, private funeral won out in the end.

The spirit of General Ben Ben continued with his son Demarte Dachala Pena who recently completed a book titled *My Royal Rebel Blood (Behind these scars)*.[75]

Demarte has continued his warrior heritage as a featherweight class extreme fighting champion in South Africa known as Demarte *The Wolf* Pena.

CHAPTER **8**

THE BEGINNING OF THE END

The unfortunate Soviet plan caused FAPLA to initiate a build up of men and equipment around Cuito Cuanavale in the Spring of 1987 in preparation for a later offensive towards the UNITA stronghold town of Mavinga. By May of that year, the alarmed UNITA commander General Demosthenes Chilingutila, who was also known as "the Devil," met with his SADF liaison Col. Fred Oelschig to clamor for increased support and assistance for the impending FAPLA attack. A few months later a similar meeting occurred between FAPLA and Cuban leadership.[76]

The South African leadership, having taken a firm position in the defense of Mavinga previously in 1985, also made their preparations by improvement of SADF's facilities in northern Namibia, particularly at Rundu. Their prompt response to the movement of FAPLA troops in the summer of 1987 suggested not only readiness but anticipation.

That August, in the heart of summer's heat, at the insistence of Soviet Lt. Gen.Pavel Gusev FAPLA forces began their advance towards UNITA positions near the Lomba River. The FAPLA attacks forced the sparse UNITA forces to retreat from their positions along the river until the SADF launched a massive counterattack named Operation Modular that turned the FAPLA advance into a rout, all the way back to Cuito Cuanavale. The FAPLA movement to Mavinga was a classic Soviet twin pincer movement, a battle plan that hadn't worked in the mountains of Afghanistan and didn't work in the bush of Angola.

Between August and September a large FAPLA force, heavily supported by Soviet advisors attached to the combat brigades, began a determined advance towards the Lomba River, where the headquarters of General Ben Ben was located, and farther east to the UNITA stronghold of Mavinga. The FAPLA forces had about ten thousand men, including the 21st Brigade, which intended to crossed the Cunzumbia river using Soviet TMM or MTU mobile bridges. The mission of the 47th Brigade, essentially a T-55 tank force, was to secure the banks of the Lomba river for the eventual crossing of reinforcing troops.

To slow down the FAPLA advance the SADF sent a team of 4th Recce soldiers with scuba and demolition capability to destroy the Cuito River Bridge for what would have been a second time on the night of 26 August. A year earlier, in August 1986, the bridge had been wrecked in a UNITA raid on Cuito supported by the SADF that also severely damaged FAPLA equipment and supplies. The SADF had first proposed the new attack on the bridge in May 1987, but it was decided that it would be better for the bridge to be destroyed after the advancing FAPLA forces were sufficiently far to the south of Cuito to maximize disruption of their supply lines as their attack was heavily dependent on receiving fuel every day. This delay allowed the 4th Recce troopers tasked with destroying the bridge to train intensely farther south at the confluence of the Cuito River with the Kavango river at Dirico where there was a similar bridge.

The teams were inserted by helicopters close to the source of the Coa River which was about 13 kilometers as the crow flies to the Cuanavale River, a substantial distance from the Cuito bridge. Here they were met by several UNITA officers: Colonel Gatow, Colonel Shangonja, and Major Calipe, who was UNITA's chief of reconnaissance. They supplied guides and guards for the infiltration team, who had to paddle in canoes for some distance. As they approached the bridge in pairs, their leader, Major Fred Wilke, came under fire by alert FAPLA sentries and he was wounded. Some of the remaining team members were able to set and explode demolition charges, but they only succeeded in damaging the bridge. In separate incidents both Major Wilke and Sgt. Antonie Beukman were attacked by crocodiles but managed to evade the giant predators. In one of the many miracles at Cuito the entire team was able to recover from the operation without fatalities despite many difficulties, including FAPLA attacks at helicopter pickup points. Team leader Fred Wilke along with Sergeants Antonie Beukman, Gerhardus Heydenrych, Richard Brent Burt, Jacobus deWet, Phillipus Herbst, Henk Liebenberg, Adriano Manuel, Johannes Oettle, Johannes van der Merwe, and Leslie Wessels as well as Cpl. Pieter Van Niekerk received the Honoris Crux medal for their valorous efforts on this mission.[77]

The bridge was only partially destroyed, about two-thirds, but this was enough to prevent vehicular from crossing for about two weeks. In 1996, as Col. Fred Oelschig worked as project manager to clear Angolan roads from landmines under contract to the U.N., he met Brig. Gen. Helder Cruz, the original FAPLA engineer officer tasked with repair of the bridge, who had a picture of the damaged bridge in his office. The former enemies shared their optimism for a peaceful future for Angola.

In August 1987 the SAAF followed upwith an attack on the bridge with a remotely-operated experimental drone bomb dropped from a Buccaneer aircraft operating within transmission range of the target. The Buccaneer crew guided this early smart bomb into the bridge causing irreparable damage that prevented its use by vehicles use until after the Battle of Cuito Cuanavale ended. In March 1989 when author Edward George visited Cuito Cuanavale he noted, "little more than one-third of the bridge's eastern section was still standing."[78]

Later that summer SADF reconnaissance troops attached to the 5th Recce Regiment, a part of the 20 Brigade battle group operating near the Lomba River area, observed movement of FAPLA troops going in the direction of the river and Mavinga. As the gathering FAPLA forces increased in size and continued toward Mavinga the SADF response was to dispatch the 32 Infantry Battalion to the Lomba River area as part of Operation Modular. The 5 Recce Commando had originally deployed in the area on 31 July 1987.

Major Pierre Franken, a forward artillery observer for P Battery, 20th Artillery Regiment, was able to clearly observe the FAPLA advance west of the Lomba River and called in a multiple rocket strike on their overnight positions. This caused many casualties and some equipment damage in what was the start of the Battle of Cuito Cuanavale, with daily artillery and rocket harassment as the FAPLA came closer to the Lomba River.

The FAPLA advance was slow in the thick bush of the area, never more than a few miles a day with late afternoon halts to dig in and prepare for night. Their movement was further retarded by concentration of their armored vehicles in the event of an attack, fear of SAAF air attacks, and the harassment of their supply lines by UNITA forces to the west and rear.

The SADF field operations commander Col. Deon Ferreira operated from tactical field headquarters near the Lomba River with Sector 20 (Rundu) commander liaison Col. Piet Muller and UNITA liaison Col. Fred Oelschig.[79]

By early September the FAPLA 21st Brigade was at the banks of the Lomba river far from home base awaiting reinforcement from the 25th Infantry, 47th Armored, 59th Mechanized and 16th Mechanized brigades. On the verge of attacking Mavinga and relatively static in the face of the Lomba River crossing, it was a propitious opportunity for the opposing forces to inflict maximum damage on the FAPLA. Commander Ferreira who was nicknamed Falcon, orchestrated a shower of aerial bombardment and artillery shells on the FAPLA forces which slowed then scattered them while awaiting reinforcement.

The SADF relied not only on hidden forward observers for artillery direction, but also performed night aerial flights in search of suitable targets. On 3 September 1987 an SAAF Atlas AM-3C Bosbok (No. 934) was shot down south of Lomba River by an FAPLA SA-8 Gecko missile system, while conducting an evening target reporting mission. The light, single-engine plane was flown by 2nd Lt. Richard Glynn with Commandant Johan Du Randt acting as a forward observer for Papa and Sierra batteries of the 20th Artillery Regiment. Both were killed in what was the first SAAF aircraft brought down by the FAPLA during the the Battle of Cuito Cuanavale. This double-seat light plane was used by the SAAF for reconnaissance and night flare missions, often flying at tree top level.

The Bosbok had been a replacement which came via the SAAF Ondangwa base, Rundu base and Mavinga airstrip for the usual plane, which was unserviceable. The regular pilot, Geoff Rogers, was near the end of his tour and due to return home to South Africa, so Richard Glynn replaced him early. During the early course of his flight Pilot Glynn reported several RPG rounds being fired at him to no effect. Nearby ground forces then reported seeing two SAM missiles overhead prior to the shootdown. The shootdown was witnessed by reconnaissance team commander Sergeant Piet Fourie from the 32 Battalion and the bodies of the two men were eventually recovered by SADF and UNITA forces led by Les Rudman and Robbie Hartslief.

Commandant Johan Du Randt was the 20 Brigade artillery fire leader and the highest ranking SADF casualty of the Battle of Cuito Cuanavale.

This was to have been a fairly safe night flight as the FAPLA SAM ground-to-air missile systems were not known to have been that far forward, near the Lomba River. While a tragedy, it was an important forewarning to later SAAF flights and gave impetus for the eventual SADF capture of a SA-8 system later on. It may also have been the first Soviet SA-8 Gecko missile kill worldwide.

Bosbok serial number 920 undergoing restoration at SAAF museum, Port Elizabeth, South Africa. In 1970 the South African Air Force ordered forty Aermacchi AM.3s, designating them the AM.3CM Bosbok. Following the end of South Africa's involvement in the Angolan War in 1989 and the subsequent downsizing of the SAAF, the Bosbok was retired from service in 1992.
—NJR ZA (Wikimedia)

About this time an SADF Military Intelligence Division liaison team, which was part of the Directorate of Special Tasks (DST) for South West Africa, was operating ahead of the main force. The DST personnel were part of a department of SADF military intelligence that coordinated special operatons forces intelligence gathering activities. This particular group at the Battle of Cuito Cuanavale was generally referred to as CSI (chief of staff intelligence) and one was led by Commandant Les Rudman. The team was comprised of DST personnel, a pathfinder squad from 1st Parachute Battalion and a handful of UNITA troops commanded by Captain Paulo.

The CSI liaison teams were allocated to the UNITA headquarters of General Chilingutila and operated under his general direction in theory, but in fact they were controlled by General Thackwray of CSI. The teams were tasked with an intelligence and training role, and to engage FAPLA forces with a high degree of autonomy. Armaments for this duty were Vickers machine guns mounted on a Blesbok vehicle, an RPG team, an 81mm mortar mounted on the Blesbok, a Casspir that caried a .50 cal. Browning and 7.62mm machine gun, a groundshout (loudspeakers for psyops) Casspir with a 7.62mm machine gun, a Gemsbok recovery vehicle, and a Kwevoel logistical vehicle. Including the four-man UNITA liaison, the CSI team numbered twenty-two men. Most of the troops were armed with AK-47 rifles or PKM light machine guns, which had great utility when ammunition was seized from the FAPLA forces. The team also had a forward observer for artillery and a forward air controller for SAAF missions. There was also a protection unit from the 32 "Buffalo" Battalion Reconnaissance under the command of Sgt. Mac de Trinidade, for a grand total of about forty men, a very small number for what ultimately confronted them.

There was also a second CSI team deployed under Commandant Bert Sachse near the Cuzumbia river, but it was not involved in the opening actions of Cuito. When these teams were initially deployed they had no great success in antitank operations as the FAPLA armored columns would move with a forward screen of soldiers on foot. A third CSI team was lead by Col. Fred Oelschig.[80]

On 5 September 1987 UNITA provided intelligence that a FAPLA battalion had crossed the Lomba River at a position west of the Lomba-Cuzizi confluence heading east. It appeared that its mission was to find the position of SADF G5 artillery guns. Commandant Robbie Hartlief quickly called Commandant Rudman to a briefing that day to discuss this information as UNITA had hastily sent troops to the area to try to contain the situation, but it was anticipated that this would take a few days. Hartlief decided to send an artillery observation team to this area as soon as possible so that he could profit from this development as they were in range of one of the G5 batteries. The report also stated that the FAPLA troops were massing in an open area, ideal for an artillery bombardment. Hartlief tasked Rudman to use his team to escort the artillery forward observers farther west to a suitable position to enable G5 shelling of the enemy battalion as soon as possible.

Rudman met with the forward observation team under Major Franken for their deployment the next day. A debrief meeting with UNITA revealed that UNITA only knew the approximate whereabouts of the FAPLA force. giving the planned deployment a greater urgency.

Early the next morning they left in convoy northwards to insert the forward observation team along with protection troops. The FAPLA battalion was entirely on foot preventing the SADF team from using their vehicles to come too close as the enemy foot soldiers were likely to hear them coming.

The entire SADF team then crossed a riverine lowland area called a shona to the tree line where they stopped at about 0600 to set up a temporary base on a small, pear-shaped rise with perimeter guards posted for security. At this point they were about nine kilometers southwest of the Lomba and Cunzumbia rivers in what is now the Coutada Publica do Longa-Mavinga Nature Reserve.

At about 1000 hours one of the perimeter guards, a UNITA mortar instructor called Kibi, came in running to report a group of FAPLA soldiers about a hundred meters away. Five pathfinders moved forward up to slightly higher ground where they observed the oncoming troops for the first time, rapidly moving towards them in a sweep-line formation. There were hundreds of enemy soldiers, and they immediately realized they were in for a massive firefight. It would be a miracle if they survived the day.

Aerial photo of Coutada Publica do Longa-Mavinga Nature Reserve, possible site of first engagement of Cuito Cuanavale, showing shell-strike marks. —*U.S. Forestry Service*

Being unsure if the oncoming force were UNITA or FAPLA one of the 32 "Buffalo" Battalion soldiers called out to the oncoming men to identify themselves. Forming a skirmish line, the men of the small observation team approached the advancing FAPLA unit of about two hundred men together with a second swath of a hundred joined in an L-shaped formation. The SADF/UNITA troops then opened fire with a fusillade that marked the opening combat of the Battle of Cuito Cuanavale.

The FAPLA unit responded promptly with mortar and small-arms fire, including RPGs, directed at the SADF positions. The SADF vehicles were left behind the skirmish line as the troops moved forwards towards the FAPLA line followed by the Casspirs under command of Rudman, who drove to the point of contact to give the ground troops supporting fire. Due to the intense fighting, the bush was set ablaze and a widespread, low-intensity fire roared through the battle zone.

Commander Rudman realized the overwhelming strength of the FAPLA unit and gave an immediate command for all the ground troops to return to the relative safety of the armored vehicles. Under covering fire from the Casspirs the troops managed to reenter and the battle was then fought from the vehicles. The raging bush fire gave the retreating troops additional cover.

At one stage the SADF mortars were adjusted to an acute elevation in order to drop bombs on the FAPLA troops who were rushing desperately close to the South African position. The aggressive FAPLA attack with numerical superiority began to encircle the SADF soldiers who started to receive fire from the rear of their position. The order was then given for all SADF troops to execute a break-out maneuver while the Browning .50 cal. machine gun from Rudman's Casspir put down withering cover fire. Making a hasty retreat over the shona the armored vehicles drove out of the encirclement picking up stranded and wounded SADF/UNITA soldiers along the way. The wounded included Sgt. S. Sterzel who was awarded the Honoris Crux for his bravery that day. The irrepressible Sergeant Sterzel returned to the liaison team and continued his work after two weeks treatment and recovery.

The SADF casualty report from that incident revealed the following helicopter evacuation cases (casevacs) except Rautenbach who stayed on:

Lance Corporal M. A. Benecke	KIA.
Sergeant S. Sterzel	shrapnel in left buttock, shot in left shoulder.
Lance Corporal W. D. Coetzee	shot in right shoulder.
Lance Corporal S. A. Summer	bullet wounds in back.
Rifleman F. Nyumba	bullet wounds upper left arm, right finger and left foot.
Rifleman Djekele	bullet wounds in right arm, shrapnel in right thigh and left calf.
Rifleman Kapakalenga	bullet wounds in neck, jaw, right lower leg and right finger.
Staff Sergeant Rautenbach	shrapnel in left breast.

The victorious FAPLA commanders massed their troops in the tree line at the edge of the shona and stated to shoot at the disappearing SADF force with all their weapons. One of the Casspir wheels was hit by an RPG-7 but managed to escape before it completely broke down. As they moved away from the site of the battle, SADF artillery observer Major Franken called in a G5 artillery strike from another vehicle as his own had been shot out.

Typical Angolan Shona.—
Richard Wiles

The FAPLA had decisively won the first engagement of the Battle of Cuito Cuanavale in a well-executed ambush, with overwhelming numerical superiority, and in which no Soviet or Cuban advisors played any part. It was to be the last taste of victory that the FAPLA would have for some time to come.

An SADF force led by Rudman returned to the battlefield the next day, 7 September, and found a number of FAPLA dead as well as a wounded FAPLA soldier who was able to give useful information about the enemy force. This soldier confirmed that he was part of the FAPLA 59th Brigade and that his group consisted of two battalions and one company, which made it at least two hundred-men strong. Six rows of tracks were found as well as ammunition for a grenade launcher and a B10 antitank gun discarded about the area. The prisoner reported that he knew of twelve FAPLA dead and twenty wounded. He confirmed that the Browning .50 cal. machine gun from Rudman's Casspir had caused many of the casualties. The FAPLA soldiers had spent the night on the edge of the shona when their observation posts had spotted the SADF vehicles of the SADF observation team crossing the shona. The unknown FAPLA commander could not believe his luck and immediately set up an ambush for the oncoming SADF troops. The hunters then became the hunted.

The FAPLA unit had failed to pursue the retreating South Africans and withdrew back over the Lomba River without attacking the nearby G5 battery position, perhaps due to the post-ambush bombardment.

The SADF commander Rudman saved many soldiers that day by his cool head and prompt actions. The capable officer remained in military service rising to the rank of major general in the postapartheid South African National Defense Force and was awarded the Army Cross.

The first SADF casualty of the Battle of Cuito Cuanavale was teenager LCpl. Melvin A. Benecke of the SADF 1st Para Battalion pathfinders who was killed by small-arms fire during the firefight. The nineteen-year-old Benecke was shot in the head. While under fire, Lance Corporals Venter and Luus bravely carried the wounded Benecke to a Casspir where he died. Venter received the silver Honoris Crux for his selfless actions.

Young Melvin came from the quiet town of Uitenhage outside of Port Elizabeth on the South African Eastern Cape and was buried in the Alicedale cemetery. Benecke's former teacher at Brandwag High School Dr. T. C. Breitenbach wrote in a newspaper: "Why did the handsome young men and others like them give up their lives?"[81]

Lance Corporal Melvin A. Benecke.
—*Marielle Ford*

Three major rivers and nine tributaries intertwine across the nearly nine thousand square miles over which the battle was fought. Not all of the rivers were large, especially during the prewinter dry season, but most were paralleled by swamps and flooded grasslands bordering the rivers or shonas. These riverine obstacles caused much of the fighting to occur around the bridges and fords where FAPLA forces tried to deploy Soviet bridging equipment. These narrow entry points became bottlenecks for slaughter once the South Africans arrived to fully contest the crossings.

Among the various equipment provided by the Soviets to the FAPLA was the TMM truck mounted bridging units that if used to cross the Lomba River could put the FAPLA 21st Brigade units a short way from Mavinga. Many of these bridging units were destroyed by accurate G5 howitzer fire as well as other bombardment, but the FAPLA still crossed the Lomba.

UNITA had kept up nightly harassment attacks on FAPLA forces massed at the Lomba River and numerous casualties were inflicted and Brazillian-made Engesa trucks destroyed. The FAPLA force was laden with vehicles that used excessive fuel because of night actions that prevented them from shutting down. The result was that they were using a vast amount of fuel that presented a difficult logistical situation, which was compounded when the Cuito bridge was partially destroyed and they were unable to freely move.[82]

Soviet TMM-6 mobile bridge.—
Anthony Turton

In the midst of these obvious preparations for a major bush confrontation there was a prisoner exchange on 7 September 1987 between Angolan and South African authorites. Hindsight would suggest that the South African government wished to complete this popular transaction involving the daring sabotage expert, Major Wynand Du Toit, before matters were to explode at the Lomba River.

The next day the equally heroic but more successful Commandant Robbie Hartslief was ordered to lead Combat Group Bravo (CGB) south of the

Lomba River. The CGB had two infantry companies traveling by Casspir armored personnel carriers from 101 Infantry Battalion and a 32 Infantry Battalion antitank squadron commanded by Major Hannes Nortmann.

Although there were some reports that the SADF force laid a chain of mines adjacent to the Lomba River at that time, nothing could have been further from the truth. The SADF did not have the resources or time to conduct such a labor intensive operation. Much later, when deployed East of Cuito Cuanavale in the Tumpu area, a large defensive minefield was laid between the South Africans and the well-fortified positions of FAPLA forces still east of the Cuito River.

On the morning of 9 September 1987 UNITA intelligence reported that several hundred FAPLA soldiers of the 21st Brigade had crossed the Lomba River to secure the opposite bank for a river crossing by their armored vehicles which had massed together in anticipation of just such an event.

The FAPLA forces were about fifteen kilometers from Combat Group Bravo, so Commandant Hartslief immediately ordered a company of mounted infantry and a troop of Ratels to locate and attack the FAPLA 21st Brigade. This SADF force with some UNITA ground support reached high ground near the crossing site.

In the first armored action of the battle, at the Lomba River a Soviet BTR 60 armored personnel carrier armed with a 14.5mm heavy machine gun and supported by infantry was fired upon and destroyed by a Ratel 90.

Captured FAPLA Soviet made BTR 60 November 1987.
—*Richard Wiles*

Soviet BTR-60 armored personnel carriers seized by U.S. military personnel during
Operation Urgent Fury, the 1983 U.S. invasion of Grenada.
—*Technical Sergeant M. J. Creen (defenseimagery.mil)*

The crew of this first kill Ratel were; Wayne Rossouw the crew commander,
F. C. Els gunner and Clinton Roberts, the driver.[83]

Ferreira's 20th Artillery Regiment, with accurate forward observation
guidance, fired several debilitating salvoes into the waiting FAPLA soldiers
causing many casualties. The UNITA forces failed to take advantage of this
action even though they were essentially at the command and control of
Hartslief's CGB. Hartslief was accompanied by UNITA liaison officer Major
Mickey who had great difficulty keeping UNITA forces in play in the face
of the fast-moving SADF tactics.

The FAPLA had responded with some desultory artillery and the CGB
forward unit withdrew about five kilometers to await the remaining units of
the combat group before commencing a full attack the next day. When Major
Nortmann arrived with the remaining forces in the darkness Hartslief split
them into the classic ambush arrow shape to face the expected morning attack by the FAPLA who were forced to push forward or retreat in ignominy.

During that night two large elements of the FAPLA 21st Brigade were
able to come across the river and a third FAPLA unit utilized a Soviet TMM
mobile bridge to come over the river at a second bridgehead.

At dawn on 9 September the FAPLA attacked with inaccurate rocket
fire from their Soviet BM multiple rocket launchers, which are similar to the
Stalin Organ of World War II, supported by artillery and mortars. Their

unknowing soldiers proceeded to advance across a river delta with little cover and no forward fire direction.

The well-positioned Combat Group Bravo slowed then stopped the FAPLA advance on the open ground. The accurate fire and mounting casualties threw the FAPLA troops into disarray in the face of advancing South African armored vehicles commanded by Major Hannes Nortmann with UNITA troops aboard. In the eventual wild retreat the SADF units maintained punishing fire and inflicted FAPLA casualties in the hundreds.

UNITA Major Mickey was on the outside of Hartslief's vehicle when they passed through the retreating lines of FAPLA infantry and was observed lying on his back on the camouflage net piled on the spare tire, shooting at the FAPLA soldiers.

The FAPLA briefly reformed across the Lomba and sent several T-55 tanks towards the TMM bridge which were then confronted by a Ratel ZT3 127mm antitank guided missile attack by Major Nortmann. After several misfires and misses they were able to severely damage or destroy three T-55 tanks.

The ZT3 antitank missile system was a third generation antitank missile system developed to sidestep international sanctions that prevented acquisition of existing systems by South Africa from foreign suppliers. It was a laser-guided missile with an effective range of four thousand meters and was on its first combat deployment, which explains some of the misfires and misses.

SADF Ratel ZT3
with antitank
missile system.
—Richard Wiles

In a fairly short time SADF operators were able to use these missiles with improved accuracy and reliability.

Artillery fire and skirmishes continued throughout the following days with the FAPLA advance slowly making progress with two large elements of the FAPLA 21st Brigade being able to come across the river. Action continued to peter out as the FAPLA, SADF and UNITA forces were caught up in a cycle of occasional action followed by artillery and strategic repose by their respective commanders, neither side having struck a knockout blow.

The FAPLA advance was slowed by withering G5 shelling and other artillery fire. At the same time the SADF played a cat and mouse game with FAPLA's T-55 tanks as well as avoiding MiG air strikes. At this point the FAPLA had a superior numerical and armored force but poor Soviet leadership, who were fast losing the confidence of FAPLA field commanders.

By the third week of September Combat Group Bravo under Commandant Hartslief was ordered to focus exclusively on the FAPLA 21st Brigade while farther south the FAPLA 47th Brigade was confronted by Combat Group Alpha (CGA) under Commandant Bok Smit and Combat Group Charlie (CGC) led by Maj. Dawid Lotter.

After extensive bombing by the SAAF and intense artillery fire, Hartslief's CGB advanced, despite a poison gas attack false alarm, and occupied a FAPLA trench system that had been abandoned following an earlier attack. The gas alarm was caused by the high detonation of a bomb from a MiG that resulted in a substantial smoke cloud drifting down. Most of the SADF and UNITA troops deployed along the Lomba River feared that this cloud contained toxic gas and withdrew from the Lomba River as a safety precaution. It eventually drifted away to the north and the forces were able to return to their positions early the next day.[84]

The FAPLA trench systems were built in according to Soviet doctrine using a zigzag layout for the trenches that would make it difficult for attackers once they entered the trench system as each corner presented an obstacle and would have to be cleared, slowing the attackers down. South African soldiers were drilled to attack a single entry point where fire would be concentrated to enable a breach for troops to use. Each leg of the trench would then be cleared by a grenade around the corner of the trench while the section was covered by other team members. Once the grenade exploded, the troops would come around the corner using an angling technique called slicing the pie, which is still in use today. This entails going around a corner slowly with weapon ready to fire while maintaining cover of the rest of the body. This

SADF training went largely unused as the Ratels avoided the problem of the zig-zags by driving straight across the trenches which usually panicked the defenders but at great risk of Ratel getting stuck, as happened on occasion.

Shortly thereafter, in the late afternoon CGB confronted a large FAPLA column of armored vehicles and infantry advancing across a river delta towards their position. A barrage of accurate MRL rockets, G5 shells, and mortars were unleashed on the unfortunate FAPLA soldiers and vehicles causing several hundred casualties as they scrambled for nonexistent cover. The Ratels and artillery accounted for several armored vehicles including T-55 tanks and BTRs, some of which caught fire.

A left front view of a Soviet BMP-1 mechanized infantry vehicle. The vehicle is on display at Bolling Air Force Base.—*Don S. Montgomery (defenseimagery.mil)*

At this point the retreating infantry and vehicle crews simply abandoned undamaged vehicles and made a run for their original river crossing. Sensing victory, the South African armored vehicles chased them with combined fire of 7.62mm machine guns, small-arms fire, and antipersonnel cannon rounds that were like giant, deadly shotgun shells loaded with two thousand some odd ball bearings.

The heavy, fast-moving vehicles added to the carnage by crushing numerous wounded and hiding FAPLA soldiers in the tall African grass. It was as if Hannibal's elephants were transported to modern times and became wheeled behemoths lurching through the bush. They were the last thing seen by the terrified soldiers before life was squeezed out of them. The remaining FAPLA soldiers and equipment were caught in withering fire when they paused at their original crossing point, which had been destroyed by accurate G5 artillery fire.

This was essentially the beginning of the end for the FAPLA 21st Brigade which was bitterly disappointing for their high command. Still, it was only a small part of a very large army. Russian officers, sensing a debacle, evacuated by Cuban FAPA helicopters leaving the remnants of the defeated force to attempt a link up with the 47th Brigade. This was the beginning of the end of Soviet advisor leadership and the start of a new era of command and control on the battlefield by tactically superior Cuban officers.

Heavy artillery fire punished the FAPLA 47th Brigade when it attempted to link up with the 59th Brigade and forced it to withdraw to its earlier position. The SADF actively sought to keep these two brigades separated from each other, which prevented them from joining to become a major force while allowing the South African combat brigades to attack them individually. The 59th Brigade had sent a substantial vanguard force in the middle of September to attempt a preliminary link up without result.

Although the SADF/UNITA forces were enjoying great success, it was not without cost. For example, Rifleman F. De Bruin was in a logistics vehicle of 61 Mechanised Battalion on 12 September 1987 when he was killed by an artillery or air strike.

Yet again Hartslief's CGB entered the fray on 13th September at a shona near the Lomba river. The combat group was supported by accurate artillery fire leading this attack, sometimes at short, but protective distances. On one

Troop of Ratels advancing through Angolan bush.—*SANDF Documentation Centre*

flank a large number of the FAPLA vanguard troops began to flee from the shelling and were chased by a troop of Ratels and Casspirs under Capt. Koos Maritz.

The unlucky FAPLA troops ended up on the wide unprotected river delta where they were mown down by withering machine gun fire and anti-personnel canister shots from the Ratels. FAPLA casualties again ran to several hundred.

South African success was not complete as the remaining Ratels ended up in another trench complex and several became stuck in the deep holes requiring evacuation under fire. Forward observer Pierre Franken, who had ordered in the first artillery strikes on the initial FAPLA advance, lurched into one such trench with his armored personnel carrier. The maze of trenches caused the Ratels great difficulty, which became critical when FAPLA T-55 tanks advanced as they were awaiting rescue.

The usual technique for crossing a trench with a Ratel was to lower the nose of the vehicle into the trench until it bottomed out on the far side of the excavation. Then the six-whee-drive differential locks would be engaged, after which the driver would floor the accelerator causing the front of the vehicle to pop up out of the trench with the rear wheels powering it over the far edge. This did not always work especially in a multiple trench scenario.

When being pursued by T-55 tanks many Casspirs and Ratels escaped by accelerating erratically through the bush. One of these tanks was taken on by Commandant Hartslief who fired several rounds into it from behind a curtain of thick protective bush before it was destroyed. Major Nortmann and Sgt. Riaan Rupping began a massive rescue effort in between the trench holes, battle smoke, signal smoke, and gunfire beginning with Pierre Franken of forward-observer fame and his armored personnel carrier. Norton and Rupping left their respective vehicles and bravely managed to extricate two of the Ratels, which were under fire. Both were awarded the Honoris Crux medal for their actions that day.

The CGB Ratels continued the action that day by drawing the T-55 tanks into deep bush where they were less maneuverable, and by using their greater speed the Ratels were able to fire their smaller cannons at the rear of the tanks causing maximum damage with minimal firepower. By this method a further two tanks were destroyed for a total of three, with several more damaged. As the light faded on the battlefield, the combat group escaped what could have been a great disaster and retreated from the FAPLA under bombardment.

Many FAPLA tanks were destroyed or critically damaged by Ratels during the Battle of Cuito Cuanavale, but South Africa's high explosive antitank (HEAT) rounds were not powerful enough to generate a first-hit kill. Even at the short ranges of the Angola bush, single 90mm rounds were incapable of destroying tanks. Ratels would have to hit their target with several volleys before knocking it out. Excellent crew drill and the cover of the thick bush saved more than one Ratel that was surprised at close range by a T-55 tank. There was of course no substitute for proper equipment, so the South Africans brought up Olifant tanks before going on the offensive towards Cuito Cuanavale.

Camouflaged FAPLA tank (center of photo), Angola 1987.—*Roland De Vries*

Later the evening of the 13th, Combat Group C under Major Lotter was dispatched to retrieve some damaged armored personnel carriers. He was ambushed by waiting FAPLA tanks and would have suffered serious casualties but for the brave actions of young Lieutenant Kooij, who led his Ratels into a fast paced and circuitous engagement of the T-55 tanks. After several attacks, feints, and eventual retreat, two tanks were destroyed without any SADF losses. Kooij was awarded the Honoris Crux for his distinguished and capable actions. This maneuver did not always work: Rifleman F. A. Muehlenbeck, the driver of a 4 South African Infantry Ratel, was killed along with his gunner while engaging a FAPLA T-55 tank on 9 November 1987.

It was a bad luck September 13th for Capt. Alfred D. McCallum and Lt. J. R. Alves who were in a Ratel armored vehicle trapped in a mud hole when it was fired on by a T-55 tank. The entire crew was killed instantly when the Ratel was hit by the 100mm tank shell, which detonated the interior ammunition causing the Ratel to explode. It seems likely that the other crew members killed in this action were Sgt. J. R. Mananza, LCpl. M. M. De

Destroyed FAPLA T-55 tank.—*SANDF Documentation Centre*

Klerk, LCpl. Waite Tchipango, and Trooper M J Kuyler. Foxtrot Company commander McCallum was the second highest ranking South African soldier killed during the Battle of Cuito Cuanavale.

One of the crew, Lance Corporal De Klerk, may very well have been the same soldier involved in a grenade throwing incident at Okalonga Base in March 1986. After a night of excessive drinking by several soldiers, including De Klerk, several grenades were thrown around the base at night causing a false attack alarm with helicopter support being dispatched to the scene. No one was killed but several soldiers were wounded by shrapnel. It was determined as a friendly fire incident and disciplinary punishments were handed out to the guilty parties.

SADF trooper Damian French was told on arrival at the UNITA base in Mavinga towards the end of 1987 that his original Ratel had been destroyed at the Lomba River and the intensity of the fire had melted machine gun and cannon shells on the floor of the machine. He subsequently was part of a Ratel attack on the remnants of the FAPLA 21st Brigade in January 1988 and confirmed the presence of South African Olifant tanks on the battlefield at that time.[85]

CSI and UNITA liaison team leader Bert Sachse was severely injured in the same encounter when a T-55 tank shell exploded over his Casspir. These FAPLA tanks only briefly wreaked havoc but caused damage and destruction of several vehicles. In the end six SADF soldiers were killed in this encounter; the greatest one incident,one day loss of life by the 20 Brigade, the 32 "Buffalo" Battalion, and by the South African Defense Force for the month of September and the Battle of Cuito Cuanavale. Eventually a withdrawal of the 32 and 101 Infantry battalions was ordered but in the confusion an officer and enlisted man were left behind. The 1 Para Battalion officer, Lieutenant Liebenberg, heroically sent his subordinate back to UNITA lines as he laid down distracting fire against advancing FAPLA soldiers. He then played dead among the dead on the battlefield until he was able to make his way back after a SADF counterattack.

The SADF attacked the FAPLA 47th, 59th, and 21st Brigades several times during September with air strikes and artillery destroying equipment and inflicting punishing casualties. Despite all this, 47th Brigade commander Silva strongly urged his superiors to allow his unit to hold its position but was refused in the strongest terms and ordered to withdraw.

On 2 October, UNITA forces under Capt. Antero Vieira, in conjunction with the SADF, attacked the remnants of the 47th who had assembled in an attempt to retreat across the Lomba and link up with the other FAPLA brigades. The concentration of FAPLA equipment provided ample targets for accurate G5 cannon fire that destroyed many vehicles. This constant bombardment prevented a river crossing that day or later that night.

The FAPLA had attempted to make a temporary track from their base about a kilometer southwest of their attempted crossing point of the Lomba River by laying tree logs on the mud of the floodplain. This force did not have the bridging equipment like the better equipped 21st Brigade, so in des-

Captured FAPLA equipment, Angola. —SANDF Documentation Centre

peration they drove flat-topped Soviet PT 76 amphibious tanks into the river in order to form a roof-top bridge for the marooned T-55 tanks. Then a T-55 slipped off this vehicular platform and blocked any following vehicles. The SADF 61st Mechanised Brigade, led from the east by a UNITA recce unit, proceeded to rush the rearguard of the 47th Brigade and finish it off. The entire 47th Brigade was caught in the open from the log road to the river banks and panic spread among the troops of the 47th who proceeded to drive their vehicles into the river or simply abandoned their equipment in a rush to escape. It was at this point that an entire Soviet SA-8 missile system was abandoned. Artillery fire from their comrades in the 59th Brigade to assist their escape was ineffective.[86]

Resistance stiffened for a short time with FAPLA artillery counterstrikes and tank attacks until arrival of the UNITA 3rd Battalion, which was the tipping point of the battle. The aggressive disposition of FAPLA tank commanders surprised the SADF commanders in the field and clearly showed they were a cut above regular troops.

Hundreds of FAPLA troops eventually fled and were mown down as they ran into a nearby shona pursued by UNITA and SADF mechanized units. The attacking forces were able to capture or destroy a huge amount of equipment, much of it new, including eighteen tanks and several Soviet armored vehicles, artillery pieces, and nearly a hundred trucks.[87]

South African estimates of FAPLA casualties for the last week of September 1987 were two to three hundred and three to six hundred for the entire month. An unconfirmed estimate of SADF casualties is eight: six ground force and two air force. This total rises to fourteen when the following are incuded:

Rudolf J. Badenhorst	died 26 September 1987 cause unknown
Rifleman William G. Beukman	died 20 September 1987 in a G5 howitzer loading accident.
Rifleman F. De Bruin	died 12 September 1987 in a motor vehicle accident while on patrol.
Lance Corporal H. A. Oosthuizen	died 4 September 1987 in a motor vehicle accident during operations in southern Angola.
Private Francois du P. Smit 1st Recce Regiment	died 4 August 1987 in a shooting accident.

Rifleman P. A. Visagie,	died 16 September 1987
61 Mechanised Battalion	accidental shooting while
	on training maneuvers.

Although a relatively primitive machine the Ratel, named after the South African badger, made a name for itself at Lomba River only because of brave and capable crews who had to flank the Soviet T-55 tanks to their rear and shoot from a standing still position. This was an immense act of self-control in the given situation as the hits had to be almost point-blank in the T-55's spots, such as, vents, turret joints, and the engine compartment in the rear of the tank chassis. The thick Angolan bush had about a ten to twenty meter visibility, which helped the Ratel crews blindly attack FAPLA T-55 tanks. The smaller, more agile Ratel could often fire several 90mm rounds into the tank before it could react. The repeated Ratel shots that it took to immobilize the T-55 tanks were a future warning for the SADF on the limited power of their 90mm gun.

Destroyed FAPLA T-55 Tank.—*Anthony Turton*

Being a small force, in the nature of a self-sustaining flying column, the SADF 20 Brigade was unable to pursue the remaining FAPLA 59th, 21st, and 16th Brigades, which were able to retreat to fight another day. They were also assisted by the SADF conscript policy which resuted in a mandatory changeover of those soldiers who had completed their tour of duty at a crucial time in December.[88]

CHAPTER 9

COMMANDANT ROBBIE HARTSLIEF

Robert "Robbie" Hartslief, the son of William P. Hartslief, was born in South Africa on 27 December 1956 in Kroonstad, which is about two hundred kilometers south of Johannesburg. It lies in what was formerly the Boer independent republic known as the Orange Free State. If there was a Boer heartland, it was here. Legend has it that the town was named after a horse called Kroon, which had belonged to a Voortrekker, who had founded the town. Kroon apparently died by drowning in a stream near where the town now stands. Voortrekkers, Afrikaans for "those who trek ahead," were Boer pioneers who moved into the interior of South Africa.

Kroonstad was also home to the famous black Jamaican geologist Isaac Barnes who founded and operated two diamond syndicates between 1903 and 1909. In 1907 the two mines owned by Barnes grossed over one million pounds. Barnes was deported in 1909 after he addressed a crowd of over ten thousand, of all races, in Cape Town on the evils of apartheid. The next black man to do this was Nelson Mandela nearly a century later. Many white Boer businessmen oppposed his deportation and several swore an affidavit in support of his character.[89]

Jannie Geldenhuys, chief of the SADF, also came from Kroonstad and Hartslief would ultimately serve under him. Robbie was educated in South Africa first at the Afrikaanse Hoerskool in Kroonstad and later at the South Africa Military Academy where he graduated in 1977 with a Batchelor of Arts (Military) from the Saldanha faculty of Military Science at the University of Stellenbosch. At the time he attended the academy it was an all male, all white institution. His SADF force number was 72427875 PE, which meant he entered the SADF as a volunteer to the permanent force in 1975. Hartslief was no conscript but a military man to his lifelong core.

The South Africa Military Academy was established on April Fools Day 1950 at Voortrekkerhoogte (Voortrekker Heights), a military base outside of Pretoria, as part of the University of Pretoria and the South African Military College, which later became the South Africa Army College. It was a unique blend of academia and warrior, which like many things South African was ahead of its time in sub-Saharan Africa but similar to the U.S. Army ROTC college programs, among others. In the English colonial period Voortrekker Heights was known as Roberts Heights after Field Marshal Lord Roberts, commander in chief of the British forces in South Africa. This area is now called Thaba Tswane in the postapartheid era and it is hoped that after two historical name changes the South African National Defence Force will resist the modern trend to rename places of distinction with corporate names.

In 1953 the academy was moved to Saldanha as part of the University of Stellenbosch where it remains today, a venerable institution of military officer corps training. Saldanha Bay is a small town with a natural harbor on the coast of South Africa, northwest of Cape Town and not far from Stellenbosch, the second oldest town in South Africa. Robbie Hartslief was first married to Petro van der Merwe, a union that followed with three sons: Perrin, Werner, and Lothar. The first marriage did not last and his second and

Colonel Robbie Hartslief March 2004.—*Dr. Marna Cilliers-Hartslief*

final marriage was in 1990 to Dr Marna Cilliers, a well-known South African environmental activist.

Robbie started his military career 1975 with the 1st South Africa Infantry and by 1977 he was a second lieutenant. He rose through the ranks becoming a lieutenant in 1979, a captain in 1981, major in 1984, lieutenant colonel in 1987, and his last promotion to colonel in 1994. He was to remain at this rank for the five years until his departure from the SADF although his evaluations rose from 83 percent in 1993 to 89 percent in 1995. All his promotions came every two to three years on the first of January and at the time of the Battle of Cuito Cuanavale he was a lieutenant colonel, although many sources refer to him as commandant. Since the nineteenth century South African armed forces had the rank of commandant equivalent to a lieutenant colonel in other countries' defence forces. In 1996 the rank of commandant was "retired" from the SANDF.

Robbie passed his basic training in March 1975, the officer course in September 1975, and graduated from university with his degree in December 1977. By January 1985 he was a major with the 2nd South Africa Infantry Battalion.

Commandant Robbie Hartslief of Combat Group Bravo, 20 Brigade, was the last casualty of the Battle of Cuito Cuanavale to not receive significant recognition for his courageous and daring actions for the SADF at the

SADF Ratels on their way to Angola to fight FAPLA 16th Brigade.—
Richard Wiles

Lomba River. On 13 September 1987 Hartslief sought to assist some disabled Ratels when he demolished a T-55 tank at dangerously close range near the Lomba River by firing several rounds from his Ratel.[90]

There was no accelerated promotion for Hartslief, or at the very least a Honoris Crux medal; action men like him are feared and rejected by the administratively and politically astute who zealously guard their leadership positions.

Robbie's last hurrah turned out to be the Lesotho incursion of 1998, referred to as Operation Boleas, which made him politically unpalatable in his home country whatever the outcome. In March 1999 when he resigned from the South African National Defence Force he was described as the country's most highly trained peacekeeper. At the time he was commander of the National Defence Force's 43rd Mechanised Brigade. Ultimately, like so many others, Colonel Hartslief left the SADF for international security work. He had been asked to make way for a younger successor recruited from the former ANC military wing Umkhonto We Sizwe (Spear of the Nation) or MK.[91]

Before his departure from the South African military, in a confidential SANDF assessment document that was highly complimentary of Colonel Harslief, he was described as having excellent communication skills with both soldiers and the media in English and Afrikaans. It went on to describe him as a capable and flexible officer who had mastered the new South African Department of Defence management and planning systems. The colonel was also characterized as a proven and capable commander who led by example from the front.

In matters of training Hartslief had a thorough background as a directing staff member of the South African army and attended peacekeeping courses abroad to broaden his knowledge and capability as a commander. Colonel Hartslief changed with the times, enhanced his professional knowledge, and performed his duties without a bad mark against him. The true loves of his life, the army and South Africa, cast him aside at the apex of his talents, and that was an unforgivable act by any measure for a man who had dedicated his life to such a singlular and honorable purpose.[92]

Robbie started as country manager for Gray Security in Angola before a promotion to regional director that required travel and work in both West African countries and Kosovo. Colonel Hartslief then joined Group 4 Securicor to manage operations in twelve countries including Sierra Leone, Cameroon, and Nigeria. His last posting was to Bratislavia, Slovakia, as regional director for the company.

As his career faded, Hartslief was consigned to the dustbin of the loyal, honorable, and brave, and Robbie decided to end his own life in July 2006. Only forty-nine years old he would find good company in the hereafter with his former Cuban foe General Ochoa and his ally, General Ben Ben.

Colonel Robbie Hartslief, March 2004.—*Dr. Marna Cilliers-Hartslief*

Robbie Hartslief committed suicide a few months short of his fiftieth birthday on 19 July 2006 suffering from posttraumatic stress disorder: gone but not forgotten.

It is often said that the brave die first but fear and confusion can be the constant sky over a life well lived with sundown, the only release.

Plutarch records such a death in *The Life of Brutus*:

Finally, he spoke to Volumnius himself in Greek, reminding him of their student life, and begged him to grasp his sword with him and help him drive home the blow. And when Volumnius refused, and the rest likewise . . . grasping with both hands the hilt of his naked sword, he fell upon it and died.

CHAPTER 10

THE RETREAT

As a result of the debacle at Lomba River and the resulting retreat, General Pedro Benga Lima, nom de guerre Foguetao or Rocket, the FAPLA commander was relieved of duty but nevertheless continued serving in the FAPLA. There was also a report that after the dust settled the commander of the 47th Brigade was executed.[93]

On 1 October 1987, during the 21st Brigade's retreat from the Lomba River Soviet officer and FAPLA translator Oleg Snitko was hit by South African artillery shrapnel that broke his leg and tore his off hand. He was evacuated by a Cuban operated FAPA helicopter but died a day and a half later. Snitko's death left many of his fellow Soviet officers shell shocked from the persistent SADF artillery and air strikes. Young Snitko's body was returned to his home town of Kiev in the Ukraine for burial.[94]

Two days later another young officer from the opposing side, 2nd Lt. Adriaan Hind of the SADF, reported on the radio that he had seen a FAPLA tank and was killed soon after when a T-55 tank or RPG round destroyed his Ratel 90 and badly wounded two of his crew. The projectile struck the left front underside and axle of the Ratel leaving a gaping hole above the axle. The projectile likely deflected off the axle before it came up into the compartment in front of Lieutenant Hind and to the left of driver Glen Woodhouse.

Adriaan Hind was able to exit the vehicle and walk away before collapsing from his injuries. A Ratel that was following came up quickly, and as driver Woodhouse flopped to the ground Rifleman Brad Saunders dismounted and dragged the wounded driver back into the undamaged Ratel.

Saunders administered first aid to Woodhouse's awful wounds while the injured driver was choking on his own blood, and had had some of his fingers blown off. After being briefly stuck on a tree trunk Woodhouse was delivered to the medics. Shortly afterwards the injured driver emerged from the Unimog medic vehicle ramp covered in bloody bandages, relieved himself, and walked back up the ramp. The other lead-Ratel crew member, Stompie, received shrapnel wounds but also survived.

The round could have been a ricochet off the ground as the FAPLA often put their tanks in earthen revetments, reversed in with their turrets at ground level. FAPLA forces thought themselves well protected with an extensive network of trenches and bunkers, which in fact made them a fixed target for the highly mobile SADF forces. The only FAPLA advantage was the rare occasion when an attacking Ratel that overran a trench became stuck, not having made it to the far side, making them a sitting duck.

Captured FAPLA officer bunker, November 1987.
—*Richard Wiles*

The Ratels also experienced many RPG hits on the ground in front and to the side sometimes bursting tires and often throwing up sand which poured into open turrets. One SADF unit thought it was under attack by MiGs that flew over so low that the South African soldiers could feel the heat of the jets' engine exhaust. Fortunately for the South Africans the MiGs did not attack them; perhaps the MiGs were flying too low and too fast to notice them.[95]

At the Lomba River, the disciplined and more experienced SADF troops found that a frequent FAPLA reaction to artillery fire was panic on their radio net. This served to assist the South African fire control as frightened FAPLA officers reported artillery shell strikes at set distances and direction from their position.

There were allegations of poison gas use by both sides. UNITA frequently complained that soldiers had been subjected to toxic gas with a number showing symptoms of poisoning. These men were evacuated for medical treatment and seen by SADF doctors whose diagnosis was posttraumatic stress disorder by those who thought they had been subjected to poison gas. However, in 1989 UNITA found what was believed to be toxic bombs near Mavinga. One of these approximately 76mm bombs, yellow with red markings in Russian, and individually packed in a sturdy container, was sent for analysis. The ultimate analysis result is still secret.[96]

SADF Ratel at temporary base in Angola. —SANDF Documentation Centre

The SADF had several false warnings about poisonous gas with the associated rush to don gas masks and issue of antidote injections. This usually turned out to be nothing more sinister than white phosphorus smoke, which was confirmed by a later inquiry at which many senior SADF officers testified.

On 8 October 1987 Frikki De Jager was a Ratel 90 driver of Charlie Squadron, 61 Mechanised Battalion, in the eastern Angola bush. After the defeat of the FAPLA 47th Brigade near the Lomba River, Charlie Squadron advanced farther north during the night to get in position for a follow-on attack. Just before dawn the squadron attempted to take cover in the trees and bush near a shona to avoid being caught in the open in the early morning daylight when FAPA MiGs were known to patrol. The soldiers followed the usual procedure when they pulled in to camp: camouflage with brush and camouflage nets and dig foxholes while maintaining radio silence. After such a long night the drivers were tired and most of them fell asleep while other crew members proceeded to disguise their vehicles.

Trooper De Jager was lying on a bench in the back of his Ratel 90 to the left side in front of the ammo racks when there was a sound like radio static followed by a loud roar as two sand colored MiG-21s approached at tree top height. De Jager's unit was about half a kilometer in front of the rest of the convoy when the MiGs must have seen the dust trail in the light of the breaking dawn. Some thought they were South African Air Force jets as there had been no warnings over the radio from SADF headquarters. Then, when the MiGs were close enough to see the red star on their sides there was panic. The aircraft were a hundred or so feet away, above the trees and the unit was still exposed when the headquarters radio warning finally came, too late. as 500 lb. parachute bombs exploded around the unit. Frikki De Jager was sound asleep when one of the bombs exploded behind his Ratel, forcing the rear end down and igniting the Ratel's ammunition to ignite. Trooper De Jager suffered multiple wounds and was evacuated out by helicopter but didn't survive the flight.

Another soldier, Pierman White, saw the bomb coming down on parachute and tried to run. His lower leg was severed above the boot by shrapnel. White would spend the rest of his life with a crutch and prosthesis in his home town of Durban. He received 10,000 Rand from the SADF for this terrible wound.[97]

Somewhat akin to the practice in World War II where rude or intimidating messages were put on bombs, the Cubans did the same but used more ideologically correct phrasing. In one case, the recovered tail fin of a MiG parachute bomb had the words"Des Tornados Puesto," The Tornadoes of Destruction.[98]

During the middle of October FAPLA Major Major Joao Domingos Baptista Cordeiro, or Ngueto as he was known, was in command of the forward command post at Cuito Cuanavale when G5 shelling started. He became involved in a frenetic coordination effort to guide remnants of the retreating FAPLA units to the relative safety of Cuito's air defences. Ngueto eventually rose to the rank of lieutenant general and Commander 6th Region. He survived Cuito but unfortunately died in a 2002 helicopter crash accompanied by former UNITA officer Lt. Col. Felisberto Mortalha while promoting the new, reunited Angolan FAA army.[99]

As the FAPLA brigades retreated, South African motorized units screened by UNITA vanguards attempted to go after them. Often this meant following the FAPLA tracks, which predictably resulted in the occasional FAPLA ambush, as the SADF combat groups discovered. In addition, specialized FAPLA units placed antivehicle mines as they departed, often in conjunction with antipersonnel mines, to catch escaping troops who might flee a damaged vehicle. This slowed but did not stop SADF movement. The small SADF force ultimately sought to prevent the FAPLA brigades from escaping across the Chambinga River bridge to the east and reaching the Chambinga high ground. It was a tall order under the circumstances, ultimately too tall. Apart from the occasional skirmish and bombardment, the FAPLA were able to reach Chambinga in late October.

By the end of October 1987 the South Africans had moved close enough to Cuito Cuanavale to begin regular G5 shelling of of the the strategic stongpoint town. These initial bombardments destroyed several aircraft as well as other equipment and buildings. Initially some aircraft were destroyed when the SAAF made feints with Mirages as if to attack Cuito and MiGs were scrambled in response from Menongue. In short order all FAPLA and Cuban aircraft activity ceased at Cuito but their antiaircraft missile defenses remained very strong.

South African Olifant tanks attacked FAPLA T-55 tanks of the 16th Brigade for the first SADF tank battle since the World War II near the Chambinga River on 9 November 1987. Over time the brigade had become substantially isolated near the Chambinga River and thereby ripe for attack by the the limited but potent South African offensive forces in the area at that time. They were also able to achieve tactical surprise by attack feints on the 59th Brigade from a southerly direction, which provided a perfect distraction at a crucial time. Credit for the first SADF tank-on-tank kill since World War II went to Lt. Hein Fourie.[100]

Olifant tank commander Roelof Voster had this to say about the conditions in the Angola bush:

One of the things about a tank, it's ironic. A tank is designed and developed in a certain way, and I'll explain to you now what I mean. When you're up on the border you get rid of those things for practical reasons. If you look at a tank sideways like that, there's what you call plate. There's some steel plates that covers the tracks. Now one of the main purposes of that is to ensure early detonation from enemy fire. Especially if you have an RPG or something shooting at you. It will first hit the cover plate before it actually penetrates the tank. But when you're up in the bush those things are just in the bloody way. It's a nuisance. So what do you do, you take them off, you move them one side, you go fight without them, so what's the point of designing a tank like that? It's not typical tank country.[101]

SADF Olifant tank in Angola.—*SANDF Documentation Centre*

A South African Defence Force tank troop consisted of three tanks, with three troops in a squadron for a total of nine Olifant tanks. Each tank had a crew of four: the driver in front who sits closed in his compartment, the gunner in the cupola or turret, the tank commander who sits behind and slightly above the gunner, and last but not least the loader on the other side of the main gun from the gunner. The Olifant's 105mm main gun rounds are very heavy, but the tank is designed to "bomb up," that is move rounds from a storage rack to the ready rack, when the rounds are loaded into the tank. There are specific places for the ammunition to be readily available, and when that supply is finished, the crew have to wait for a lull in the fire to turn the turret to access the other storage compartments. The noise in the tank was bad during firing but dust and sand were more a problem for tank crews in Angola.

The SADF did not win this part of the Battle of Cuito Cuanavale without loss, including one of a pair of twins. Sergeant Pierre Digue of the 61st Mechanised Battalion was killed on 9 November 1987 leaving behind his twin brother Andre. Pierre was killed when his vehicle encountered a Soviet 23mm AAA gun deployed in a ground-firing role. Sergeant Digue is buried at Durbanville Cemetery located in the northern suburbs of Cape Town. Depressingly, this cemetary is listed as one of the top hundred attractions for out-of-towners visiting Cape Town.

SADF Ratels attacking FAPLA 16th Brigade camp, November 1987.
—*Richard Wiles*

Five other SADF soldiers were killed that day. Ratel No. 12B gunner Rifleman A. M. Thom and his driver F. A. Muehlenbeck of the 4 South African Infantry were killed with crew member Rifleman P. G. Claasen when they were surprised by a T-55 tank just a few hundred feet away. Prior to this Thom had fired several 20mm armor piercing rounds at another T-55, which had exploded inside the tank.

Rifleman Adriaan Thom was awarded the Honoris Crux posthumously for his bravery that day. Thom and Claasen were only nineteen years old while Muehlenbeck was not much older at twenty when they were all killed.

Burning SADF Ratel 21B of Thom, Muehlenbeck, and Claasen.
—*Richard Wiles*

The burning Ratel had its hatches blown out and it was two days before remains could be recovered.[102]

Corporal T. A. Duvenhage of the 4 South African Infantry and Pvt. A. Steward were also killed as a result of contact with FAPLA forces. Duvenage was hit by mortar shrapnel after he dismounted from his Ratel. This second, one-day loss of six South African soldiers speaks to the ferocity of battle that day between the Chambinga and Lomba rivers, although one source puts the total at seven. And, the SADF casualties did not stop there.[103]

FAPLA T-55 destroyed by two armored-piercing shots from SADF Ratel 90.
—*Richard Wiles*

By the end of the day the FAPLA was left with nearl at least a hundred casualties with at least thirteen tanks and various other equipment destroyed, abandoned, or captured by the UNITA/SADF force. The SADF had an Olifant tank damaged and one Ratel destroyed and another damaged. While this was a brief, fierce engagement, the FAPLA 16th Brigade was able to withdraw and remain intact, unlike the earlier decimation of the 47th Brigade at the Lomba River.

Two days later the South Africans, supported by UNITA troops, mounted a further attack on elements of FAPLA that were west of the Chambinga River, again with a two-prong force with one part being utilized to distract the 21st and 25th brigades to the south of the actual objective. The attack was mounted in thick bush and after an initial advance of several tiring kilometers without contact, the SADF/UNITA force paused for a rest whereupon they began to take FAPLA fire. A confusing battle ensued with the attackers running into a known minefield causing massive damage to an Olifant tank and a Ratel. With all the casualties and equipment damage the advance ground to a halt and the FAPLA forces withdrew. An disinterested observer might have described this scene as a well-planned FAPLA ambush of over-confident attackers, although the FAPLA also took some losses including several tanks and armored vehicles.[104]

That same day it was raining when John Howes, Marius Mitton, and Pieter Schutte were ambushed on open ground while riding in Ratels of the 61st Mechanised Battalion. They were driving through thick bush and an-

SADF Ratel advancing through Angolan bush.—*SANDF Documentation Centre*

other Ratel carrying Rifleman Evan Lyon kept breaking down, causing it to fall behind which likely saved his life.

After some time the Ratels came into a clearing where they received a barrage of small arms fire and mortar fire. John Howes exited the Ratel next to Rifleman Lyon and was shot through the heart. He died instantly. Lyon, who was the tail gunner, immediately went to the front of his vehicle and began to fire the .50 cal. Browning heavy machine gun. Under the cover of Lyon's fire the Ratel's retreated from the ambush, but Lyon's vehicle got stuck, so the crew jumped out with the bullets still zipping past their heads.

Rifleman Marius Mitton of the 4 South African Infantry Battalion and part of Combat Group C was able to destroy a FAPLA T-55 tank that same day by striking the turret rim several times with fire from his Ratel. Shortly after, Mitton's Ratel was hit by a 100mm shell from another T-55, wounding him severely and killing his driver, twenty-year-old Rifleman Pieter Schutte. Gunner Mitton was seen to climb out the Ratel turret and fall to the ground. He was evacuated but died of his wounds on 25 November 1987. There were three other SADF casualties that day: Rifleman Ernest Kapepura, 32 "Buffalo" Battalion ; Rifleman Fernando Mauricio, "Buffalo" 32 Battalion; and Rifleman D. W. Van Zyl, 4 South African Infantry.

The two Buffalo soldiers were apparently killed by a mortar round that struck the Olifant tank upon which they were riding in their usual position, on the outside. Van Zyl was recovered from the battlefield after having been shot in the neck. One source has the casualties as five that day, not the actual six. (Or eight if the two unknown G5 bombardier casualties mentioned by Brig. Gen. Dick Lord are included.) It was the third time the SADF had suffered losses of six soldiers in a single day.[105]

Total South African ground losses for November 1987 alone were twenty, increasing to twenty-one with SAAF pilot Andre Stapa. And there were four more KIAs in October. If the total of fourteen for September is added in, this would be thirty-nine South African deaths for the three months. This accounting casts grave doubt on SADF chief General Geldenhuys's report that thirty-one South African soldiers were killed during the eight month period July 1987 to February 1988. Perhaps this was an attempt not to add fuel to the fire of the End Conscription Campaign.[106]

One SADF miscalculation that didn't involve casualties was on the night of 14 November when the entire FAPLA 21st Brigade was able to slip past a force sent to ambush them. The South African force had been deployed to the wrong area and the FAPLA troops crossed over the Vimpulo River to safety with other FAPLA units. The next day UNITA General Ben Ben was highly critical of this error in discussions with the SADF officers. At night in the thick bush with incomplete intelligence and fairly long distances, it was an understandable mistake. There was also the occasional friendly-fire incident such as during an attack in December when a 4 South African Infantry Ratel mistakenly shot out the rear of Ratel No. 12B that crossed its line of fire in the dense bush before destroying a FAPLA BTR 60.[107]

During this uncertain period the FAPLA brigades experienced frequent mass desertions in the face of poor logistical supply, incompetent or absent leadership, and the threat of wide-ranging UNITA forces in difficult terrain. One of the largest desertions of FAPLA soldiers was from the 59th Brigade in December, which in addition to weakening the brigade also gave the benefit of additional intelligence collection to SADF/UNITA. In many cases, crucial FAPLA equipment was abandoned by its drivers only to be taken over by the UNITA forces. Repeated efforts to send large FAPLA advance parties to sweep for the SADF forward observers who who were calling in punishing artillery strikes came to naught.[108]

The SADF minimized battlefield deaths by having a superior field medical system provided by medics from the South African Medical Service (SAMS). Prior to joining their units medics received thirty-six weeks of training including medical theory, trauma management, and nursing skills. The SADF force also included the armored, mine-resistant Rinkhals ambulance (an Afrikaans name for the snake curling around the medical emblem) that could carry a medic, six litter patients, and two ambulatory cases. Also, smaller Unimog vehicles were often used in Angola with medical crew. The ambulances would evacuate casualties to the nearest medical post where they were stabilized prior to evacuation, by air if necessary. Typically a team comprised of a doctor and medic rode the medevac, or *casevac* as soldiers called them, in SAAF Puma helicopters to continue treatment enroute to the hospital. Because of the FAPLA dominance of the air during daylight a seriously injured casualty in the morning was unlikely to survive the wait to nightfall. The SAMS medics operating in combat zones were also quite susceptible to being caught in firefights or ambushes. They were some of the most highly decorated and brave South African troops of the Battle of Cuito Cuanavale.

On 15 November LCpl. J. Redelinghuys of the South African Medical Service was severely injured in a firefight near the Hube River and died shortly after his twentieth birthday. While being recovered, Redelinghuys's disabled Rinkal medic vehicle had been surprised by a FAPLA BM-21 rocket launcher. The Stalin's Organ (German soldiers had dubbed a predecessor to the BM-21 "Stalin's Organ" while they were under Soviet bombardment.) fired a rocket that hit the tow bar and the shrapnel struck young Redelinghuys in the abdomen and hip. Two older, more experienced soldiers were also wounded with Medic Redelinghuys, who died several days later being evacuated to the SADF base at Rundu in Namibia.

SADF Wit Hings Recovery Vehicle with Unimog in background.
—*Gary Smith/ sa-soldier.com*

That same afternoon there was another confused running firefight that left casualties and equipment destroyed on both sides. Again, this had its genesis in the inaccurate deployment of an SADF unit, which prevented execution of a successful ambush. At the height of the action the South African forces were forced to withdraw for replenishment, which allowed the FAPLA 21st Brigade to safely withdraw. This was the first occasion that the FAPLA had battled a major SADF force to a standstill, and it was the beginning of harder-fought encounters the they moved closer to Cuito Cuanavale and the farther the South Africans were from home.

One source puts SADF casualties at four with no account given of UNITA casualties. Two of those unidentified are likely Sgt. Arsenio Baptista and Rifleman Joaquim Pedro, both members of the famed 32 "Buffalo" Battalion, who were reportedly killed on 16 November. Baptista was one of the highest ranking Buffalo soldiers killed during the Battle of Cuito Cuanavale. A third was 4 South African Infantry Cpl. J. Van Heerden who was instantly killed by mortar shrapnel as he walked through a deserted FAPLA camp.

The following day, 17 November, elements of the SADF expeditionary unit led by UNITA troops decided to pursue FAPLA forces who were heading to the Chambinga bridge and fords that had been secured despite frequent artillery strikes.

SADF tactics normally generated a greater operational tempo than the FAPLA, which had brought them early to the jump-off point. The ensuing movement only resulted in some minor skirmishes due to a delay in maneuvering through difficult bush conditions in an effort to attain the best attack position. During this confused maneuvering the remnants of the 21st Brigade slipped away while the SADF resupplied their forces. The FAPLA escape allowed it to reach the Chambinga high ground and join in the defence of the Tumpo bridgehead. This was the sole instance during the Battle of Cuito Cuanavale when FAPLA forces achieved a tactical success through superior speed of movement albeit in retreat.

The lucky but depleted 21st Brigade was able to reach this important river crossing much to SADF dismay but some grudging regard. This became a significant milestone in the events of the battle when the tide began to turn against UNITA and the SADF as the Cubans arrived to intercede and with South African logistical superiority beginning to diminish. It is clear that these harassing attacks with few resources showed no great commitment by the SADF to either destroy the retreating FAPLA forces *or* attack Cuito Cuanavale. At best it was a tactic to keep FAPLA on the run and prevent substantial counterattacks.

Almost a week later, on 21 November 1987, it was the Cuban turn to shed blood, except this time the victim fell from the sky. Veteran MiG-23ML pilot Lt. Ernesto Chavez Marrero of the Cuban FAPA 25th Air Combat Fighter Regiment, operating out of the former Portuguese Serpa Pinto Air Base at Menongue, was killed by his own antiaircraft fire. He had been scrambled to intercept unknown radar targets and had been mistakenly vectored into prohibited airspace over Cuban antiaircraft units near the Lomba River. The young pilot was killed when his neck broke on ejection. There was also a report that Marrero was shot down by UNITA antiaircraft fire.[109]

An aborted SADF attack on 25 November towards the Tumpo River resulted in the death of an unknown Ratel gunner when a mortar shell fell through the open hatch. The attacking force had become bogged down by difficult navigation in thick bush and became subject to accurate FAPLA bombardments, some of it from Cuito. The tables were beginning to turn and the South African forces advanced no farther for some time. This frus-

trated attack would give a morale boost to FAPLA troops now being reinforced by experienced Cuban troops.[110]

During the African winter of 1987 the FAPLA forces were in retreat
under constant harassment by the UNITA and SADF forces towards Cuito
Cuanavale. The FAPLA leadership realized that the loss of Cuito Cuanavale
and its airfield would mean a further retreat to Menongue which was several
hundred kilometers from Mavinga and a quantum leap for UNITA controlled territory. This also meant that UNITA, and more so the SADF supply lines, would start to be severly stretched. With the FAPLA retreating
in disarray westward, mostly without Soviet advisors, the leadership requested
urgent Cuban military assistance. Prior to this disaster the Cubans were maintaining the Lubango-Menogue southern front against UNITA to prevent
the SADF from moving deeper into Angola.

The Lomba River debacle was a severe blow to the FAPLA forces who
lost several thousand soldiers and valuable Soviet supplied equipment. In an
outbreak of frankness in December 1987, Gen. Antonio Dos Santos Franca,
FAPLA army chief of staff, also known by his nom de guerre N'Dalu, confirmed in a newspaper interview that they should never have crossed the
Lomba River. The cracks in their relationship with their Soviet benefactors
were beginning to show and a more pro-Cuban approach quickly developed
in the upper echelons of the FAPLA, many of whom were disgusted with
the indecent haste that the senior Soviet officers fled the field of battle,

A Russian BM-21 Grad rocket launcher (Stalin's Organ) on a Ural-4320 chassis (2B17) in Saint Petersburg in 2009. —Robert Wray (Wikimedia)

frequently with the speed of helicopter evacuation.[111] A month prior to this revelation N'Dalu confirmed to Mozambican journalist Carlos Cardoso that FAPLA losses were 242 dead, 16 missing, and 728 wounded. Equipment destruction included 27 tanks, 126 other vehicles, 4 helicopters, and 2 MiGs.[112]

A right side view of six Soviet 122mm BM-21 multiple rocket launcher systems. The BM-21 consists of a Ural-375D truck chassis with a 40-round rocket launcher mounted on the rear of the hull.—*defenseimagery.mil*

Unfortunately, Journalist Cardosa joined the teeming ranks of the African dead when he was murdered in 2000 for doing the unimaginable: revealing the truth. In southern Africa they obviously follow the Greek tragedy Antigone by Sophocles to the letter: "No one loves the messenger who brings bad news" or the modern equivalent, shoot the messenger.

It was not the finest hour for the nation of Stalin, which followed up its cowardly performance in Angola later with an even more stinging retreat from Afghanistan. It seemed that the great steel of the Soviet war machine proudly publicized during and after World War II rang hollow in the ebb tide of the following years. To add insult to injury, it is reputed that the SADF took one of its captured Soviet T-55 tanks and melted it down to use as a campaign medal for its soldiers in Angola.[113]

A fair and possibly objective assessment was made by American Chester Crocker, former assistant secretary of state for African affairs in the Reagan administration who succinctly stated in his book *High Noon In Southern Africa*:

SADF Ratel Crew
Medal, Operation
Modular, Angolan
winter 1987.
—*Richard Wiles*

In early October the Soviet-FAPLA offensive was smashed at the Lomba River near Mavinga. It turned into a headlong retreat over the 120 miles back to the primary launching point at Cuito Cuanavale. In some of the bloodiest battles of the entire civil war, a combined force of some 8,000 UNITA fighters and 4,000 SADF troops destroyed one FAPLA brigade and mauled several others out of a total FAPLA force of some 18,000 engaged in the three-pronged offensive. Estimates of FAPLA losses ranged upward of 4,000 killed and wounded.[114]

Crocker went on to to help negotiate the peace in Angola in 1988 for a war that his country had helped to finance, encourage, and proliferate before waltzing away from the mess of mines, poverty, and AIDS. The U.S. policy at the time utilized the valuable lesson of Vietnam that it was cheaper to finance guerillas in a low intensity conflict such as Angola or Afghanistan. The Soviets were then stuck with the multibillion ruble bill of shoring up foreign governments, which ultimately may have contributed to the disintegration of the Soviet Union. In Angola, the dollar was mightier than the ruble.

Yet in all this South Africa remained an economic giant to adjoining and nearby southern Africa countries, who maintained strong economic ties to Johannesburg despite conflicts, attacks, invasions, *and* apartheid. In southern Africa, the rand was even mightier than the dollar.

When the FAPLA suffered heavy losses at the Lomba River the Soviets meekly withdrew their advisors from the fluid battlefield which severely hampered the FAPLA field leadership and contributed further to general confusion and retreat west. Igor Zhdarkin, a Soviet translator to the 21st Brigade revealed in his memoirs of Angola that FAPLA troops were under continual bombardment by the SADF along with sniping, mining, and other harassment by UNITA forces on the ground in the retreat from the Lomba River. Even the Russians who had served in Afghanistan never experienced such horrors as the barrage of SADF artillery across the Lomba River. Zhdarkin confirmed that under fire from the G5 guns with Mirage and Buccaneer aircraft bombing sorties, the FAPLA brigades panicked and deserted the field in flight, leaving behind a Soviet graveyard of tanks, armored personnel carriers, trucks, ammunition, and miscellaneous equipment. He also alleged that during the retreat to Cuito Cuanavale they were even bombed with chemical munitions containing poisonous gas against which they had no gas masks for protection. There has been no confirmation of this from any other source and this claim seems doubtful. Finally, and after nearly two months of retreating under fire, Zhardkin was able to join the 59th and 16th Brigades awaiting the defense of Cuito Cuanavale. This suggests that in fact it was the FAPLA 21st and 47th Brigades that were substantially destroyed at the Lomba River and not the 16th Brigade.[115]

Translator Zhdarkin, a part of the Soviet officer cadre that decamped in the face of adversity, went on to make bizarre racist remarks that Angolan soldiers were unsuitable for war, afraid to take part in combat actions and unwilling to take the Russians' advice. Zhdarkin fails to mention that it was the Soviets who were the architects of the Lomba River disaster. Further and as was later observed at Cuito, the FAPLA soldiers generally fought better alongside the Cubans than the Soviets. In contrast he accurately states that the South African fought well and competently. He was also apparently enamored by SADF propaganda messages delivered by artillery shells that the Soviets leave Cuito Cuanavale to the SADF. Contrary to expectations, similar FAPLA messages directed to their opponents only provided comic relief for SADF soldiers in the field.

Many accolades were also given by Zhdarkin to the Cubans who saved the day at Cuito Cuanavale as he retreated with the remnants of the 21st Brigade.[116]

The Cuban expeditionary forces carried on a code of conduct established since their first incursion to Algeria where astutely Raul Castro required the Cuban soldiers act with humility, to be modest and not act like experts. The Soviets would have done well to follow this example, which was already practiced by the SADF with UNITA.

In an immense piece of good fortune, and to Russian chagrin, the SADF 61st Mechanised Battalion captured a Soviet SA-8 antiaircraft missile system from the 47th Brigade as well as various other advanced Soviet hardware left behind in the hasty FAPLA retreat to Cuito. Not all of this equipment was captured as a result of being abandoned by FAPLA soldiers. The change in SAAF 250 kg bombs to larger ball bearings resulted in greater damage to FAPLA vehicles rendering them inoperable by damage to tires, radiators, and engines. Proof positive was that much high value captured equipment had to be towed from the battlefield and to this day much remains rusting away in the bush beyond repair. Also, some early SADF attempts to capture Soviet equipment were discouraged by small-arms fire from remaining FAPLA troops who stood firm despite the horrors of South African aerial and artillery bombardment.[117] Although pressured by UNITA commanders to keep all the captured Soviet equipment, the SAM system was retained for inspection by the SADF and their allies Israel and the United States.

Captured
FAPLA T-55
tank with UNITA
crew, November
1987.
—*Richard Wiles*

There was an agreement between senior SADF liaison Col. Fred Oelschig and Savimbi that the SADF could keep any equipment that was captured it wanted despite UNITA misgivings. Savimbi was also quite open and willing to show the Stinger and TOW missiles supplied to his forces by the CIA to SADF analysts who visited UNITA bases on a regular basis. Certainly UNITA did not get enough credit for the result of these actions which were a significant military achievement even with the substantial SADF support.[118] SAAF liaison officer Maj. Johan Lehman received the Honoris Crux for capturing the first SA-8 missile system under sporadic fire. It was the first system of this type taken by Western forces but was in fact left behind by the retreating FAPLA. This took place in the first week of October 1987 at the end of the Lomba River skirmishes. In a November 1987 report it was estimated that the FAPLA lost twenty T-55 tanks, six SAM missile systems, and another two hundred military vehicles.[119]

Less successful was the South African diplomatic mission to the United Nations, which on 25 November was reduced to being mere spectators by the passing of Resolution 602 that demanded that South Africa cease the attack and respect the sovereignty of Angola. This resolution amounted to a rejection of the prior South African offer to withdraw its troops from Angola if Cuba did the same. Already facing international ostracism and sanctions, the South Africans ignored the resolution, much like Iraq in Kuwait during the first Gulf War, and continued their aggression.

There was also the occasional surreal incident that often occurs during a protracted conflict. In early December there was a scene reminiscent of the World War I football (soccer) game between enemies on the Western Front when SADF Ratel Driver Richard Wiles witnessed the following:

Early December we were called into battle for the first time. We were all excited and eager to "get on with it." We advanced on 25 Brigade I think. As we advanced we took heavy mortar fire and had to close all hatches. Not easy to do when it is 37 deg, 90% humidity and sitting in a steel coffin. I could hear small arms fire hitting the side of the Ratel, I could see mortars explode a few meters way but could not see where it was all coming from. We just shot wildly into the bush ahead in the hope of hitting something. I had been struggling with the Ratels diesel filter for a few days and was down on power. Our Ratel was then called upon to go and rescue another Ratel that had got stuck in a Shona. There was no bush around and the Shona was about 200m wide and 1km long with no vegetation in it. I jumped out, secured my tow bar to the other Ratel, got back in and started to pull back. That's when the diesel filter decided it had enough and the motor died and would not restart. Another Ratel came along and tried to pull us both back, he got stuck. Eventually there were 5 of us all attached together and all stuck and very vulnerable. I was scared for the very first time. I remember looking out my right hand side screen and seeing two T55 tanks about 700m away crossing the other side of the Shona. They definitely saw us as the stopped and turned their turrets on us. The Ratel that I was trying to pull out was an antitank Ratel and he had put up his Milan missile launcher ready to fire. I think they were scared to fire and attract attention and we were too. So for about 20 sec we just stared at each other waiting to make the first move. The T55 then turned their turrets back and proceeded ahead. To this day I have no idea why they didn't fire. Maybe their guns misfired or broke. An Oliphant recovery tank was called and pulled all 5 Ratels out with one pull."[120]

CHAPTER 11

THE SIEGE OF CUITO CUANAVALE

On Sunday 15 November 1987 there was an emergency meeting chaired by Cuban Commander in Chief Fidel Castro with his brother Raul, then Minister of the Revolutionary Armed Forces, Gen. Ochoa Sanchez, and others at a house in Miramar, Havana, which lasted for more than ten hours. Eventually a decision was taken to reinforce Cuito Cuanavale by Cuban troops, codenamed Maniobra XXXI Anniversario and prevent a further debacle. The code name was a reference to the anniversary of the creation of the post-Batista Cuban army, Fuerzas Armadas Revolucionarias or FAR.

This was a reluctant but necessary decision to prevent a wide scale break down of the southern Angola front beginning with the potential loss of Cuito Cuanavale. It was further decided that General Leopoldo (Polo) Cintra Frias, an experienced tank commander from prior Cuban operations in Ethiopia, was to be placed in command of the defense of Cuito Cuanavale.[121] Frias enjoyed the particular confidence of his commander in chief in what was to be his third mission in Angola with the Cuban/FAPA forces. As it turned out this confidence was well founded.

Major General Leopoldo "Polo" Cintra Frias.—*Fred Oelschig*

The Cuban Military Mission Angola (MMCA) was thus increased from about fifteen thousand to fifty thousand troops and support staff as well as substantial amounts of equipment. This required a massive air and sea mission which in itself was a substantial logistical military accomplishment in view of the limitations of aircraft, ships, and ports available to MMCA.

The first Cuban task force members, a majority from the elite FAR 50th Division, arrived in Cuito Cuanavale on the morning of 5 December 1987 by MiG-protected helicopters. Among them was Col. Alvaro Lopez Miera, Cuban Military Mission in Angola (MMCA) chief of operations, his deputy Lt. Col. Jose Senen Viamonte, and a dozen other support staff including air force and radio specialists, with a special forces squad from the feared Ministry of Interior to act as security. They were briefed by Lieutenant Colonel Batista, then head of the FAPLA at Cuito, on the status of the FAPLA brigades. information was quickly forwarded to Havana and FAPLA leadership in Luanda.

Other MMCA soldiers, officers and technical personnel followed by air to Cuito Cuanavale early that December and later by ship. They provided much needed competent middle and upper leadership that had been absent from the FAPLA side of this theater of operations until then.

The Cuban delegation inspected every position to appreciate the overall tactical situation and by their very presence brought confidence to the demoralized FAPLA troops. Their first order of business was to organize a wall of artillery to slow the SADF advance, which began slowly but steadily within a week of the Cubans' arrival. Although much of this artillery fire was inaccurate especially from the Soviet BM-21 Katyusha rocket launcher commonly known as Stalin's Organ, it served as harassing fire and slowed the South African advance.

Cuban soldiers quickly began to occupy positions near the bridge, the forward command posts, and radio stations as well as work continuously with the FAPLA commanders to organize artillery and improve accuracy without being exposed to punishing SADF counterstrikes. This part of the operation was led by the chief of the MMCA artillery, Col. Guillermo Diaz, whose efforts began to bear fruit later in January. One important directive was to push forward observers several miles out to provide more accurate intelligence. Among this frenetic activity roamed Cuban film crews tasked with sending Commander in Chief Castro footage to support the written appraisals he received, which included the conclusions by his commanders in the field that Cuito Cuanavale could repel the SADF.

Bridges and damaged equipment were repaired in preparation for the FAPLA retreat from an SADF advance that was eventually halted in February 1988 in the vicinity of the Tumpo River. The men of the MMCA directed by their energetic commander Cintra Frias, began an immediate, intense, and brief schooling of the FAPLA in the sophisticated Soviet weaponry that had been mishandled and misapplied to date. Complex and extensive trench systems were hurriedly prepared with bunkers for living and storage. These bomb resistant shelters were, for the most part, defenseless, against delayed fuse G5 howitzer shells, which on a direct hit had a devastating impact on any soldiers sheltering within.

This was when the similarities with Stalingrad began to appear as the defenders of Cuito Cuanavale went underground, a signal for a long and arduous resistance. Strengthened hangars were also prepared for FAPA helicopters operating out of the nearby airfield which could not be used by the MiGs due to constant G5 artillery harassment.

The Cuito River bridge, damaged by the SADF commando attack and then destroyed by an unmanned drone on 3 January 1988, was replaced with a wood bridge named *Patria o Muerte (Fatherland or Death)* by the Cuban builders. Eventually a self-propelled ferry was brought up to support FAPLA logistical movement into Cuito Cuanavale but this too was hit by SADF artillery. Later, a Soviet mobile bridge was brought up to cover the Cuito bridge gap caused by earlier damage.

It was a warning for the forthcoming South African attacks that the FAPLA defenses were beginning to harden and there would be no strategic retreat. The SADF and UNITA forces had yet to confront such a force in a fixed battle at a fixed location. The advantages to the experienced and well-equipped attackers of a fluid bush war were beginning to disappear on the plains around Cuito Cuanavale. It was vitally important for Commander Frias to hold or delay this advance until reinforcements arrived and for this arduous duty, within the precincts of Cuito, he delegated Commander Venancio Avila Guerrero.

The defenders of the town were organized on the ground by Col. Venancio Avila Guerrero and even began using damaged equipment by burying immobile T-55 tanks to be used as fixed cannon positions aimed towards the direction of expected SADF assaults. The most important preparation as it turned out was the layers of antitank and antipersonnel minefields that caused the demise of many South African Olifant tanks while forcing a narrow entry for any attacking forces.

The majority of Cuban reinforcements and equipment were to come by road from Menongue because of limited FAPA air capability at the town's sole airport. It was a slow, torturious transport due to wet weather, UNITA mines, and attacks ending up with SADF G5 artillery bombardments as they came in range on the approach to Cuito Cuanavale. Mines were so effective that the Cubans took to placing a medical unit near the vanguard of each column in anticipation of casualties. These columns were purposefully divided into smaller units so as to be less vulnerable to bombardment damage as they proceeded to Cuito.

The SADF also began to bring in reinforcements via the SAAF Rundu base with Hercules C-130 aircraft, and then they were driven over the Cubango River by Kwevoel cargo trucks into southeastern Angola to a transit camp for acclimatization before starting frontline duty. The first thing that hit arriving soldiers when they landed at Rundu was heat that felt like a massive outdoor oven. The heat slowed midday outdoor activities for soldiers who found the it so intense they would lie on camp beds drenched in a pool of sweat. They were soon introduced to a local insect called a pissmoth that squirted a liquid that caused skin blisters.

After a couple weeks of this, the troops would be flown at tree top level at night to the UNITA stronghold of Mavinga by a smaller version of the C-130 called the C-160 Transall. Soldiers who were in Angola always remember the flies that would crawl into nose, ears, or even worse openings while using the toilet necessitating a branch used like a jockey whip. While at Mavinga, four soldiers were wounded on 14 December 1987 by shrapnel from a defective 81mm mortar round and had to be evacuated by air or casevaced. The survivor with the worse wounds ended up on crutches and some brain damage.

On 2 January 1988 the SADF deployed armored vehicles to harass FAPLA 21st Brigade troops who were entrenched northwest of Cuito near the Cuatir River. That night in what was mainly a psychological exercise to see if they would withdraw, tanks, artillery, and mortars hurled hundreds of rounds at the position. In addition, groundshout Casspirs equipped with broadcast equipment were brought up to make horrendous noises. Unfortunately these were all used without the desired effect as the FAPLA Brigade held steady with some artillery counterstrikes. A UNITA attack on the brigade was also repulsed by a clever FAPLA force that withdrew and called in an artillery bombardment on the attackers who were now in a known position, before successfully returning to their original positions. The attack did draw a sustained but inaccurate attack by MiGs out of Menongue without any UNITA Stinger antiaircraft missile fire.[122]

In the second week of January the SADF were in the process of bringing up reinforcements to begin the first of what would prove to be several major ground assaults on the entrenched FAPLA positions east of the river. Also at this time the G5 howitzers were firing a couple hundred shells a day in almost round the clock fire on FAPLA forces at Cuito. As this SADF counteroffensive progressed there were frequent SAAF C-130 Hercules night flights to the Mavinga airfield carrying 155mm G5 howitzer ammunition and other supplies as the only alternative was a four hundred kilometer bush route, which was used for less urgent supplies. The airfield was a difficult landing at night with kerosene lamps as runway lights the only landing guide. Despite FAPLA SAMs and MiGs the able SAAF pilots managed to avoid any cargo plane losses during the winter of 1987 and spring of 1988.

The FAPLA 21st, 25th, and 59th brigades being without substantive armor or artillery,were essentially marooned east of the Cuito and Tumpo rivers. The Tumpo to the west was the only barrier between the beleaguered units and the opposing forces. They also met a bottleneck at the bridge over the Chambinga River as it was the only route back to Cuito Cuanavale. This provided the SADF G5 artillery fire with a bombardment box from which very few FAPLA soldiers escaped. Pressure began to build on both sides to act at Cuito as the SADF had an imminent tank unit change and FAPLA had a convoy due that required urgent repairs to the damaged bridge.

Serious fighting broke out on the afternoon of 13 January 1988 with a massive South African bombardment of 127mm multiple rockets from their Valkiri-22 Mk 1 or "Vorster Organ." This was joined by a choir of 155mm G5 howitzer shells and 120mm mortar shells mainly focused on the beleaguered FAPLA 21st Brigade south of the Cuatir River. The rockets from the Valkiri missle launcher had eighty-five hundred small metal balls that exploded outward on impact for a thousand to fifteen hundred meters. One of these metal balls had hit Soviet Col. Andrei Gorb in the throat, killing him, during a night Valkiri attack in November 1987 on the retreat from the Lomba River debacle.[123]

An attack was eventually launched by the SADF with two battalions, 4 South African Infantry and 61st Mechanised, supported by the UNITA 3rd Battalion. Again the attacking force met stiff resistance from FAPLA artillery counterstrikes and a surprising last stand by a fearless group of soldiers in a bunker firing on an SADF tank that eventually demolished the structure.

The SADF and UNITA pushes were under the cover of bad weather that it was hoped would protect them from MiG attacks. Unfortunately the weather cleared by afternoon and the attacking force was repeatedly struck by a squadron of FAPA planes led by Col. Humberto Trujillo who took advantage of the situation but with limited results. The MiGs were joined by reinforcements rushed from surrounding FAPLA units but this only slowed the advance to the brigade headquarters which was the usual complex of bunkers and trenches that trapped some vehicles temporarily as they traversed it in pursuit. Eventually this sustained battle was brought to a halt by night falling and the disappearance of FAPLA resistance.

Captured FAPLA T-62 tank, Angola 1987.
—Roland De Vries

The next day found a much reduced and punch drunk FAPLA 21st Brigade skeleton force completely out of position with numerous FAPLA tanks, multiple rocket launchers, and assorted vehicles destroyed or abandoned as well as hundreds killed. The SADF and UNITA troops had ended up next to the Dala River and the road to Cuito. Landline communication, which was so helpful in preventing intelligence eavesdropping by the South Africans became disastrous in a mobile engagement and led to the temporary disarray of FAPLA local command. The 21st Brigade became the second FAPLA brigade almost completely obliterated by the SADF and UNITA.

Yet again, however, the victors failed to advance forward and capitalize on the FAPLA retreat. This was probably due to force-size limitation or lack of diesel fuel from the logistical problems for such long distances through the African bush. It was to be the last hurrah for the UNITA and SADF offensive with much credit to the UNITA forces who provided a necessary ground element and screen while bearing significant casualties in this role.

Within a few days FAPLA units attacked and began to reoccupy the original 21st Brigade position somewhat by default as the South African command decided against immediate action. Morale would have been low for the loss of all that effort and life for naught. To further exasperate matters, the two SADF commanders of that theater of operations, Liebenberg and Malan, had to be replaced for illness in the middle of the continuous conflict.[124]

UNITA troops on SADF Olifant tanks in Angola.—*SANDF Documentation Centre*

SADF commander Col. Paul Fouche recalled that four FAPLA brigades occupied terrain from the Dala River down to the southern tip of the nearby high ground, the Chambinga heights, on the Tumpo plain east of Cuito Cuanavale. They were deployed in defensive positions with the 25th in the south, 59th Brigade in the center, and the reinforced remnants of the 21st Brigade to the northwest. The 16th Brigade was held in reserve at the center and eastern section of the bridge over the Dala River. The demolished 47th Brigade had ceased to exist as a fighting unit.

The stress of an extended campaign on the SADF soldiers began to reveal itself in many ways like an incident on the night of 14 January 1988. An SADF soldier called Wortel, carrot in English due to his red hair, had ordered

SADF Olifant tanks and Ratels advance towards Cuito Cuanavale.—*SANDF Documentation Centre*

his driver to make his food. The driver had refused, so he ordered the gunner to make the food and he had also refused. Wortel then retrieved his R4 assault rifle and shot the gunner in the leg while he sat in the turret of the Ratel. The gunner was casevaced and Wortel arrested but the incident was later described as an accidental shooting by his commander.[125]

SADF 2nd Lt. M. S. McCann of the 101 Battalion was killed on 4 February 1988 as was Sapper Michael C. Suter at an unknown location in Angola. Suter was traveling in an armored personnel carrier that was ambushed and was killed by FAPLA armor-piercing rounds.

A split attack led by UNITA units followed by the 61st Mechanised Infantry Battalion under SADF Commandant Mike Muller and the 4 South African Infantry Battalion made a determined assault on 14 February against the FAPLA 59th Brigade and remnants of the 21st Brigade, reinforced by other brigades, west of the Dala River.

After a time, his numerically superior Olifant tanks faced a FAPLA T-55 tank counterattack led by Cuban Lt. Col. Ciro Gómez Betancourt. The FAPLA lost five tanks but managed to damage a SADF Olifant. It was reported by Cuban sources that fourteen Cubans died in this battle between FAPLA T-55 tanks and SADF Olifant tanks. The FAPLA lost several hundred soldiers and substantial equipment. Although a decisive result, the SADF attack lost momentum and they withdrew without any substantial territorial gain. The FAPLA-Cuban combination was proving to be discernibly more difficult and tactically able than previous encounters. This attack was meant to be a prelude to a further attack on the Tumpo area, but this was called off in the face of such determined opposition.[126]

Under SADF command directives the expeditionary force was to minimize casualties. It is unknown why the FAPLA did not attempt targeted attacks on SADF troops to give pause to their commanders similar to those of insurgents Iraq and Afghanistan. Perhaps it was due to a lack of special operations forces or the effectiveness of UNITA troop screens.

Four South African casualties of this attack were Riflemen Andre Groenewald, Pieter Groenewald, Vincent Nieuwenhuizen, and Cpl. (Jan) Hendrik Kleynhans who were all killed on Valentine's Day 1988 when their Ratel No. 22C was struck by 23mm fire from a FAPLA ZSU antiaircraft gun from the 59th Brigade being used in a ground attack mode. The Ratel had become

SADF Olifant tanks on the move in Angola.—*SANDF Documentation Centre*

stuck on a tree stump. One eyewitness saw four holes on one side and a massive hole on the opposite side of the Ratel. Corporal Kleynhans was the commander of the Ratel which was part of Bravo Company, 61st Mechanised Battalion. Andre Groenwald was eighteen years old and Pieter's nephew. Five other soldiers were injured in the attack.

Other Ratels were damaged but with no casualties including one commanded by Captain van Zyl when it was hit under the gearbox which put the Ratel out of action. It was eventually recovered about two days later.

By this time the Angolan FAPA air force ruled the skies and the SAAF was wary of committing their few Mirages to a gauntlet of radar, SAM missile systems, shoulder-fired MANPADS (man portable air defense systems) and MiGs. That morning an SAAF Mirage piloted by Ed Every was shot down as it attacked a supply convoy on the way to Cuito.

During January and February 1988 artillery batteries attached to the 32 Battalion attacked several convoys on the Menongue to Cuito road. This culminated with an artillery bombardment of the FAPA Menongue airfield on 13 February by a force commanded by Robbie Hartslief. This attack did not have any great result and the task force returned to Rundu by the end of February.[127]

The FAPLA bridgehead at Tumpo, east of Cuito Cuanavale was a formidable obstacle to any attacking force by February 1988. The positions had been fortified over a period of months with trenches, bunkers and minefields with embedded artillery that had prepared strike zones. Most important was that the west bank of the Cuito was higher than the surrounding area, which afforded it a clear and superior observation platform for any prospective attack. It was a lowland African Masada manned by a unified force of Angolans and Cubans ready to meet any attack. The minefields would slow or stop the opposing force who would feel an unremitting rain of shells and rockets on armor and flesh alike.

On the early morning of the 25 February the SADF attacked with a full complement of armored vehicles consisting of Olifant tanks supported by Ratels and Casspirs that resulted in the early loss of many UNITA troops due to the strong light of FAPLA flares in the predawn sky. The newly laid minefields combined with heavy and sustained cannon fire from artillery, Stalin's Organ multiple rocket launchers, and T-55 tanks delayed the attack. The FAPLA had earlier retreated from forward positions, luring the SADF into the minefields that sowed confusion and damage.

Commandant Muller fell victim to this trap and entered deep into a minefield before having to reverse out under a strong FAPLA bombardment. A path was bravely cleared under fire that allowed the armored column to cautiously advance but troops came under numerous MiG attacks that caused many casualties. Bombardier Clinton Hendricks, a member of an antiaircraft missile team of the 61st Mechanised Battalion, was killed during this action by shrapnel from a MiG bombardment when he tried to use his SA-7 MANPAD. Lance Corporal Leon F. Van Wyk was also killed in the same attack. He left behind a wife and two daughters aged one and four years old. He was killed by a 122mm FAPLA rocket strike on his tank hatch.[128]

As night fell the SADF and UNITA forces retreated, despondent and defeated, dragging their damaged equipment as they left the battlefield. They had been foiled by the now tried-and-true Cuban led FAPLA formula for defense success: minefields, artillery fire, T-55 tank fire, and MiG bombing attacks. Two SADF vehicles were destroyed by explosives as they were not in a recoverable state. Cuban commander Venancio Guerrero had wisely decided to reduce the effectiveness of the SADF artillery fire by dispersing his troops into smaller staggered units along the defensive line that helped reduce the number of casualties from the G5 shelling. This was not to be an all FAPLA and Cuban day. The MiG aerial hunt for the SADF G5 howitzers that continuously harassed the FAPLA troops in Cuito were embarrassingly unsuccessful. Effective camouflage, movement, MiG early warning, and ceasing fire when MiGs were in the air prevented any damage to the SADF guns except that caused by their own incompetence.

A second SADF advance with reduced equipment moved forward on the morning of 29 February although a night attack was the original intention. By afternoon they were yet again trapped in a zone of minefields and artillery fire combined with unexpected withering fire from the Soviet ZSU 23mm antiaircraft guns deployed in a ground-fire mode. Cloud cover militated against repeated MiG attacks but the SADF armored vehicles still suffered several hits and damage from mine explosions. There was another retreat by Commandant Muller in the face of rapid deployment of FAPLA tank reinforcements. The leap year brought no luck to the depleted SADF force or the many UNITA soldiers left on the battlefield. The arduous task of recovery of abandoned SADF equipment took place under the cover of darkness.

One account has the Cuito defenders planting over four hundred antivehicle booby traps made with BM-21 rockets and MiG bombs for a total of over fifteen thousand mines. Attempts were made to clear the extensive antitank and antipersonnel minefields around Cuito Cuanavale at various times to prepare for SADF attacks. These activities were often as dangerous as the attack itself being under poor weather or light conditions with frequent harassing fire if the minesweepers were observed. SADF Capt. Tai Theron blew off his right foot while conducting a mine exercise on 9 March. He lived to talk about it, being promoted to colonel and to lead Project African Warrior for the modern postapartheid South African National Defence Force. Later on 24 May, SADF engineer Piet Kock also reaped the whirlwind when he blew off a foot while laying mines east of Cuito Cuanavale.

The South Africans laid a chain of mines at the Tumpo River after the conclusion of the SADF operations during a holding phase under Operation Displace. This minefield was surveyed and marked according to normal convention and was laid as a barrier against a possible FAPLA breakout.[129]

Over two decades later the mine clearing charity Halo Trust had great difficulty in attempting to remove these mines with a mine-clearing supervisor saying:

> One of the mine belts was laid by the South African Army over 8 months, from April 1988. It is an extensive cordon that runs for several kilometres to the east of the town, blocking land from cultivation and other useful purposes, and preventing safe transit. It continues to claim victims. Professionally laid by military engineers, it consists of minimum-metal mines which are very difficult to detect, and there is also evidence of booby traps and other unpleasant surprises.[130]

A knowledgeable former member of the SADF confirmed, however, that comprehensive maps of the minefields were drawn up by the 2nd Field Engineer Regiment. During the mid 1990s the Angolan government requested these maps and they were made available through the military attaché of the South African Embassy in Luanda. The SADF mines at Cuito follow a pattern of center row antitank mines five meters apart protected by two antipersonnel mines nearby in the ten and two o'clock positions towards the likely approach. The antitank mines were fitted with an antilifting device and two rows of antipersonnel mines a few meters on either side. Some antipersonnel mines were connected by detonation cord to claymores that would explode and disperse numerous ball bearings for maximum havoc.[131]

Corporal Greg M. Stewart of the 44th Parabat Regiment was killed on 20 March. This elite parachute trained soldier had completed two years as a Parabat Pathfinder and had been wounded in the leg during a previous deployment. He had been called up in March 1988 to go to Angola. He died doing a night practice jump north of Pretoria. It was a Sunday and he had not reached his twenty-first birthday.

After several unit and commander changes on the morning of 23 March 1988, the SADF made a third attack on the Tumpo redoubt. It was essentially an armored vehicle assault led by experienced tank officer Commandant Gerhard Louw and supported by a couple hundred of the remaining

SADF armored tank recovery vehicle in Angola. —*SANDF Documentation Centre*

UNITA troops who bravely showed up in the face of the two previous South African debacles. There was also a diversionary attack to the south and once again this final attack was planned to coincide with weather conditions that would keep the FAPA MiG aircraft grounded. There were artillery and aircraft bombardments during the attack, which made good progress until a vast minefield was encountered. SADF soldiers equipped with an experimental minefield-clearing device called a Plofadder then went into action. The Plofadder was a rocket that pulled a string of explosives across the minefield that detonated when it landed and the shockwaves of the explosion were supposed to detonate any mines in the vicinity. Unfortunately for the attackers the device proved to be less than reliable, and out of the four or five Plofadders deployed only one detonated as it was intended and cleared a path through the minefield.

None of the attacking SADF tanks were struck directly by a tank projectile but three tanks were lost and abandoned. They remain to this day east of the river in a minefield. One tank was destroyed by a huge boosted mine that blew off the suspension rendering it immobile as a tortoise on its back. (A boosted mine is one laid with extra explosive, usually an artillery shell, to increase the power.) In the process of passing around this tank two other tanks threw their tracks and could not be recovered under circumstances of heavy and unusually accurate FAPLA fire.[132]

Commandant Louw and his brave crews tried several times to extract the damaged tanks without success. The SADF leadership decided to withdraw in the face of this adversity hoping to recover the tanks later. Significantly Gerhard Louw was a last minute replacement for the original tank regiment commander who failed to show up for duty in Angola. It is unknown if that absent commander ended up in Pollsmoor Prison (maximum security prison near Cape Town) for failing to show up.

The later recovery never happened. It was a humiliation of the SADF and a propaganda victory for the defending FAPLA and Cuban troops who posed and paraded with their conquests. The simmering SADF commanders could only look on in dismay. The South African forces had been brought to their knees by conventional war at a fixed location; bound by the political directives to prevent mass casualties; understrength in soldiers and units; and hampered by rotation of field commanders: there was plenty of blame to distribute and reasons to ponder for years to come. This chagrin was lessened by the equally devastating, previous capture of a Soviet SA-8 missile system at the Lomba River. History was indeed repeating itself. The demise of the famous Custer's Seventh Cavalry at the Little Bighorn underscored the danger of fighting columns with insufficient firepower to prevail once the the target is located. The balance between mobility and firepower remains a challenge in contemporary expeditionary operations. There was also the earlier and very similar experience of the Boer army at the siege of Mafeking in October 1899, which was a forgotten lesson nearly a century later.

On 25 March 1988 Rifleman Nicolas J. Vermeulen of the 101 Battalion was killed. The SADF released a public statement that an unidentified soldier had died during a stand-off bombardment on a small base in the operational area in the early hours of the morning.[133]

Commandant Gerhard Louw received the Honoris Crux for actions that day in attempting to remove the three disabled Olifant tanks under fire. Corporal D. H. Maritz and Trooper H. B. Smit were the first recipients of the South African Army Cross, awarded in 1992 for actions of bravery to recover a disabled tank under fire during the Battle of Cuito Cuanavale near Tumpo in 1988.

Why, however, was the SADF so keen on trying to recover three severly damged Olifants? One theory was that the repeated tank recovery efforts under fire was to ensure that the advanced gyroscope targeting mechanism that allowed shots on the move would not fall into FAPLA, Cuban, or Soviet hands. Another was the sophisticated night vision equipment used by the driver with interchangeable periscopes to enable the gunner's night vision sight and the commander's night vision goggles. It's unclear if it was South African engineered technology at the time or had been smuggled into the country in breach of sanctions.

The SADF Olifant tanks were larger and louder than the Soviet T-55, easy to detect, and with a slow but excellent cannon. The Olifant armor protection was less than that of the T-55 but nevertheless respected by the FAPLA forces who were still wary of this powerful weapon.

On the day of this final SADF attack the Cuban newspaper *Granma* announced the institution of the Medal of Merit for the Defense of Cuito Cuanavale upon the direct order of Commander in Chief Fidel Castro. Commander Miguel Lorente recently arrived in Cuito Cuanavale awarded nearly a hundred Cuban, Soviet, and FAPLA soldiers with this Medal of Merit on April Fool's Day 1988.[134]

Second Lieutenant J. H. Diederichs of 101 Battalion was killed by a land mine on 2 April 1988. The vaunted 101 Battalion was second only to the 32 "Buffalo" Infantry Battalion in the number of Honoris Crux awards to its members.

South Africa had originally purchased about two hundred Centurion tanks built in Great Britain, but some of these tanks had been acquired from countries like Jordan in anticipation of an arms embargo. These tanks went through a series of modifications to create the Olifant, which ended up being manufactured in South Africa.[135]

Only thirty-four of the remaining tanks were actually ever used in combat in Angola against an estimated five hundred FAPLA T-55 tanks. There were never more than two Olifant squadrons of fourteen tanks each in Angola during 1987–88. Some broke down or became damaged in action but were usually recovered and repaired. The SADF loss of three Olifant tanks on 23 March 1988 to mines at Cuito Cuanavale helped stiffen opposition and encourage the defenders of a ruined city with a restricted operational airfield.

In an interview Col. Venancio Avila Guerrero, the Cuban commander credited with organizing the crucial defense of Cuito Cuanavale, said, "One day, we took over one thousand shells. We just had to sit through it in our foxholes." Colonel Avila was one of the first Cubans to arrive in Cuito Cuanavale at the end of 1987 to prepare for the expected attacks by the SADF and UNITA from the east. He was the Cuban MMCA commander who actually led the troops during the horrendous months to follow and has never received the full public acknowledgement that he deserves. He was only forty-three at the time of the battle.[136]

In a brief period the Cuban assisted FAPLA were able to create an impregnable defensive arc around Cuito by the time the SADF attacked in January 1988. Herein lay the limited but important achievement of the Cuban military assistance. After long transatlantic journeys to a foreign country, in a matter of weeks they were able to blunt the might of the best army on the African continent. This segment of the Battle of Cuito Cuanavale was correctly described as a Cuban-Angolan defensive victory by Ronnie Kasrils, the South African Minister for Intelligence Services, in a 24 April 2008 speech in Havana. Kasrils then went on to qualify this by correctly stating that undoubtedly wars are not won by defensive engagements.

In the course of this historical record, references have been made to Cuban Gen. "Polo" Frias, Angolan FAPLA Gen. "N'Dalu" Franca, and General Ben Ben. No picture has been secured of the valiant Avila and posterity has not rewarded him with a published nickname. To this brave, unrecognized, and capable military leader it could only be Col. Venancio "Acero" (steel) Avila Guerrero.

Coincidentally at the same time that the SADF began to pull back from Cuito Cuanavale in April 1988, the Soviet army began its journey home from Afghanistan. As the SADF retreated closer to their borders their leadership became increasingly threatened by the Cuban gains towards the Namibian border. One subsequent report stated that the South African government came close to activating its nuclear weapons in 1987 when fears were rife in the inner circles that Cuban MiG jets were set to strike South African territory. It is believed that a joint South African-Israeli nuclear test had been previously conducted on 22 February 1979 in the South Atlantic with some confirmation from a U.S. Vela satellite from the A-bomb's signature double flash of light.[137]

The state-owned arms firm Armscor reopened a nuclear test site that had been closed down in 1977 after intense international pressure, a serious move in light of President de Klerk's disclosure that Pretoria possessed six Hiroshima-size nuclear bombs. Nuclear weapons experts had pointed out that the most likely target of a South African nuclear attack would have been Luanda, the Angolan capital of one million people. Renfrew Christie, now a dean of research at the University of the Western Cape, was sentenced to ten years in jail in 1980 for passing on South African nuclear secrets to the African National Congress. He had said that it was clear indication that they were getting ready to use the bomb. Ironically, it is now known that Iran acquired six hundred tons of uranium yellowcake from South Africa towards the end of the reign of the Shah of Iran for their nuclear ambitions that now draw nigh.[138]

The six nuclear warheads were stored at the National Accelerator Centre near Stellenbosch in 1987 and only required the Jericho surface-to-surface missile delivery systems developed by Armscor and an Israeli company. The Jerichos were kept at an SAAF base ready for transport to the launch site. The missing link was an accurate guidance system for missile delivery which was beyond South African capability at the time, so it is likely that this would have been supplied by the Israelis and transported through another international pariah state such as Taiwan.[139]

On 28 November 1987 a South African Airways 747 combination passenger freighter, known as the Helderberg, departed from Taiwan and later caught on fire and crashed into the Indian Ocean. It is thought that the crash was caused by volatile equipment or material for various weapons that the South African government was using the aircraft to smuggle. The real cause of the fire was never determined and 159 people died, many more than SADF casualty claims for the Battle of Cuito Cuanavale.

In November 1989 five persons were charged with trying to illegally export American missile technology to South Africa. The plot involved several unsuccessful attempts in 1987 and 1988 to export missile gyroscopes manufactured by the Northrop Corporation to South Africa's state-owned arms corporation. The plot for this important component in missile guidance systems was thwarted by U.S. Customs agents.[140]

The only SAAF aircraft capable of a nuclear bomb airborne delivery would have been the aging twin-engine Buccaneer bomber which had a two-man crew, sufficient range for the contemplated task, and good navigational equipment. There were very few operational Buccaneer aircraft available and they would soon be phased out.

Nevertheless the nuclear capabilty and security of South Africa should be of continuing concern to the nuclear community. A gang of gunmen recently attacked the Pelindaba nuclear facility in November 2007 and shot an employee. It is believed that they gained access to the building by using a ladder to scale a wall and force open a window. Pelindaba is regarded as one of the country's most secure national key points and is surrounded by electric fencing, CCTV surveillance, security guards and checkpoints. The attack came as the country prepared to preside over an International Atomic Energy Agency convention on nuclear safety.[141]

CHAPTER 12

THE AIR WAR

The South African Air Force was only prepared to risk their few Mirages on brief occasional sorties against FAPA MiGs operated by experienced Cuban pilots. The South Africans were also concerned about possible attacks on their operational bases and required many pilots to experience the boredom and extreme heat of being strapped in their jets waiting for a call. Despite this, there were many volunteers for the standyby position in early September after the first MiG encounter. The SAAF radar at Rundu was severely limited in its coverage over the Lomba River forcing many pilots to enter the war zone with many blind spots, which was not a problem for their counterparts on the other side of the battlelines.

The Angolan FAPA advantage increased with sophisticated Soviet air defence system comprised of early warning radars, acquisition radars, SA-8 missile systems and antiaircraft guns. The province of Cunene near the border with Namibia was particularly dangerous due to the network of Soviet early warning radar stations.

The Cuban Air Force (DAAFAR) 12th and 13th Fighter squadrons combination in Angola was called the FAPA 25th Air Combat Fighter Regiment and operated during the Battle of Cuito Cuanavale from Serpa Pinto Air Base near Menongue in central Angola. Serpa Pinto was named after Alexandre de Serpa Pinto, a Portuguese explorer of southern Africa and former colonial administrator.

The first dogfight over Cuito Cuanavale pitting a MiG-23ML against an F1AZ Mirage occurred on 10 September 1987 between SAAF 3 Squadron pilot Captain Anton van Rensburg and an unnamed FAPA aviator. Van

Rensburg fired two French Matra 550 air-to-air missiles but failed to score a hit.

The first SAAF ground attack was on 16 September 1987 when FAPLA's 47th Brigade was hit by multiple air-burst bombs near the Lomba River that if on target would have caused an immense number of casualties and vehicle damage. However, subsequent attacks by the SADF found many well-developed bunker and trench systems that would have offered some protection to FAPLA soldiers from South African aerial bombardment but not to their vehicles.

On the morning of 27 September 1987 the SAAF sent three pairs of Mirage fighters in over the battlefield at low level; the first pair were flown by Captain Carlo Gagiano and Captain Arthur Piercy. The two Mirages were vectored towards a pair of MiG-23MLs from the FAPA 25th Regiment on a mission escorting several helicopters. piloted by Maj. Alberto Ley Rivas and his wingman 1st Lt. Juan Carlos Chavez Godoy The jets turned to face each other near the Lomba river and at a low altitude and acute angle Rivas fired a Soviet AA-8 Aphid missile at Piercy's Mirage No. 206 that hit the target. The South African pilot's plane was only damaged and eventually made it back to the SAAF Rundu air base.[142] Unfortunately, Captain Piercy was permanently paralyzed as a result of the ground level operation of his ejection seat when the drogue parachute failed to deploy and stop the plane from running off the end of the runway on to rough ground. According to old established protocols of air combat this did not count as the first Mirage kill of the Battle of Cuito Cuanavale because the stricken aircraft successfully made it back to its base.

This was one of the more heroic deeds of the Battle of Cuito Cuanavale for Piercy to fly a damaged aircraft to his home base of SAAF AB Rundu in Namibia more than 300 kilometers from Mavinga and the Lomba River. It is testimony to his skill that the plane landed in one piece.[143] The rear portion of Piercy's No. 206 was used to repair another Mirage and his aircraft is now on display at the School of Mechanical, Industrial and Aeronautical Engineering, University of the Witwatersrand, Johannesburg.

On 28 October 1987 Lt. Col. Manuel Rojas Garcia, the pilot of a two man MiG-21UM, and Capt. Ramon Quesada Aguilar of the 25th FAPA were shot down and captured by UNITA, likely hit by a Stinger MANPAD, at Luvuei, Angola. Both men ejected safely and were captured by UNITA ground troops without a fight.

This MiG-21 Fishbed variant was essentially a trainer fighter jet, so why

FAPA MIG-21 Fishbed single seater crash landed by FAPA pilot Lieutenant Vinez due to navigation error and recovered from Namibia 1989. This MiG-21 Fishbed variant was mostly used as a trainer. —Dr. Peter Hammond

was it flying in a combat area. This can only be attributed to command error, a shortage of aircraft, or a shortage of trained pilots. Apart from the MiG kill it was a massive propaganda coup as well: Lieutenant Colonel Garcia was the most senior Cuban officer ever captured in Angola. It was the second tour of duty in Angola for Captain Aguilar who had completed his first in 1983.[144]

Cuban MiG commander Eduardo Sarria decided to instruct his pilots to strap a foldable AKM assault rifle in the cockpit on every combat flight with a chestpack of four magazines. This was based on the experience of a Cuban pilot in Ethiopia who ejected after being hit by antiaircraft fire. The pilot hit the ground with his rifle because it was not strapped to the seat but to the pilot with a harness. In the Angolan environment when pilots became infantry, surviving was a tough task. One downed Cuban helicopter pilot reportedly spent twenty-six days walking to the FAPLA lines with burnt hands and wounds infected with worms while eating all manner of things to survive. The AKM could help the pilot hunt for food and otherwise help keep him alive in such situation and all pilots carried one. Contrary to various propaganda statements issued during the course of the Battle of Cuito Cuanavale, the AKM policy is proof that the Cuban FAPA pilots feared being shot down, even if they didn't expect to be.[145]

Some SAAF pilots also carried small arms but they had a reasonable expectation of prompt and experienced search and rescue. The Cubans did not have such a benefit east of Cuito, hence the expectation was of delayed rescue while a downed pilot engaged in escape and evasion. Nevertheless there were many lucky escapes and safe landings with potentially lethal damage, including small-arms bullet strikes, by some MiG pilots during the war.

FAPA MiGs were not the only aerial casualties that wet African winter. SAAF Capt. Andre Stapa, who was flying the Italian designed Atlas Impala Mk 2 light jet No. 1024, was shot down on 14 November 1987 near Cuvelai, several hundred kilometers west of Cuito Cuanavale, on a night ground-attack mission. (Impalas were also frequently used as airborne radio relay stations called Telstar that allowed communication between troops deep in Angola and their headquarters.) According to a colleague, Stapa was involved in a bomb run with a steep profile and was unable to pull out of the dive. The bombing processor was linked to the aircraft's altimeter, and relied on the pilot setting it up correctly to give a two-tone warning: the first tone started at 1,700 feet from weapons release with a higher pitched tone starting at 300 feet prior to/above the weapons release point. The audio tone stopped at the weapons release height, whereupon the pilot would press the firing button on his control stick to release the bomb or fire other ordnance. This was followed by an immediate pull out due to the low altitude of the weapons release. Typically the entry into the dive started above 20,000 feet with weapons release as low as 2,000 feet. Pilots were trained not to rely solely on the bomb-release processor, but also to watch the normal altimeter very carefully in the dive, anticipating the altitude at which the tone should start in case of failure or incorrect settings. Standard operating procedure required the processor to be working before flight dispatch. The processor was typically set up during the flight enroute to the target.

Only one large explosion was observed by Stapa's wingman, which was probably the impact of the Impala.

Pilot Stapa was the commanding officer of the Impala squadron operating out of the SAAF Ondangwa air base and his body had not been recovered at the time of his memorial service. An eyewitness to the recovered wreckage confirmed that Stapa's survival kit was missing, but this is likely due to the impact. The wreckage also showed evidence of bullet damage, possibly from an antiaircraft ZSU. The Angola News Agency subsequently reported that the South African pilot's remains had been discovered by FAPLA forces. Andre Stapa was originally from Rhodesia and received his pilot wings from the Rhodesian/Zimbabwe Air Force in August 1980 in one of the last pilot-training courses (No. 34 Pilot Training Course) conducted before the country became Zimbabwe.[146]

Flight International magazine of 28 November 1987 had this brief report: "A South African Air Force Atlas Impala MK2 is missing, presumed shot down in Angola, after failing to return from night operations in early November. The pilot was Capt Andre Stapa."

SAAF Atlas Impala Mk 2.—*Jens Frischmuth/hangartalk.co.za*

The FAPLA command soon realized that the South Africans would stop firing the G5 howitzers when the FAPA MiGs were active in order to hide the powerful cannons from Cuban aircraft. This also meant that FAPLA equipment could then be moved free from artillery bombardment, but it would be extraordinary use of sophisticated fighter aircraft to only facilitate the relatively safe movement of equipment for a short period of time.

The inability to control the airspace over Cuito because of the Cuban MiGs turned out to be a most effective but limited solution in preventing G5 fire. It is reported that on one particular day there were nearly a dozen Cuban MiGs overhead searching for the hated G5s. Prior to a MiG attack there would usually be several calls over the SADF radio net of approaching FAPA aircraft with Afrikaan warning shouts of "Victor Victor! or Vyandelike Vliegtuie!" The MiGs could drop 500 lb., 1,000 lb., or cluster bombs, which were the most feared by SADF soldiers as the bomblets were small enough to get into foxholes. The cluster bomb could clear an area of about fifty meters with no vegetation left higher than knee level height while the craters left by larger bombs could swallow up a Ratel. These bombs were normally parachute retarded when dropped from high altitude, so the SADF troops would watch to see which direction they would be fall, taken either by the wind or the release trajectory. This method of release bought them time to decide best cover in the furthest foxhole away from the bomb site or inside a Ratel with consequent limitation on casualties.

At the Battle of Cuito Cuanavale the SADF tried different ways to deceive MiGs and other FAPA aircraft into firing on fake equipment in order to ambush them in a prepared antiaircraft kill zone. One such way was to use tree trunks and smoke grenades to resemble cannons. The SADF G5 howitzers that terrorized Cuito Cuanavale were high priority targets and the deception often worked, but the SADF were unable to capitalize on this due to poor performance of their French made Cactus antiaircraft missiles. On one occasion the only casualty was an SADF soldier scorched by the rocket blast of the rotating missile platform before release.

An earlier deception method was developed with some success by SADF Col. Deon Ferreira and Maj. Mossie Basson of the SAAF. This utilized fake helicopter crashes on ambush sites where SAAF helicopters at visible altitude would appear damaged by showing smoke from smoke grenades and then leave a simulated burning site at very low height. UNITA troops waiting at the site would then attack any FAPLA troops that came to investigate. Another ruse was balloons with aluminum strips that simulated aircraft on FAPA/DAR radar systems causing the SAM missiles to fire on nonexistent targets.

SADF Spanish-speaking intelligence officers, some from Chile, were able to listen to FAPA radio communications of the Cuban pilots as they talked to each other. A 120mm mortar group detachment with phosphorus rounds would deploy to strike a FAPLA position. As MiGs were flying in that area, a shell was fired at the target and the jets would attack their own troops as soon as they saw the smoke, mistaking it for a G5 firing. This happened several times.

The SA-8 antiaircraft missile system was what Soviet advisors in the field called the Osa-AK. The FAPLA fired several expensive SA-8 missiles at the weather balloons released by G5 howitzer crews at night, which were mistakenly taken to be SAAF Puma helicopters. No SAAF helicopters were lost during the Battle of Cuito Cuanavale although there were also several SAM strikes on remotely operated observation aircraft, an earlier version of today's unmanned aerial vehicle (UAV) more commonly known as the Predator.

The SAAF used their Raptor stand-off or smart bomb on 3 January 1988 to destroy the center portion of the Cuito Cuanavale bridge when previous attempts the month before had failed. This was the second time the South Africans had destroyed the bridge having already done so in 1986 during Operation Alpha Centauri. FAPLA vehicles could not use the bridge thereafter and were reduced to utilizing pontoon bridges that were regularly damaged by artillery bombardment. There was a third attempt to attack the bridge by SAAF Buccaneers escorted by Mirages on 6 February 1988. The SADF also used the earlier versions of the unarmed UAV Predator, with Israeli design help on a limited basis, to locate FAPLA units in the field. An earlier attempt on 25 November 1987 to bomb the FAPA Menongue air base with a similar device was aborted due to technical difficulties that suggest this was a weapon in progress.[147]

Major Ed Every who was on his second tour of duty was killed in SAAF Mirage F1AZ No. 245 on 20 February 1988 by a FAPLA SAM missile while on a bombing mission of a FAPLA convoy with several other Mirages.

South African pilots used a flick-type bombing method on FAPLA targets whereby they flew in low and then pulled up steeply several kilometers away while dropping the bombs. In theory the bombs would lunge at the targets without exposing the planes to danger. FAPLA ground troops who had grown wise to this method had started to deploy SA-7 MANPADs to anticipate this tactic and nearly downed two Mirages on 4 October.

The thirty-one year old Major Every was part of a four plane sortie that attacked a FAPLA convoy with the airburst fragment bombs near Cuito Cuanavale in this fashion. The SAAF antimissile evasion tactic failed to work that day. Every's South African aircraft was reported by a Cuban soldier to have come past the area once and then returning a second time to drop his bomb load when the waiting troops fired on him. This was a risky act by an experienced combat pilot.[148] There had been several attacks in the same area previously, which may have called for greater caution in pursuing this sortie or ordering that it be carried out. Shortly after the bomb release Every's plane was seen to crash and black smoke rose from where pieces of his aircraft were later observed and collected by FAPLA troops. When he was killed Major Every had been standing in for another pilot who was on leave to be married.[149]

An SADF Valkiri multiple rocket launcher supposedly fired numerous rockets at the crash site later that would have further destroyed the wreckage as well as any FAPLA and Cuban troops doing an intelligence inspection.

In all of this, nowhere has anyone in the leadership at that time with the restricted radar cover, improved antiaircraft tactics on the ground, and dominance of the air by FAPA MiGs acknowledged openly that this raid was a bad idea; the closest to an admission was the decision not to repeat this type of raid.

An SA-7 Strela is believed to have struck Capt. Willie van Coppenhagen in SAAF Mirage F1AZ No. 223 after a night strike on 19 March 1988 at Longa north of Cuito Cuanavale in what was described as a diversionary raid. Captain van Coppenhagen did not survive the encounter and his remains were only discovered several days later by a search team. He had been led on the flight by another Mirage F1AZ flown by Commandant Johan Rankin who reportedly saw a flash of light coming back from the attack and later never saw his wingman return. (Commandant Rankin was an experienced pilot famous for shooting down two MiG-21s in the early 1980's. The first of these, on 6 November 1981, was the first confirmed air-to-air SAAF kill since World War II.)

The SAAF later described it as a low-level flameout and that there was no distress or missile-strike radio call. Clearly missile-strike or distress calls are few and far apart when a low-flying jet is hit by a missile. Prior to this,

on 18 February, van Coppenhagen had a near mishap at the limited Rundu airstrip with a drag-chute failure after a bad weather diversion landing in poor light conditions. In an admirable display of courage, two days later he returned a second time after an aborted strike on a target at Lubango in southwest Angola to accurately deliver his bomb load. This was described by Brig. Gen. Dick Lord: "Probably the most dangerous act in warfare is to carry out a repeat attack on a target." Captain van Coppenhagen was buried at Hero's Acre in the Goede Hoop Cemetery near Cape Town.[150]

A view of a Soviet SA-7 Grail surface-to-air missile.—*defenseimagery.mil*

Not all aerial encounters were so

deadly. On 10 September 1987 a pair of MiGs were engaged by two SAAF Mirages. One of the Mirages fired a Kukri air-to-air missiles without result. The same thing happened again on 27 September 1987. Later, on 25 February 1988, a flight of three Mirage jets led by SAAF fighter ace Johan Rankin chased two MiGs. The South African ace fired Kukri missiles and his cannon at Cuban Capt. Orlando Carbo Galvez without a hit.[151]

The problem with all of these air battles was that the Mirages often approached high-flying MiGs at tree top levels to beat FAPLA radar and missiles. The SAAF ground control was hundreds of kilometers away with the result that the aircraft were directed to climb in an imprecise manner. The SAAF fighters would end up adjacent to or in front of their targets instead of behind the MiGs.

Ultimately that's how SAAF pilot Piercy ended up in a pickle with the Cuban MiGs astern and in prime shooting position. The MiGs, although less maneuverable than Piercy's Mirage, possessed superior armament and acceleration. That meant even when taken by surprise, Cuban pilots could usually outdistance Mirages with ease. All these Battle of Cuito Cuanavale air encounters had few maneuvers with one or two high-speed turns for pointing weapons at opponents followed by high-speed disengagements.[152]

The Cuban pilots of FAPA and their numerous daily air strikes were only taking a small, albeit deadly toll of SADF forces under the difficult circumstances of terrain, target size, and the mobility of their experienced foes. Nevertheless, MiG strikes were still feared and often instilled panic in the SADF troops trying to avoid them. Lance Corporal Marius J. Lecuona of the 61st Mechanised Battalion was the commander of a Ratel that fled for cover from approaching FAPA MiGs on 3 February 1988. A tree branch caught his heavy Browning .50 cal. machine gun, which struck Marius in the head and killed him.

Sergeant G. M. Maritz and nineteen-year-old Signalman Jacques De Lange of the 5th Signals electronic intelligence collection unit were killed by shrapnel in such an air strike on 21 February 1988. Signals vehicles were a particular target of FAPA MiGs looking for high value SADF intelligence gathering and foreign language speaking units.

On 14 January 1988 While on a second bombing run for the day led by Lt. Col. Armando "El Guajiro" González under cloudy conditions, a FAPA MiG-23ML flown by 1st Lt. Alfonso Doval was hit by UNITA 20mm anti-aircraft fire near the Chambinga Heights overlooking Cuito forcing him to make an emergency landing near Longa. His MiG started to vibrate and fuel began to spray out of the plane from shrapnel holes. Doval landed the plane on an emergency strip but the impact fractured his lower face requiring extensive surgery. A veteran of some sixty-seven combat missions in Angola, Doval returned from hospitalization as a flight instructor in Luanda and became a lieutenant colonel in the Cuban Air Force.

That following month FAPA MiG-23ML pilot Capt. Juan "Capri" Perez Rodriguez operating out of Menongue was killed by friendly fire on 2 March 1988. A fellow pilot reported that he was shot down by Cuban antiaircraft units as he descended through the clouds near Longa when he was returning from a combat sortie at Cuito Cuanavale. His wingman's warning that they were over a Cuban antiaircraft prohibited zone came too late to save him. Over time these self-inflicted friendly-fire casualties became sufficiently common that they ultimately outnumbered SAAF kills.[153]

The last Cuban MiG casualty of the Battle of Cuito Cuanavale was pilot Carlos "El Gordo" Rodriguez Perez who was killed on 4 May 1988 while on a routine visual reconnaissance mission. The Cuban FAPA radar controller lost his signal and he is presumed to have been shot down by a UNITA missile.

Two things appear to be certain at the time of the Battle of Cuito Cuanavale where the air war was concerned. The Cuban FAPA forces ruled the sky with more sophisticated aircraft and antiaircraft measures while the South African Air Force did not lose as many aircraft as their foes nor had any of their pilots captured. Despite their lighter losses, the SAAF cannot point to much success over Cuito Cuanavale. Cuban MiGs dominated the airspace during the battle and flew far more sorties than the SAAF.

South African flying time from their base at Rundu in Namibia left their Mirages with only two minutes of combat flying time near Cuito Cuanavale while MiGs could loiter around the skies seeking targets of opportunity. The almost constant overhead MiG flights had a demoralizing effect on SADF ground troops who were besieging Cuito Cuanavale. The SAAF planes had to fly extremely low and blind until the last few minutes of attack for any sortie near Cuito, which made it a most perilous though not impossible endeavor. Mirage In flight, midair refueling of Mirages by SAAF tanker aircraft was prevented by the effective FAPA-DAR radar network and interception by MiGs. Former SAAF Brig. Gen. Dick Lord confirmed that the Soviet MiGs were superior to the Mirages but the jury remains out on pilot ability with so little action to assess. There was no evidence that either Cuban or SAAF fighter pilots were reluctant to engage in aerial combat and to the contrary were likely eager but for their respective operational directives.[154]

MiG pilot Eduardo Gonzalez Sarria felt no plane was superior to another in absolute terms. The MiG-23ML had better weaponry, radar, acceleration, thrust/weight ratio, and lower wing loading, but it was a short-range flyer that had atrocious visibility from the cockpit. Parity was lost when the theater of operations moved into Cuito Cuanavale and the SAAF lost their radar cover.

Despite vast expense and extensive pilot training invested by the SAAF, their Mirages mostly sat out the Battle of Cuito Cuanavale safely on the ground. As American author John Augustus Shedd (*Salt from My Attic*, 1928) wote, "A ship in harbor is safe, but that is not what ships are built for." A similar situation would be the Iraqi dispatch of its aircraft to neighboring countries or burying them to prevent destruction or capture by U.S. forces during the Gulf War.

The last SAAF attack in Angola took place on 23 March 1988 with a theater deployment that lasted several months. It is estimated that the Mirages flew 794 sorties during the Battle of Cuito Cuanavale and delivered nearly four thousand bombs to the battlefield. The same source has over one hundred SAMs fired at the Mirages, which resulted in only one South African fatality.[155]

The SAAF lost three Mirage F1AZ's (Nos. 206, 223, and 245) as well as Bosbok No. 934 with five fatalities and one severely wounded.

During the Battle of Cuito Cuanavale the hard working and able SAAF Hercules cargo aircraft crews flew supplies onto the sand runways of the Mavinga airstrip at night, lit by improvised fuel lights to avoid air or ground attack. Testimony to this was the lack of accidents during the seven months of operation and the rapid turnaround of cargo aircraft on the ramp. The usual pattern was for the plane to come into final approach after a low level trip from Rundu before landing and return after a quick unload. Cuban-piloted MiGs dominated the Angola airspace and occasionally were able to bomb the Mavinga area but were unable to effectively put the landing strip out of action. They were never able to down any Hercules cargo craft during the Battle of Cuito Cuanavale.

There were no SAAF helicopter losses during the battle and only five Pumas were shot down during the entire conflict. This was substantially due to the lock down of helicopter operations to avoid sophisticated Soviet radar, SAM missiles, FAPA MiGs, and FAPLA handheld MANPADS. No evidence has been found to support Cuban researcher Ruben Urribarres claim of a Puma shoot down on 27 September 1987 by an R-60 missile from a MiG. The SAAF helicopters were mostly in action for medical evacuation, but only at night, to the unfortunate luck of anyone wounded in the early morning.

In early 1988 the FAPA aircraft were able to extend their range by the construction of airbases at Cahama and Xangongo near the Namibian border. The Cahama strip had two twenty-five hundred meter runways completed in just over two months in an exemplary display of Angolan-Cuban construction management. This increased the pressure on the South African leadership to seek a quick resolution of ongoing peace talks.[156]

Cuban Gen. Ulises Rosales del Toro told a Prensa Latina correspondent on Cuban television that from December 1987 to March 1988 there were more than four hundred SAAF attacks in Angola while the Cuban pilots made more than fifteen hundred combat sorties.

On 28 April 1988 the last Cuban FAPA aircraft loss of the Battle of Cuito Cuanavale was an Antonov-26 transport plane shot down on approach to Techamutete in southern Angola when it was hit by friendly antiaircraft fire and an SA-7 missile. The Cuban antiaircraft batteries were on high alert because of the reported presence of SAAF planes in the immediate area. The plane went down with twenty-six soldiers and three crew including Brig. Gen. Francisco Cruz Bourzac, the highest ranking Cuban casualty of the Battle of Cuito Cuanavale.[157]

In 1997 Cuban Gen. Nestor Lopez Cuba confirmed the delivery of six MiG-29 fighters shortly before Russia discontinued widescale military support of Cuba. Later when they attempted to sell the Cubans more MiG-29s at a cost of $20 million each, they were told that the Cubans would sell them back the six fighters they already had at that price. General Cuba went on to say that they were making efforts to sell the MiGs.[158] Perhaps some of these recently showed up in the hold of a North Korean ship in Panama.

CHAPTER **13**

CASUALTIES OF THE BATTLE
OF CUITO CUANAVALE

The excellent SADF 155mm G5 howitzers with an accurate range of forty kilometers were never destroyed despite best efforts by the FAPLA and FAPA. However, there was extensive self-inflicted damage to a G5 that exploded upon improper loading at the Lomba River in September 1987. Rifleman William G. Beukman of the 61st Mechanised Battalion was killed on 20 September near the Lomba River in this incident. Gunner K. A. Roberts died on 12 January 1988 from injuries he received after being struck by a G5 recoil on a misfire.[159]

Gunner Tyrone Heyl recalled that he flew into Mavinga with a replacement G5 in early September for Sierra Battery, which was attached to the 4 South African Infantry, when a howitzer exploded and killed several gunners. Replacement parts also had to be flown in by air to keep the SADF artillery compliment full. In his book *From Fledging to Eagle* Dick Lord reported two further G5 breech-block deaths on 11 November 1987 that suggest that more G5 artillery was damaged by the SADF than FAPLA. The identities and details of these deceased artillery soldiers are unknown.[160]

Not all training and operational conduct by SADF soldiers was professional and above reproach. Rifleman Pieter A. Visagie of the 61st Mechanised Battalion was killed on 16 September 1987 before he reached the battlefield. While on live fire training maneuvers Visagie was shot in the back of the head by a 7.62mm light machine gun at point blank range by another soldier trying to switch on the weapon's safety.

Rifleman Johannes Barnard a 1 South African Infantry soldier died on 19 January 1988 in Angola near the Lomba River when he was accidentally shot by a fellow soldier examining an AK-47 war trophy taken from the battlefield. Barnard was just eighteen years old and had been a member of the SADF contingent that had routed the FAPLA 21st Brigade. Johannes was shot in the head by a FAPLA AK-47 assault rifle mishandled by his driver who was playing with the rusty rifle while sitting on the jump seat on the right hand side of the vehicle. Barnard was standing in the doorway of the vehicle when the driver accidentally shot off a three-round auto burst. The wounded soldier was attended by Medic Russell Jones who found Johannes lying on his back on the ground in a pool of blood by his head. The medic found a small entry wound just below and slightly to the left side of his lower lip with no pulse or breathing. Medic Jones attempted to insert an IV but there was no blood pressure to raise a vein, whereupon a doctor arrived and stopped further effort. He pronounced Barnard dead and the body was temporarily covered with a mosquito net before being put in a body bag with his dog tags in a windowed exterior pocket for shipment back to South Africa.[161]

Gunner A. W. De Villiers of a G5 howitzer battery was killed on 8 October 1987 after falling asleep in the path of a mechanized convoy that subsequently ran over him near the Lomba River. Private A. T. N. Sadler was also crushed by a vehicle on 29 November 1987. Sergeant M. G. Pienaar the commander of an Olifant tank from the Pretoria Regiment was accidentally crushed by a tree in the tank hatch on 1 November 1987. The tank column was proceeding at night towards Mavinga in an effort to make up lost time when the tank struck a tree that fell on him. Although severely injured he did not die immediately as an attempted rescue failed.

One casualty from a friendly-fire incident was Sapper Steven Lelong of the 1st Para Battalion who was killed by mortar fire on 22 February 1988 in what the SADF called a blue on blue incident. This unfortunate accident occurred due to a command error in location of the rendezvous and operational areas. Shamefully, many of his fellow soldiers were not allowed to attend his funeral.[162]

The Cubans were not without their share of embarrassing military moments such as the 28 April 1988 shootdown related earlier of Brig. Gen. Francisco Cruz Bourzac a vice minister and member of the ruling Cuban Central Committee among others. The Central Committee paid tribute to the general at a meeting the following July and was later honored by having a military-industrial company in San José de las Lajas named after him. By one stroke that Cuban antiaircraft battery killed more Cubans, twenty-nine, than in any other land or air encounter during the entire the Battle of Cuito Cuanavale.

Cuban provincial newspapers published the names of each province's fatalities around 7 December 1989, the day when Cuba conducted almost simultaneous memorial services for the Angola dead around the island. Cuban, FAPLA, Soviet, and UNITA losses are not accurately known except for the recent release of 2,106 names of Cuban MMCA combatants at Freedom Park, Pretoria.

Over a thirteen-year war in Angola this means the Cubans lost about thirteen men a month, comparable to the reported SADF losses but unrealistic for this conflict. In a single encounter on Valentine's Day 1988 in a small part of the Angola war theater of operations the Cubans admitted to losing fourteen men in a tank battle. The best estimate comes from the well-researched Edward George book *The Cuban Intervention in Angola, 1965-1991: From Che Guevara to Cuito Cuanavale* of five thousand Cuban fatalities over the entire Angola intervention. Both the Cubans and the South Africans underreported their KIAs, the Cubans by about a factor of two and the South Africans by a factor of at least three.[163]

The Cuban forces certainly led in the number of high-ranking casualties with the deaths of Generals Francisco Cruz and Arnaldo Ochoa Sanchez, although the latter was caused by but after the Battle of Cuito Cuanavale.

Cuba also lost six aircraft and nine aviators in the battle, but only seven KIAs as pilots Lt. Col. Manuel Rojas Garcia and Capt. Ramon Quesada Aguilar were captured after successfully ejecting from their stricken aircraft and were eventually released by UNITA. Three crewmembers of an Antonov-26 cargo plane were lost on 28 April 1988 and four fighter pilots were also killed in action: Capt. Lorenzo Morales Ramos (28 October 1987), Capt. Carlos "El Gordo" Rodriguez Perez (4 May 1988), Capt. Juan "Capri" Perez Rodriguez (2 March 1988), and Lt. Ernesto L. Chavez Marrero (21 November 1987).

Parachutist Pedro Ernesto "Coco" Subiaurre Carmenate was part of an MI-17 helicopter search-and-rescue crew or Busqueda, Salvamento y Rescate(BSR)that operated in Cuito Cuanavale. In an interview with the Cuban Escambray News he related participating in the rescue of four downed Cuban aircraft. He also stated that he observed a MiG shoot down a South African Plane. He could only recall the nickname of the Cuban pilot as "el Pez" (the "Fish).

One report puts the number of Cuban ground troops lost at thirty-nine although fourteen of these alone would have had to come from the tank battle mentioned earlier. Despite their best efforts and caution the Cuban MMCA forces in Angola must have suffered a few hundred casualties during the Battle of Cuito Cuanavale when the continuous South African bombardment of their fixed positions as well as the courageous frontline leadership they displayed is factored into a realistic estimate.

The four SAAF pilot fatalities were Maj. Ed Every (20 February 1988), Capt. Willie van Coppenhagen (19 March 1988), Capt. A. A. Stapa (14 November 1987), and Lt. Richard Glynn (3 September 1987).

In summary the Cubans had nine aircrew shot down to four SAAF pilots as well as six aircraft lost to four South African planes. The Cubans suffered seven fatalities and the SAAF only four, not couting the forward artillery observer in Glynn's plane. They were evenly matched with the Piercy and Doval intercepts that resulted in injuries and aircraft damage but no kills by accepted standards. Unlike prior conflicts neither side managed an aircraft to aircraft kill, likely due to the poor performance of missiles on both sides.

By any accounting method the Cuito Cuanavale air war would have been a victory for the SAAF but for the mistaken and accurate Cuban antiaircraft crews of Techamutete, Angola.

Claims, counterclaims, propaganda, and spin are naught for these warriors joined together in death will not be returning from Angola. No barroom salutes, no posters, no headlines, no dedications, and no headstones will ever bring them back to friends and loved ones. Cream of the crop curdled by war, created by leaders, fought by others, and now forgotten to time.

The SADF claimed losses for the Battle of Cuito Cuanavale of forty-three men killed and two Mirages, one Bosbok light aircraft, three Olifants, and four Ratels destroyed. Their claim for the FAPLA was heavier and unconfirmed at 4,768 men killed and ninety-four tanks, twelve MiGs, and nearly a hundred armored vehicles and trucks destroyed.

In April 1988 the SADF stated that thirty-one young conscripts were killed in Angola during the prior six-month period although other information suggested that at least seventy-one soldiers had been killed during that period, seventy-six if the air force deaths are included. (Note kk)

SADF Gen. Jannie Geldenhuys confirmed that thirty-one South African soldiers were killed and ninety wounded in the eight months between July 1987 and February 1988. Helmoed-Romer Heitman provided a more realistic assessment of twenty-five fatalities between September and 20 Novem-

ber, almost three months. Brigadier General Dick Lord gave the Cuito Cuanavale losses as forty and has never included the SAAF pilots Andre Stapa
or Willie van Coppenhagen as combat losses in his two books on the SAAF
having determined their loss as a result of aircrew or maintenance errors and
not FAPLA fire. There is no reference to Stapa's body being recovered in
Angola but a member of the SAAF remembered seeing the recovered wreckage of the Impala being dumped near the bomb storage on the north side of
the Ondangwa air base. The inquiry on the destroyed Mirage No. 223 of
Willie van Coppenhagen was inconclusive.[164]

A SADF press release in June 1988 reported 69 deaths for the previous
six months in the entire Border War and all operational areas. Another source
has 249 deaths for the SADF in 1987 and 1988.[165]

The SAAF casualties for the Battle of Cuito Cuanavale from September
1987 to May 1988, were four killed and one severely wounded with SADF
casualties being seventy-five including five accidental deaths from shooting
accidents and howitzer explosions for a total of 79 South African dead. There
was an increase to eighty-one with the death of two unnamed soldiers in G5
explosions of 11 November 1987 reported by Dick Lord. There are also a
further three additional unnamed casualties on 15 November, one on 25
November and a sapper on 23 April reported in the Helmoed-Romer Heitman book, which added together make it eighty-six deaths. This is almost
triple the casualty report by General Geldenhuys.

Thirty-six, nearly one-half of these casualties were young men no older
than twenty-one. SADF Casualties aged 17–21:

NAME, UNIT	DATE KIA	AGE
Private F. du P. Smit, 1st Recce	11 August 1987	age 17
Rifleman J. P. Barnard, 1 South African Infantry	19 January 1988	age 18
Rifleman A. S. Groenewald, 61st Mechanised	14 February 1988	age 18
Lance Corporal M. A. Benecke, 1st Para	6 September 1987	age 19
Rifleman W. G. Beukman, 4 South African Infantry	20 September 1987	age 19
Rifleman F. De Bruin	12 September 1987	age 19

Rifleman P. G. Claasen, 4 South African Infantry	9 November 1987	age 19
Corporal T. A. Duvenhage, 4 South African Infantry	November 1987	age 19
Bombadier C. Hendricks	25 February 1988	age 19
Second Lieutenant Adriaan Hind, 61st Mechanised	3 October 1987	age 19
Trooper F. De Jager, 61st Mechanised	8 October 1987	age 19
Signalman J. De Lange, 5th Signals	21 February 1988	age 19
Rifleman P. H. Groenewald, 61st Mechanised	14 February 1988	age 19
Rifleman J. M. Howes, 4 South African Infantry	11 November 1987	age 19
Corporal J. H. Kleynhans, 61st Mechanised	14 February 1988	age 19
Lance Corporal M. J. Lecuona, 61st Mechanised	3 February 1988	age 19
Sapper S. E. Lelong, 1st Para	22 February 1988	age 19
Lance Bombadier P. Mansfield, 4th Artillery	16 October 1987	age 19
Rifleman A. M. Thom, HC, 4 South African Infantry	9 November 1987	age 19
Second Lieutenant J. R. Alves, 32 Infantry	13 September 1987	age 20
Lance Corporal M. M. De Klerk, 32 Infantry	13 September 1987	age 20
Gunner A. W. De Villiers, 4 South African Infantry	8 October 1987	age 20
Trooper M J Kuyler, 32 Infantry	13 September 1987	age 20
Rifleman F. A. Muehlenbeck, 4 South African Infantry	9 November 1987	age 20
Rifleman M. J. Mitton, 4 South African Infantry	12 November 1987	age 20
Lance Corporal J. Redelinghuys, South African Medical	17 November 1987	age 20

Private A. T. N. Sadler	20 November 1987	age 20
Private A. Steward, 4 South African Infantry	9 November 1987	age 20
Corporal G. M. Stewart, 44th Parabat	20 March 1988	age 20
Rifleman P. M. Schutte, 4 South African Infantry	11 November 1987	age 20
Corporal J Van Heerden, 4 South African Infantry	16 November 1987	age 20
Lance Corporal H. J. Venter, 7 South African Infantry	3 May 1988	age 20
Corporal V. Z. Venter	21 February 1988	age 20
Rifleman Rudolf J. Badenhorst	26 September 1987	age 21
Second Lieutenant M. S. McCann, 101 Battalion	4 February 1988	age 21
Sergeant M. G. Pienaar, Pretoria Regiment	1 November 1987	age 21[166]

For every officer SADF officer killed in Angola during the Battle of Cuito Cuanavale, there were more than ten soldiers.

A further and perhaps better enquiry should be directed as to why a country like South Africa would send inexperienced young conscripts to frontline duty in Angola when it had such a large pool of professional career soldiers in various units at its disposal marking time in the relative safety of border patrols and absolute safety at the rear. The size of the SADF in 1986 was estimated at 43 thousand in the permanent force, 265 thousand part-timers, and 67 thousand conscripts. Of this substantial force only about 5 thousand were sent to the inferno of Angola, and it was unforgivable to use young conscripts seeing combat for the first time. Surely, at the very least, the SADF leadership could have given permanent soldiers the opportunity to replace the inexperienced conscripts heading for frontline duty in Angola. Given the history, heritage, bravery, and professionalism of the South African soldier corps, not one young conscript would have reached Angola in that event. Post-action explanations of the logistical difficulties with long distances to Angola and extended period of the conflict do not surmount this view.[167]

The South Africans were fighting a conventional war in Angola, a counterinsurgency war in Namibia, an unconventional war in Mozambique, and localized civil disturbances within South Africa. All good reasons to recruit professional soldiers attracted by proper compensation, especially when the permanent force was mostly officers. Proof positive would be the substantial voluntary participation of former soldiers in well paid mercenary work in the years that followed the Battle of Cuito Cuanavale.

South Africa leads the number of private security contractor deaths in Iraq after the United States and United Kingdom. On one day alone, three South African contractors were killed as a result of an IED explosion on Haifa Street, Baghdad on 14 November 2005. Two were killed instantly and the third died three days later. They were Naas Du Preez, Johannes Poltgieter, and Miguel Tablai, who worked for Dyncorp International. They joined the thirteen killed in 2004 and another seven killed in 2005.[168]

More SADF troops were killed accidentally, the majority in vehicular mishaps and shooting incidents, than were killed by the FAPLA during the battle. There were even fatalities caused by lightning and an elephant attack in Kruger Park, and a few such as Pvt. F. du P. Smit of the 1st Recce Regiment were killed during training accidents. By comparison, in October 2007 nine soldiers were killed and fifteen injured at the SANDF Lohatlha battle school in Bloemfontein, South Africa, in a single training accident involving a 500-round automatic 35mm antiaircraft gun. This was believed to be the worst accident suffered by the South African National Defence Force in its entire history.[169]

According to FAPLA General "Ngongo" Soviet casualties in Angola for the entire intervention were fifty-one Russians killed and ten wounded, including two Soviet officers, Colonel Gorb and Lt. Oleg Snitko, who were killed at Cuito.

Recently Colonel Sergey Kolomnin, the press secretary of the Russian Union of the Veterans of Angola, claimed that only three Soviet soldiers, two officers and one enlisted man were killed in Angola during the time of the battle of Cuito Cuanavale in 1987–88. He went on to state that ten more Soviet soldiers were also injured. This assessment is without any capability of belief.

Estimates of UNITA and FAPLA losses run from the hundreds to the thousands and cannot be confirmed. These soldiers were sufficiently dispensable that no one even recalled or published their names or unit numbers; their only memorial is the faceless tomb of the unknown soldier at the Santana cemetery in Luanda and the geometric edifice at Cuito Cuanavale. One thing was for certain, there was no apartheid on the battlefield, the medical evacuation, the hospital, the mortuary, or final resting place in the porous

African earth. Soldiers were killed and wounded without note of skin color, for bullet and blast are indiscriminate killers.

During the attack in the Tumpo River area in March 1988 several hundred UNITA soldiers, some of whom were mounted on SADF tanks, ran into a well-prepared FAPLA position supported by Soviet ZU 23mm guns. The vulnerable UNITA forces were decimated by these guns and suffered terrible casualties. About four hundred UNITA combatants were killed in this single action and were buried in a mass grave. This grave was subsequently unearthed and the UNITA remains mistaken by some for SADF soldiers as they were also dressed in SADF uniforms known as Army Browns.[170]

The FAPLA forces were also capable of thinking outside the box when it came to killing, even in an act of kindness. In an incident reminiscent of Vietnam, LCpl. W. A. F. Price of the 61st Mechanised Battalion was killed on 17 February 1988 by a booby-trapped water bottle given to him in a plea to be filled with water by a masquerading FAPLA soldier. Despite a roll call of UNITA soldiers and perimeter search the FAPLA soldier survived this daring trick. Price's arm was blown off by the explosion and his body was put in a sleeping bag as no body bags were available.[171]

Taking another page from Viet Cong tactics, the FAPLA would set mines with a backup explosive device if removal were attempted. A variation of this would be the secondary IED explosions commonly seen in Iraq.

At a higher level Cuban Gen. Raúl Menéndez Tomassevich confirmed that UNITA leader Jonas Savimbi was a high-value target being pursued by the FAPLA and that he, Tomassevich, was the only man capable of finding Savimbi. It appears that the Cuban leadership were intimately familiar with the concept of targeted assassination to decapitate UNITA leadership.

The now deceased Tomassevich said, "He and I both know that. I never saw him, but I was pretty close. If you knew that Savimbi had a crew escort of several men, including a highly-educated female secretary, who we captured and later changed to the MPLA side." These nasty thoughts were subsequently replaced with necessary nicety for the later Cuban prisoner release by Savimbi in August 1988. The secretary referred to by Tomassevich was reportedly Savimbi's wife Ana, who unfortunately was killed in Luanda in 1992 after the aborted reconciliation elections. In December 2001 captured UNITA Lt. Col. Pedro Nunda claimed to the media that Ana Savimbi had been killed upon the assassination order of her husband.[172] Savimbi appeared to strike first on 3 November 2001 when there was an assassination attempt on defence minister and well respected general Kundi Paihama at the Hotel

Tropico in Luanda. His car without him inside was blocked and shot up but only the driver and a bystander were hurt.[173]

General Tomassevich's quest was ultimately assisted by Gen. Geraldo Sachipengo (Nunda) who was a crucial advisor and tactician for the FAPLA Savimbi elimination team led by Brig. Simao Carlitos Wala. General Nunda had defected from UNITA in 1990 and became deputy chief of staff of FAPLA in 1994, rising in 2010 to chief of staff. The general had defected with his family from UNITA in 1992 using FAPLA assistance. Satisfying as this was, it is believed that his ultimate target in the hunt was UNITA Gen.Esteves Pena also called Kamy, who was the alleged mastermind of the 1995 brutal killing of Nunda's cousin Pedro "Tito" Chingunji, the UNITA foreign affairs secretary and his family. Kamy who was never far from Savimbi has not been heard of since.

UNITA Commander in Chief Jonas Savimbi was killed in February 2002 with a few tattered diehard remnants of his army in the former UNITA heartland, Moxico province. He crossed and recrossed rivers, divided up the few followers left in distraction groups, all of which failed against hardened pursuers determined to end Angola's bleeding years. The heroic handful of hunters brought a just end to Angola's national nightmare.

A further casualty was Savimbi's deputy Gen. Antonio Sebastiao Dembo, who died a few weeks later from lack of medication for chronic diabetes. Common for Angola, Dembo had a brother that did not share his dedication to the UNITA cause and became a major in the unified Angolan armed forces. Dembo was from the Mbundu tribe and was a rare exception to the Ovimbundu dominated UNITA, which could explain his extreme loyalty to Savimbi. Prior to this, in January 2002, UNITA security services chief Gen. Samuel Martinho Epalanga was captured by the FAPLA along with communications chief Brig. Domingo Sopite.[174]

As the South African aid expert and author Leon Kukkuk (*Letters to Gabriella: Angola's Last War for Peace, What the UN Did and Why*) astutely noted:

> It is a common perception and opinion that every time the Angolan government does something good or well it is because somebody has compelled it to do so, and every time the military does something good or well it is because somebody helped them, either Israelis, or Americans or even South Africans or Namibians. The fact of the matter is, whatever the faults and failings may be, neither the An-

golan president, Jose Eduardo Dos Santos, nor FAA Chief of Staff, Joao de Matos are lightweights. They cannot afford to be, because neither is their adversary, Jonas Savimbi. One should not, however, demean the maturity of the government approach to reconciliation; the sincerity of their offer of amnesty and the success with which this was implemented. For years Savimbi had told his supporters that the government will kill them if they are captured, he even told them that they would be killed by the people in the cities should they ever appear there. It was the sort of thing that the government had to overcome in order to entice the UNITA soldiers out of the bush.[175]

National reconciliation was eased by the lack of ethnic cleansing common to other regional civil conflicts like Rwanda as well as the growing cross tribal content of the unified Angolan armed forces.[176]

The large, thirty-meter-long bunker prepared and occupied by Savimbi with all necessary facilities earlier in the conflict at Andulo, some hundred miles north of Kuito failed to protect him. It had been abandoned to the elements as the FAPLA forces advanced to victory and today only remains a tattered symbol of his self-centeredness or the utter futility of war.[177]

Another casualty of the Battle of Cuito Cuanavale was the highly decorated hero of the revolution Gen. Arnaldo Ochoa Sanchez who was commander of the Angola southern front until replacement by the favored but able commander Leopoldo "Polo" Cintra Frias. Ochoa was executed for treason on 12 July 1989 in Havana for alleged drug smuggling. Perhaps there were no postrevolution crowds crying *"Paredon!"* at the execution wall, but that is where he ended. Ochoa was unlucky that the leadership did not follow the example of Stalin who simply sent World War II hero Field Marshal Zhukov into obscurity. The general was unable to call for the Beretta and three hundred bullets he brought to Column No. 2 under the able leadership of Commandante Camilo Cienfuegos during the Revolution.[178]

Polo for his part, wisely continues to deny any comparison to Zhukov, as he did recently at a 2006 Cuban war memorial dedication at Freedom Park, South Africa of the 2,106 dead Cuban soldiers.[179]

Caribbean shipping magnate Michael Chastanet recently recalled his involvement in shipping food supplies to Angola for two years during the Angola war and that he would "never forget seeing the Cubans shipping their dead soldiers on special refrigerated boats back to Cuba. It was a harrowing sight."[180]

Two other commanding generals involved in the Battle of Cuito Cuanavale died prematurely of various illnesses: FAPLA General Pedale in 1995 and UNITA General Ben Ben in 1998 of cerebral malaria. Neither would see the fruition of their leadership or Angola at peace.

A former SAAF helicopter pilot had this to say about his combat experiences: "It's the most depraved kind of behavior. But I think all it does,whilst I think it's depraved, I think that it's the way, all it does is to highlight the fact that we're still linked to the primates. All we've done is to find another way of killing each other. Not ripping each other's throats out and biting and, we just do it with ammunition now."[181]

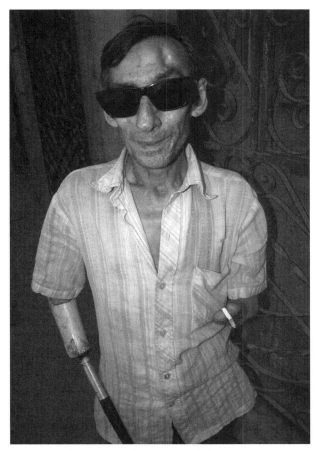

Angolan War veteran Havana, Cuba, 2001.
—*Tommy Huynh/TommyImages.com/*

CHAPTER 14

PRISONERS OF WAR

A significant aspect of the Battle of Cuito Cuanavale was that neither side held large numbers of prisoners at the conclusion of the conflict. There are several instances of UNITA captures of Cuban, Soviet and Eastern Bloc soldiers earlier in the war often presented by photographic evidence or documentary reports but no forward information as to what happened to many of them.

Shortly before the Battle of Cuito Cuanavale, on 7 September 1987, there was a well publicized prisoner exchange when SADF Maj. Wynand Du Toit was exchanged for 133 FAPLA and 2 Cuban soldiers. Sabotage specialist Major Du Toit received his promotion from captain to major during his more than two-year incarceration in an FAPLA Angolan prison.

On 11 November 1987 Eugene Kayumba, an artillery reconnaissance scout from an artillery battery attached to the UNITA 4th Battalion, was captured by the FAPLA near the Chambinga River and interrogated. He was from the province of Huambo and had been with UNITA three years. Later on 15 December, a FAPLA second lieutenant was captured by UNITA and interrogated by the SADF at their headquarters. Their fates are unknown.[182]

The two MiG-21UM FAPA Cuban pilots, Lt. Col. Manuel Rojas Garcia and Capt. Ramon Quesada Aguilar, shot down in October 1987, were released by their UNITA captors in August 1988 as part of secret talks held in the Ivory Coast between the Cubans and UNITA rebels. Little is known about these two pilots after their release. Prior to providing their freedom UNITA leader Jonas Savimbi, apparently sensing a change in the tide, said that the two pilots were released, "to show Cuba that we are also men, revolutionaries and human." Savimbi would not go on to show equal compassion for his UNITA comrades-in-arms in later years.

The Cuban pilot release may also have been a good-faith gesture in response to the July 1988 overture for a prisoner exchange made by Jorge Risquet of the Cuban government at a Lisbon news conference.[183] In May 1988 SADF soldier Johan Papenfus was wounded and captured when his Casspir armored vehicle was hit by an RPG near Donguena, Angola, less than a hundred kilometers from the Namibian border. He was taken to Havana and hospitalized at the foreigners only Hospital Hermanos Almejeiras before eventual return to Ruacana for the prisoner exchange. It is the same hospital where dissident Cuban political prisoner Orlando Zapata Tamayo, who had been arrested in 2003, died after eighty-five days on hunger strike in February 2010.

This was what some modern day critics of the war on terror call extraordinary rendition as South Africa was not formally at war with Cuba. Papenfus was eventually permitted a visit by the International Committee of the Red Cross in Havana in February under the Geneva Convention. Further, the South African soldier was paraded before Cuban television, Hanoi Hilton style. To Papenfus's credit, one Cuban observer reported that he maintained the Boer warrior spirit and cursed several times requiring censorship bleeps when filmed. To be fair, the captured Cuban pilots received no such exposure before Western media by the SADF.

A prisoner exchange took place on 31 March 1989 at Ruacana, Namibia, when fourteen FAPLA Angolans, including a pilot, and three Cubans were exchanged for Papenfus. It is unknown if the Cuban group included twenty-seven-year-old Miguel Garcia Ensmorado, who was interviewed by a journalist in November 1986 and described as a deserter although his presence in Angola, the UNITA camp, interview replies, and the close presence of minders suggest that none of the foregoing was voluntary.[184]

Papenfus's Casspir was destroyed by Cuban soldier Bernardo "Shogun" Heredia Perez who received the Order Camilo Cienfuegos and the medal of courage Calixto García among others for his extraordinary bravery. Papenfus was the first SADF soldier captured alive by Cuban soldiers around the time of the Battle of Cuito Cuanavale. Cuban soldier Eliecer Duran of the 40th Anti-Tank Brigade was killed in the 4 May 1988 encounter and likely returned to Cuba in the refrigerated containers seen by Michael Chastanet.[185]

Perez and his Cuban-FAPLA scout unit led by Lt. Geomar Fernández of the 40th Tank Brigade was alerted to the presence of the SADF soldiers of the 101 Battalion by the sound of rock music, band unknown, in the African bush. By the end of the engagement 3 Casspirs were destroyed and I captured.

An eyewitness to the event gave this account:

It was the afternoon of May 3, 1988 when I was with B Company 101st Battalion at the shore by Calueque that I met Capt Dewald Hattingh (201st Battalion) when he was pulling out of the area north of Calueque. B Company had to maintain presence, locating and destroying enemy. Data indicated that there was activity in the vicinity of Donguena and north-west from there. Capt Hattingh has swept from the road south of Donguena to Calueque and B Company had started to move. At the point where 201Bn began a sweep, I let the soldiers of 7 SAI sweep in a northerly direction, passing by the ruins at Donguena by 500m. We moved in a westerly direction over rough and smooth veld for approximately 5 kilometers and then turned north for a temporary base. The night was very quiet and no incidents of strange noises were heard. Shortly before dawn we heard droning and were convinced that they were vehicles. The roads were in disuse and the droning was of big machines. I sent out a section in the direction and they began to follow. As the day progressed, we momentarily lost the sound and at 11h00 the sound was lost. In the process we moved most of the time in a northeastern direction. I cancelled the follow orders and turned east in the direction of the north-south road that runs north from Donguena. It was hardly a km when we discovered tank tracks. It was clearly heavy tanks with infantry. The tracks were very old. The muddy tracks were already dried. It has not rained recently. I wanted to return south to Donguena and then work west between lines indicated on the map. In order to save time, I would not drive on or sweep the roads, with the result that we had to move through rough and smooth veld east of the road. When we moved over the road on the east side we turned in a southerly direction, we found a lot of fresh tracks. I thought it was the tracks from yesterday morning so we spread out in a line. The tracks were so obvious that we didn't require any trackers on the ground, we had the formation shifting left and right of the track to keep the formation centered on the track. After a time

I contacted 51BN's ops room over the radio and reported the situation to Capt Tobie Mynhardt. He indicated that the gunships were inbound. I thought it was premature as the tracks were not so fresh. Capt Mynhardt in any event ordered the gunships to standby. I think it was about 15h30 when the tracks disappeared again. At first, it was as if a bombshell had gone off. The entire formation was at a standstill and trackers and I were on the ground. Before the formation stood a dense forest, which looked very rugged. Suddenly we were under small-arms fire. It was chaos. The drill was to immediately attack and in went the Casspirs. I had troops on the ground while the Casspirs rode forward. I had trouble with my vehicle's back door. The troops tried to open the door from inside while I opened the door from outside. I could just put my arm in the door, then I wormed my way in. The shots have hit against the plating on the side of my vehicle's tower. I radioed in and yelled some words. We responded heavily to the fire. We fired at any movement in the forest. Suddenly it felt as if someone hit my nose with their fist. The impact of the RPG burst my ears. I felt something against my chest. I felt and looked but saw nothing. I found out later that I was hit under the arm by shrapnel. Everything seems to be in order. The chaos lasted for an unknown length of time. When I got back into the vehicle, I saw that Corporal Venter was lying with a bloodied chest and face. I realised for the first time that we were in big trouble. The Casspir was on fire! Through a side window I could see an enemy trench with movement. He was not black. He was very dark-skinned and had straight black hair. I climbed over the wounded Venter as he lay in my path. The RPG or something else had him on his chest on the webbing. I could see moving bowels as he breathed. I knew he was not going to make it. Immediately, the words of Commandant Leon Lambrechts came to me: "Boys, we must not leave bodies behind!" I wanted my R4 [rifle], but the flames had already burned high in the bin right next to the gun. At the diamond mesh of the bin white phosphorus grenades hung. The flames had already started licking them. I grabbed Venter by his webbing. Isaac Hamutanya was the driver and he helped the man outside the vehicle to the furthest wheel and let him sit. I made sure that all the troops from the Casspir were out and then closed the doors. Small-arms fire receded. Corporal Coenie Van Zyl came alongside our vehicle to help. We again drew fire and the driver then drove forward. I dragged Venter [LCpl. H. J. Venter] for a short distance to the Casspir and we loaded him. I shouted to Coenie that he must instruct the other vehicles over the radio to withdraw to the South. We were not far from there when we met and set up defence. In my wildest dreams could I imagine as much chaos on the battlefield as I saw that day. We were short 4 Casspirs. Corporal Du Preez was nowhere to be seen and I know we could not lose bodies. We had many flat tyres to change. The troops were anxious and struggled in setting up defence, most wanted to stay near the vehicles. I made contact with 2nd Lieutenant Coetzee's vehicle again. Captain Meinhardt has confirmed that the gunships were 10 minutes out and that Pumas were inbound for casevacs. Impalas would begin bombing in 5 minutes. I contacted them with the A72 and had tried giving detailed information. I think the sortie was successful. They turned and flew away. The gunships had arrived and asked for formation intelligence before attacking. There were simply no vehicles whose wheels were not all un-damaged. I think 3 were all right to drive. We were led by the gunships a few miles east to the place where a Samel stood with a flat front tire. The rim was hit by an RPG. I think the record for the fastest wheel change ever was broken. I must now say, we only put on 3 wheel nuts and then we rode.

We now drew fire, but from an artillery cannon. The gunship reported that an olive green vehicle was creeping along in the northeastern direction. The fire was certainly indirectly and not accurate. We went back to the other vehicles. Du Preez suddenly made his appearance. We loaded the wounded and Venter's body into the Puma helicopters. How much time had elapsed, I don't know. Capt Hattingh arrived with 17 Buffels with 201 Battalion troops. We tried to regroup. At this stage Corporal Coenie van Zyl informed me that Johan Papenfus was missing. We had to rush under the trees when Migs appeared in the air. They never saw us. By night fall, we had 2 columns entering the combat zone. There was still a lot of smoke and flames around the burning vehicles. Capt Hattingh launched 81mm mortars into the combat zone. We could not get much back and moved back to the temporary base. At dawn we approached the combat zone. There were holes dug in the ground in the shape of landmines. There was a lot of visible ammunition. Level trenches with blood and Casspir tracks proved that the enemy also suffered casualties. 5 of our own troops were found dead, but not a single foe. The five found dead were:

Rifleman L. Haifiku
Rifleman H Haimbodi
Rifleman W Robert
Rifleman J Petrus
L/Corporal F Petrus

It was serious for me that I did not see enemy dead. There were no weapons left behind. It was a big shock to only see 3 burned vehicles. I was just gone. We looked and there was no sign of Papenfus. According to Corporal van Zyl he did not have his bush-helmet, but wore a neutral cap with a black rear. We speculated that he must be dead. The whole area was filled with balls as big as pebbles. I think that it was something to do with the Air Force bombs. It could have been shrapnel. We also found the tank tracks from the previous day. Some of them were 40cm wide. There were already 3 recovery vehicles there to retrieve the Casspirs. The vehicles were in the process of leaving when a Buffel ran over a mine left by the Cubans. I do remember 2lt Duvenhage's back was injured, I cannot clearly recall having to airlift him to base, although I think we did. There were no deaths anyway. The vehicle was totally buggered with the wheel blown away. To make a long story short, everything was sent to Calueque. The Casspirs were dumped in the river and blown up. Brigadier Serfontein had come to fetch me in a helicopter and flew me to Ruacana to debrief. I think it was May 20 when the radio announced that Papenfus was imprisoned in Cuba. We suspect that he was in the vehicle was hit by an RPG and he wasn't severely injured. We know that his hip was seriously injured as he was hit by the RPG."[186]

It is not known if the Ruacana group of exchanged FAPLA soldiers included 47th Brigade tank commander Silva, reported to have been captured by the SADF on 14 October 1987 after a tank battle near the Chambinga River, or UNITA scout Eugene Kayumba, captured by the FAPLA.[187]

There was no published information by the direct foes of the Angolan civil war for prisoner collection or assistance in repatriation of remains. Part of the rationale would be that both the FAPLA and UNITA, being essentially ground troops in a fast-paced bush war, were simply unable to accommodate any prisoners whether high value or otherwise over the extensive period of the conflict.

As one SADF commander put it, "We didn't take any prisoners. Not one. They were either killed or they ran away, but we never encountered any prisoners." Further, the UNITA forces disintegrated on the death of Savimbi in 2002 with the limited available resources being devoted to integration of the remaining live soldiers into the existing national army.

One curious exception to this was two ANC operatives captured by UNITA in June 1987 and held at their Jamba headquarters. On 15 September 1987 John Battersby of *The New York Times* reported on what was believed to be the first capture of South African rebels from the outlawed African National Congress (ANC) by National Union for the Total Independence of Angola (UNITA), South African-backed, anti-Communist guerillas who had been fighting for ten years to overthrow the Soviet-backed government in Luanda.

The two rebels were thirty-two-year-old Michael Mkona and twenty-five-year-old Mthunzi Mnguni. Mkona left South Africa in 1978 and Mkona "studied in Cuba, East Germany and Bulgaria after leaving South Africa in 1978. Mr. Mnguni said both men had been based at an African National Congress camp at Novo Catengue near Quela in Malanje Province." Documents captured with the rebels indicated that Mr. Mkona is a commander in the Congress's military wing and Mr. Mnguni is a commissar, although the prisoners refused comment on their ranks or positions within the ANC.

UNITA intelligence officers said "the Novo Catengue camp is one of about 16 Congress guerrilla bases and refugee camps spread across the northwestern quarter of Angola." Twelve hundred ANC guerrillas are believed to be in Angola.

"Last week, in their first interview with journalists since they were captured June 25 near the southeastern guerrilla base, about 300 miles east of the Angolan capital of Luanda, the two men said they feared they would be turned over to the South African Government for interrogation. But Jonas Savimbi, the Angolan rebel leader, said in an interview last Monday that he had refused a South African request to hand over the two guerrillas. The prisoners are members of the Congress's military wing, Umkhonto We Sizwe, or Spear of the Nation."

In the interview neart Mavinga Mr. Savimbi emphasized that UNITA opposes apartheid, the South African policy of racial separation, but didn't see any point in criticizing the white South African government saying, "I don't want to lose my influence with President P. W. Botha.[188]

Their fate is unknown.

CHAPTER 15

CEASEFIRE

The formal ceasefire was connected to the withdrawal of the Cubans and South Africans from Angola as well as the implimentation of U.N. Resolution 435. A number of talks took place in May 1988 in London, Governors Island in New York harbor in July, Brazzaville in August, New York in October, and Geneva in October. It was only after these talks that the tripartite agreement was signed on 22 December 1988 where it was agreed that the Cubans would withdraw from Angola, the South Africans would withdraw from Angola, and U.N. Resolution 435 would be implimented on 1 April 1989. All parties met at Ruacana, Namibia, on 22 August 1988 with Cuban representative Gen. Leopoldo Cintra Frias, SADF representative Maj. Gen. Willie Meyer, and FAPLA Col. Antonio Jose Maria. It was only after this process that the Joint Monitoring Commission was established using senior officers from the former foes who met daily, often over lunch with the exchange of souvenirs and gifts of South African wines.[189]

The South African team was lead by Director General of Foreign Affairs Neil van Heerden with Gen. Jannie Geldenhuys and other SADF officers. They met the Cubans and FAPLA teams at various times in Sal Island, Cape Verde, and Brazzaville, the capital of Congo. The discussions took place on Sal Island for three days in July 1988 with the Cuban military only, and included Gen. Rosales del Toro and Gen. Cintra Frias among the large Cuban contingent.

It was only at the last day of the meetings that Gen. Arnaldo Ochoa Sanchez appeared. It was likely a last international public appearance before his untimely execution. The discussions in Brazzaville took place in August

1988 with the Cuban and FAPLA delegations. It was at this meeting that Colonel Oelschig finally met his Cuban counter-part Colonel Morejon, commander of the Cuban Special Forces.[190]

In June 2007 Jorge Risquet of the Central Committee of the Communist Party of Cuba made the comment that Cuba did not have any further ambitions of military intervention in Africa but an army of white coats instead referring to Cuba's medical missions. This is perhaps prescient on the part of the geriatric Cuban leadership who will require the best medical care in their dotage, a true gerontocracy.[191]

UNITA did eventually capture Cuito Cuanavale without South African assistance in January 1993, after the aborted U.N. sponsored elections. This came about in the power vacuum created when the MPLA party of Dos Santos substantially committed to the electoral process and set up a unity army joined by many UNITA officers. When election results did not favor Savimbi, he proceeded to put in motion what many thought was a pre-arranged plan to take over the country. He nearly succeeded.

By the end of 1994 some former South African veterans of the the Battle of Cuito Cuanavale, including pilots, were employed by the notorious Executive Outcomes firm of mercenaries to train elite antiguerilla units for the FAPLA army against their former ally. This was task-for-trade by former SADF soldiers from units that had previously fought the FAPLA and Cuban soldiers. The Angolan war slogans and rhetoric about South African mercenaries previously dismissed as propaganda would gain some traction by this behaviour. It would have been inconceivable and nigh impossible for former Cuban soldiers to train UNITA soldiers had UNITA achieved victory.

Of all the things to happen this must have been the greatest insult to UNITA soldiers who had fought and died in their thousands in front of South Africans, but like many things, it was always about the money. The high ground of morality and principle in this regards remained with the Cuban internationalist forces after the conflict as well as grist for the victors punditry mill. One voice of disapproval came from former Lomba River SADF combatant and Sandline mercenary commander in Sierra Leone Bert Sachse who said, "If you switch sides at the end of the day then what do you have? That is why I could not fight in Angola against UNITA. I helped train UNITA. I knew Jonas Savimbi."[192]

South African soldiers had the distinction of fighting for both sides in a relatively short period, which would support warrior tradition in that country not unlike the Hessian mercenaries of the American Revolution.[193]

The estrangement of former allies culminated in December 1995 when Angola abstained from voting in favor of the fourth consecutive U.N. resolution with 117 countries against the embargo on Cuba preferring to join 38 countries that abstained. It was a gesture towards a warming of relations with the United States predictably predicated on money. Nevertheless the two countries continued to maintain good relations. Perhaps Angola will one day soon start its own internationalist monetary mission and supply Cuba with free oil and finance to lift it out of the doldrums that its people now endure.

Cuban veterans of a the Battle of Cuito Cuanavale had a difficult time integrating back into society but none were able to turn to mercenary work for compensation. There were many bureaucratic obstacles put in the way to even receive the gestures of appreciation encompassed in medals of service and valor such as the International Combatant Medal. Cuban military pensions only provided for rank and responsibility on retirement. Later on Cuban Decree No. 101 of 1988 took account of a third parameter, length of service, but not for combat service.

There is no compelling evidence of Cuito Cuanavale being the initial objective at the start of the SADF expedition in Angola during the summer of 1987 to assist UNITA forces repel FAPLA attacks directed at Mavinga. Cuito Cuanavale became a target of opportunity upon the rapid retreat of FAPLA troops and the unexpected successes by the UNITA and SADF joint force that pursued an eventual attack on the town.

The real winners of the Battle of Cuito Cuanavale were the Angolan people who were able to say goodby to their Soviet and Cuban patrons so that the earnest business of peace and prosperity could begin while dodging the deadly inheritance of a countryside despoiled by mines. In hindsight the United States and the former Soviet Union prolonged the inevitable and should thereby bear some accountability in reconstruction aid.

Angola has one of the highest percentages of landmine victims in the world. A reported 70 thousand Angolans have suffered horrifying injuries and many thousands have been killed. Nobody knows exactly how many mines were laid during the last thirty years or where they are all located.

One South African officer found that FAPLA would place mines randomly in the area around the Lomba River without any real pattern, hoping for the best, which happened on a few occasions. However, there are still mines in that area waiting for some unsuspecting driver. In December 1998 UNITA Lt. Col. Joao Chiwisi and ten soldiers were killed while laying mines in Bie province.[194]

The heaviest concentrations are found where major battles or sieges took place like Cuito Cuanavale. Forty-eight different types of landmine have been found in the country. A capable mine-removal expert can clear five square meters a day by hand in Angola's long grass.

Removal of landmines is complicated by use of automatic ambush or anti-lifting methods used when laying mines. In these situations the larger anti-tank mines are often fitted with an antilifting mechanism that will cause them to explode on removal. The automatic ambush occurs when lifting the mine causes a reaction via detonation cord to claymore mines that then explode and shower the immediate area with lethal ball bearings.[195]

Kuwait, which was mined using traditional methods during the Gulf War, is smaller than Angola's Luanda province and a partial demining of Kuwait took three years and more than $750 million. The Namibian infantry group that served with the U.N. in Huambo demined roads using vehicles that could withstand antitank mine blasts without serious injury to their occupants. In areas they believe are heavily mined soldiers leave the vehicle to check the road with mine detectors.

The Namibians have verified and declared safe seven hundred kilometers of four major roads: Huambo to Caconda, Malange to Mussende, Malange to the River Lui, and from M'banza Congo to Tomboco. Between peace-keepers and a private company contracted by the, U.N. some 8,750 kilometers of road have been demined in Angola thus far.

In a chilling interview of Cuban Gen. Nestor Lopez Cuba in October 1997 he stated that landmines were the weapon of the poor, hence Cuba's objection to the banning of landmines. In this he echoed the prior published sentiments of Cuban Gen. Luis Perez Rospide, head of Cuban Military Industries for the Recvolutionary Armed Forces.

―――――

All is not lost and hope springs eternal as an active and vigilant Angolan media surveys the ongoing political and economic development of Angola. In Cuito a new bridge stands between the old and new, crossed daily by the growing young population for whom the war must become a distant but unforgettable memory. A former combatant who visted Cuito in October 2010 reported:

> Cuito Cuanavale during our visit in October 2010 was still war torn and the people remain extremely poor. The roads are in a pitiful con-

dition. The people are resilient and friendly beyond belief. Minefields still surround the town and erstwhile defensive positions. It is extremely dangerous to leave the trodden roads. Two people were killed by mines whilst we were there."[196]

Eventually time, even measured in decades, brings peace.

The future of Cuito Cuanavale, October 2010.—*Roland De Vries*

To every thing there is a season, and a time to every purpose under the heaven: A time to be born, and a time to die; a time to plant, and a time to pluck up that which is planted; A time to kill, and a time to heal; a time to break down, and a time to build up; A time to weep, and a time to laugh; a time to mourn, and a time to dance; A time to cast away stones, and a time to gather stones together; a time to embrace, and a time to refrain from embracing; A time to get, and a time to lose; a time to keep, and a time to cast away; A time to rend, and a time to sew; a time to keep silence, and a time to speak; A time to love, and a time to hate; a time of war, and a time of peace.

—*Ecclesiastes 3:1-8 (King James Version)*

GLOSSARY

Bateleur: SADF mobile Multiple Rocket Launcher with forty launch tubes mounted on an armored Samil 100 6x6 truck.

Blesbok: Casspir variant logistical vehicle often with Vickers machine guns.

Bosbok (antelope or bush buck): SAAF light single engine airplane with four underwing hardpoints for machine gun pods, light bombs and smoke-rocket pods.

Brigade: military unit of several battalions numbering from three to five thousand troops.

BM-21: Soviet truck-mounted 122mm multiple rocket launcher.

BMP: Amphibious tracked Soviet infantry fighting vehicle with a 73mm semiautomatic gun with a forty-round magazine.

BTR: Soviet eight-wheeled armored personnel carrier with machine gun.

Buffel: SADF wheeled, armored, mine-resistant personnel carrier

Cactus: SADF French made short-range missile air defence system originally called the Crotale.

Casspir: SADF armored mine-resistant personnel carrier

Crotale: See Cactus

CSI: Chief of Staff Intelligence

DAAFAR: Defensa Anti-Aerea y Fuerza Aerea Revolucionaria or Cuban Air Force and Antiaircraft Defense

FAR: Cuban Revolutionary Armed Forces

FAPA: Forca Aerea Popular de Angola or Angolan People's Air Force

FAPLA: Forcas Armadas Populares de Libertcao de Angola or The People's Armed Forces for the Liberation of Angola, which replaced the Exercito Popular de Libertação de Angola (EPLA), or People's Army for the Liberation of Angola, the earlier guerrilla forces of the MPLA. Now simply called the FAA (Forcas Armadas de Angolanas) or Armed Forces of Angola.

FAPA-DAAFAR: FAPA 25th Air Combat Fighter Regiment Cuban Air Force/FAPA with 12th Fighter Squadron.

G5: SADF 155mm artillery howitzer with range of forty kilometers

Kwevoel: SADF 10-ton armored truck with mine and bullet protection.

MANPAD: Man-portable-air-defense, shoulder-launched surface-to-air missile.

MiG: Soviet jet fighter/bomber called chorizos (sausages) by the Cuban pilots.

Milan: antitank weapon

Mirage: French-manufactured SAAF fighter nicknamed Vlamgat or flaming hole.

MRL: multiple rocket launcher

MTU: Soviet mobile bridge

Mortar: small muzzle-loading cannon that fires shells at low velocities, short ranges, and high-arc trajectories.

Olifant: South African modification of the British Centurion tank.

Parabat: elite SADF parachute-trained troops

PB: Soviet Amphibious armored personnel carrier

PT: Soviet armored amphibious light tank with 76mm cannon.

Ratel: Wheeled armored vehicle named after South African honey badger.

Rinkhals: SADF mine protected ambulance

SADF: South African Defence Force

SANDF: Postapartheid South African National Defence Force created in 1994

SA-13: Soviet mobile surface-to-air missile launcher

SAMIL: SADF 10-ton truck

Strela: Soviet MANPAD surface-to-air missile

T-55: Soviet tank.

TMM: Soviet mobile scissors bridge

Valkiri: "Vorster Organ" or Vorster Orrel 127mm mobile multiple rocket launcher.

Vyandelike Vliegtuie: SADF Afrikaans warning shout and radio call for incoming FAPA aircraft

Withings: SADF recovery vehicle from Afrikaans for white horse.

Ystervark: SADF single-barrel 20mm antiaircraft gun.

ZAS: Soviet satellite, scrambled communication unit

ZRK: Soviet mobile SA-6 missile air defense system

ZT3: SADF Ratel with antitank guided missile system.

ZSU: Soviet mobile 23mm antiaircraft gun often used in a ground mode.

THE CUBAN FORCES

General Abelardo "Fury" Colome Ibarra, Deputy Minister of Defense (now Minister of the Interior)

General Raul Menendez Tomassevich, (died August 2001)

Division General Ulises Rosales del Toro, Chief of the General Staff, Revolutionary Armed Forces (FAR)

Division General Ramon Espinosa Martin, Deputy Defence Minister

Division General Arnaldo Ochoa Sanchez, overall Cuba commander in Angola (executed for treason 12 July 1989, in Havana)

Colonel Alavaro Lopez Miera, Chief of Operations, Cuban Military Mission in Angola (MMCA), Army Corps General and Chief Deputy General Staff of FAR

General Rogelio Acevedo, MMCA Deputy Chief of Operations

Major General Rogelio Acevedo, President, Civil Aeronautics Institute

Colonel Amels Escalante Colas, Chief of General Staff, MMCA (now brigadier general, Chief of Center for Strategic Studies)

Brigadier General Patricio de la Guardia Font, MMCA Angola (sentenced to thirty years following 1989 Ochoa trial, released March 1997)

Colonel Antonio de la Guardia Font, MMCA Angola (sentenced to death and executed following 1989 Ochoa trial)

Commander Leopoldo "Polo" Cintra Frias, Commander Angola Southern Front (now commanding general of Cuba's Western Army)

Leopoldo ("Polo") Cintra Frías, First Vice Minister of the Revolutionary Armed Forces

Commander Miguel Lorente Leon, MMCA Cuito Cuanavale (now brigadier general)

Colonel Venancio Avila Guerrero, Commander Cuito Cuanavale
Colonel Morejon, Commander of the Cuban Special Forces.
Lieutenant Colonel Jose Senen Viamonte, Deputy Chief of Operations
    MMCA
Commander Miguel Lorente Leon, MMCA Cuito Cuanavale
    (now brigadier general)
Colonel Jorge Luis Guerrero
Lieutenant Colonel Cuban Ciro Gómez Betancourt
Lieutenant Colonel Fermin Sosa Borrero, Advisor 25th FAPLA Brigade
Lieutenant Colonel Reynaldo Hernandez
Lieutenant Colonel Héctor Aguilar, Commander of T-55 Tanks
Commander Jorge Fernandez Marrero, MMCA 3rd Battalion
    (now brigadier general)
Commander Ramon Valle Lazo
Major Gonzalo del Valle, MMCA 2nd Battalion
Captain Milagros Martinez Garcia, woman medical officer
Lieutenant Geomar Fernández, 40th Anti-Tank Brigade
First Lieutenant Vickie Fuenteseca Herrera
Second Lieutenant Víctor Batista, 40th Anti-Tank Brigade
Eliecer Duran, 40th Anti-Tank Brigade ((KIA 4 May 1988)
Bernardo "Shogun" Heredia Perez, 40th Anti-Tank Brigade (Order
    Camilo Cienfuegos and Calixto García medal)
Ritha "Chamacos" Miguel, 40th Anti-Tank Brigade
Rubén Jiménez
Jorge Luis Villazón, Anti-Aircraft Defense and Revolutionary Air Force
    (DAAFAR)
Brigadier General Francisco Cruz, Vice-Minister (killed 28 April 1988)
Brigade General Rubén Martínez Puente, Chief DAAFAR in Angola
    (now division general)
Colonel Humberto Trujillo Hernandez, Squadron Leader, 25th Air Combat
    Fighter Regiment (MiG-23ML pilot)
Colonel Colonel Colonel Luis Alonso Reina, 25th Air Combat Fighter
    Regiment (MiG-23ML pilot)
Commander Rafael Alemany, Antiaircraft
Lieutenant Colonel Manuel Rojas Garcia, 25th Air Combat Fighter Regiment
    (MiG-21UM pilot, shot down and captured by UNITA at Luvuei Angola
    28 October 1987, released August 1988)
Lieutenant Colonel Armando "El Guajiro" González, 25th Air Combat
    Fighter Regiment (MiG-23ML pilot)

APPENDIX A — THE CUBAN FORCES • 193

Major Alberto Ley Rivas 25th Air Combat Fighter Regiment (MiG-23ML pilot, first to damage SAAF Mirage in dogfight during the Battle of Cuito Cuanavale, 27 September 1987)

Captain Ramon Quesada Aguilar, 25th Air Combat Fighter Regiment (MiG-21UM pilot, shot down and captured by UNITA at Luvuei Angola 28 October 1987, released August 1988)

Captain Lorenzo Morales Ramos, 25th Air Combat Fighter Regiment (MiG-21 pilot, KIA 28 October 1987)

Captain Carlos "El Gordo" Rodriguez Perez 25th Air Combat Fighter Regiment (MiG-23ML pilot KIA 4 May 1988)

Captain Juan "Capri" Perez Rodriguez, 25th Air Combat Fighter Regiment (MiG-23ML pilot, KIA 2 March 1988)

Captain Orlando Carbo, 25th Air Combat Fighter Regiment (MiG-23ML pilot)

First Lieutenant Juan Carlos Chavez Godoy, 25th Air Combat Fighter Regiment (MiG-23ML pilot)

First Lieutenant Juan Francisco Alfonso Doval, 25th Air Combat Fighter Regiment (MiG-23ML pilot, damaged and crash-landed 14 January 1988, now lieutenant colonel Air Force of the Revolutionary Armed Forces)

Lieutenant Ernesto L. Chavez Marrero 25th Air Combat Fighter Regiment (MiG-23ML pilot, KIA 21 November 1987)

Lieutenant Eduardo Gonzalez Sarria, 25th Air Combat Fighter Regiment (MiG-23ML pilot)

First Lieutenant Eladio Avila, 25th Air Combat Fighter Regiment (MiG-23ML pilot)

Parachutist Pedro Ernesto Subiaurre Carmenate (Coco), MI-17 helicopter Busqueda,Salvamento y Rescate (BSR) (Search and Rescue), Cuito Cuanavale 1988.

Sergeant Vivian Hernandez Caballero, Women antiaircraft battery

APPENDIX B

THE SOUTH AFRICAN FORCES

SADF

General Jannie Geldenhuys, Chief of the SADF (retired 1990)
General Andre "Kat" Liebenberg, Chief of the SADF after General
    Geldenhuys (retired 1993, died 1998)
Major General Willie Meyer
Brigadier General Fido Smit, Division Commander
Lieutenant Colonel Hutchinson, Army Directorate Operations HQ
Colonel Renier Coetzee, Divisional Headquarters Mavinga
Colonel Deon Ferreira, 20 Brigade Battle Group (later lieutenant general
    and first Chief of Staff Joint Operations, retired 2000)
Colonel Roland de Vries, Second-in-Command
Colonel George McLachlan
Colonel Jock Harris, Senior Staff Officer, 20 Brigade
Colonel Mucho Delport, 32 Infantry Battalion
Colonel Paul Fouche, 20 Brigade Battle Group
Colonel Mucho Delport, Commander 32 Infantry Battalion
Colonel Jean Lausberg, Artillery commander
Colonel Fred Oelschig, Senior UNITA liaison
Colonel Coen van der Berg, SAAF liaison
Colonel James Hills, Antitank commander
Commandant J C Du Randt (KIA 3 September 1987)
Commandant Flip Genis, 32 Infantry Battalion
Commandant Jan Hougaard, 32 Infantry Battalion
Commandant Koos Liebenberg, 61st Mechanised Battalion

Commandant Gerhard Louw (Honoris Crux), Regiment President Steyn
Commandant Jan Malan, 62nd Mechanised Battalion (4 SAI)
Commandant Leon Marais, Commander 62nd Mechanised Battalion (4 SAI)
Commandant Mike Muller, 61st Mechanised Battalion
Commandant Les Rudman, CSI UNITA liaison team commander
    (later major general in SANDF)
Commandant Bert Sachse, CSI UNITA liaison team commander
Commandant Cassie Schoeman, 62nd Mechanised Battalion (4 SAI)
Commandant Kobus 'Bok' Smit, Commander 61st Mechanised Battalion
Commandant Dougie Stern
Commandant Andre Wagener, Intelligence
Commandant Jan van der Westhuizen
Commandant Robbie Hartslief, 20 Brigade
Major Mike Bourne
Major Sarel Buijs
Major L. L. du Plessis
Major Vim Grobler 61st Mechanised Battalion, Tank Squadron Commander
Major Pierre Franken, Forward Artillery Observer, G5 Battery
Major Gert Kotze
MajorJohan Lehman (Honoris Crux), SAAF liaison
Major Dawid Lotter, 1 South African Infantry Battalion
Major Servaas Lotter
Major Laurence Maree, 61st Mechanised Battalion
Major Hannes Nortmann (Honoris Crux), 32 Infantry Battalion
Major Jako Potgeiter
Major Andre Retief
Major Tim Rudman, 61st Mechanised Battalion, Tank Squadron Commander
Major Christo Terblanche, 61st Mechanised Battalion
Major Riaan Theron, Artillery Battery Commander, 62nd Mechanised Battalion
Major Robert Trautman, Forward Artillery Observer
Major Butch Williamson
Major W. van Ryneveld
Major Cassie van Merwe, Forward Artillery Observer
Major Thinus van Staden, 32 Infantry Battalion
Major Clive Wilsworth, 32 Infantry Battalion
Major Andre van Zyl
Captain Anton Boshof, Forward Artillery Observer, G5 Battery
Captain P. J. Cloete, 61st Mechanised Battalion
Captain Eckard

Captain Human
Captain Joubert
Captain Koos Maritz
Captain A. D. McCallum, 32 Infantry Battalion (KIA 13 September 1987)
Captain John Mortimer
Captain Mulder
Captain Rendo Nell
Captain Potgeiter
Captain Starbuck
Captain Steynberg
Captain Tai Theron
Captain Terreblanche
Captain A. de Wit
Captain Johan van Zyl (Honoris Crux)
Captain Petrus Van Zyl (Honoris Crux), 32 Infantry Battalion
Captain Piet van Zyl
Lieutenant Koos Breytenbach
Lieutenant Coetzer, 4 South African Infantry
Lieutenant Gawie Combring
Lieutenant John Cruse
Lieutenant Tobias De Vos (Honoris Crux), 32 Infantry Battalion
Lieutenant H. J. R. Gerding, South African Medical Service (KIA 1988)
Lieutenant Hein Fourie
Lieutenant Kooij (Honoris Crux), 61st Mechanised Battalion
Lieutenant Libenberg
Lieutenant Johnny Lombard
Lieutenant Werner Lotter, 4 South African Infantry
Lieutenat Malherbe
Lieutenant N. J. A. Prinsloo (Honoris Crux), 101 Battalion
Lieutenant Abrie Strauss
Lieutenant Corne van Schoor
Lieutenant Van Heerden
Lieutenant Nico van Rensburg
Lieutenant Vosloo
Second Lieutenant J. R. Alves, 32 Infantry Battalion (KIA 13 September 1987)
Second Lieutenant D. A. C. Bock (Honoris Crux), 101 Battalion
Second Lieutenant H. Martin Bremer (Honoris Crux), 61st Mechanised
    Battalion
Second Lieutenant J. H. Diederichs, 101 Battalion (KIA 2 April 1988)

Second Lieutenant Adriaan Hind, 61st Mechanised Battalion
  (KIA 3 October 1987)
Second Lieutenant M. S. McCann, 101 Battalion (KIA 4 February 1988)
Sergeant Major Jacques de Wet, 4 South African Infantry
Staff Sergeant Spikkels Terblanche, Olifant Tank Squadron
Sergeant Arsenio Baptista, 32 Infantry Battalion (KIA 16 November 1987)
Sergeant J. R. Mananza, 32 Infantry Battalion (KIA 13 September 1987)
Sergeant Major Koos (Crocodile) Kruger, 32 Infantry Battalion
Sergeant Riaan Rupping (Honoris Crux), 32 Infantry Battalion
Sergeant Sterzel (Honoris Crux), CSI liaison team
Sergeant Manuel Ferreira, Intelligence 20 Brigade HQ
Sergeant P. J. Digue, 61st Mechanised Battalion (KIA 9 November 1987)
Sergeant Piet Fourie, 32 Infantry Battalion
Sergeant Labuschagne
Sergeant G. M. Maritz, 5th Signals Regiment (KIA 21 February 1988)
Sergeant M. G. Pienaar, Pretoria Regiment (KIA 1 November 1987)
Sergeant Mac da Trinidade, 32 Infantry Battalion
Corporal J. J. Bronkhorst (Honoris Crux), 101 Battalion
Corporal T. A. Duvenhage, 4 South African Infantry (KIA 9 November 1987)
Corporal F Frederick (Honoris Crux), 101 Battalion
Corporal J. H. Kleynhans, 61st Mechanised Battalion (KIA 14 February 1988)
Corporal T Stander (Honoris Crux), 101 Battalion
Corporal G. M. Stewart 44th Parabat Regiment (KIA 20 March 1988)
Corporal J Theunissen (Honoris Crux), 101 Battalion
Corporal J Van Heerden, 4 South African Infantry (KIA 16 November 1987)
Corporal V. Z. Venter, (KIA 21 February 1988)
Lance Corporal M. A. Benecke, 1st Para Battalion (KIA 6 September 1987)
Lance Corporal R M Coetzee, (KIA 1 March 1988)
Lance Corporal M. M. De Klerk, 32 Infantry Battalion (KIA 13 September 1987)
Lance Corporal M. J. Lecuona, 61st Mechanised (KIA 3 February 1988)
Lance Corporal J. Redelinghuys, South African Medical Service
  (KIA 17 November 1987)
Lance Corporal H. A. Oosthuizen, (KIA 4 September 1987)
Lance Corporal W. Tchipango, 32 Infantry Battalion (KIA 13 September 1987)
Lance Bombadier P. Mansfield, 4th Artillery Regiment (KIA 16 October 1987)
Lance Corporal C. T. Moon, 2nd South African Cape (KIA 7 April 1988)
Lance Corporal F Petrus, 101 Battalion (KIA 3 May 1988)
Lance Corporal W. A. F. Price, 61st Mechanized (KIA 17 February 1988)
Lance Corporal L. F. Van Wyk (KIA 25 February 1988)

Lance Corporal H. J. Venter, 7 South African Infantry (KIA 3 May 1988)
Rifleman C. Dala, 32 Infantry Battalion (KIA 31 December 1987)
Rifleman J. W. L. Johannes, 5th Recce Regiment (KIA 3 December 1987)
Rifleman Ernest Kapepura, 32 Infantry Battalion (KIA 11 November 1987)
Trooper M J Kuyler, 32 Infantry Battalion (KIA 13 September 1987)
Rifleman Fernando Mauricio, 32 Infantry Battalion (KIA 11 November 1987)
Trooper Johann R. Meyer, 32 Infantry Battalion (KIA 25 September 1987)
Rifleman Joaquim Pedro, 32 Infantry Battalion (KIA 16 November 1987)
Private F. du P. Smit, 1st Recce Regiment (KIA 11 August 1987)
Rifleman B Zumba, 32 Infantry Battalion (KIA 31 December 1987)
Rifleman Rudolf J. Badenhorst (KIA 26 September 1987)
Rifleman J. P. Barnard, 1 South African Infantry (died 19 January 1988)
Rifleman W. G. Beukman, 61st Mechanized (died 20 September 1987)
Rifleman P. G. Claasen, 4 South African Infantry (KIA 9 November 1987)
Rifleman G. W. Green (Honoris Crux), 61st Mechanized Battalion
Rifleman A. S. Groenewald, 61st Mechanized Battalion (KIA 14 February 1988)
Rifleman P. H. Groenewald, 61st Mechanized Battalion, (KIA 14 February 1988)
Rifleman L. Haifiku, 101 Battalion (KIA 3 May 1988)
Rifleman H Haimbodi, 101 Battalion (KIA 3 May 1988)
Rifleman J. M. Howes, 4 South African Infantry (KIA 11 November 1987)
Rifleman F. De Bruin, (KIA 12 September 1987)
Trooper F. De Jager, 61st Mechanised Battalion (KIA 8 October 1987)
Signalman J. De Lange, 5th Signals (KIA 21 February 1988)
Gunner A. W. De Villiers, 61st Mechanized Died 8 October 1987)
Gunner L. M. C. Havenga, 4th Field Regiment (KIA 20 November 1987)
Bombadier C. Hendricks (KIA 25 February 1988)
Sapper S. E. Lelong, 1st Para Battalion (KIA 22 February 1988)
Recruit J. R. Marlow (died 31 December 1987)
Rifleman S. A. Masina (died 31 December 1987)
Rifleman P. D. Matroos, 54 Battalion (KIA 23 January 1988)
Rifleman M. J. Mitton, 4 South African Infantry (KIA 25 November 1987)
Rifleman F. A. Muehlenbeck, 4 South African Infantry (KIA 9 November 1987)
Private D. Ngubani, 121 Battalion (KIA 17 January 1988)
Rifleman V. V. Nieuwenhuizen, 61stMechanised Battalion
    (KIA 14 February 1988)
Rifleman J Petrus, 101 Battalion (KIA 3 May 1988)
Rifleman W Robert, 101 Battalion (KIA 3 May 1988)
Gunner K. A. Roberts (KIA 12 January 1988)
Private A. T. N. Sadler (died 29 November 1987)

Rifleman P. M. Schutte, 61st Mechanized (KIA 11 November 1987)
Rifleman A. Snyders, 1 South African Infantry (KIA 23 January 1988)
Private A. Steward, 4 South African Infantry (KIA 9 November 1987)
Sapper M. C. Suter (KIA 4 February 1988)
Private P. Thobejane, 21st Battalion (KIA 11 March 1988)
Rifleman A. M. Thom, 4 South African Infantry (Honoris Crux)
    (KIA 9 November 1987)
Rifelman P. L. H. Van Dyk, 1st Para Battalion (KIA 11 March 1988)
Rifleman D. W. Van Zyl, 4 South African Infantry (KIA 11 November 1987)
Rifleman N. J. Vermeulen, 101 Battalion (KIA 25 March 1988)
Rifleman P. A. Visagie, 61st Mechanised Battalion (KIA 16 September 1987)
Rifleman P. Warma, 31st (Bushman) Battalion (KIA 18 April 1988)

SAAF

Lieutenant General Denis Earp (SSA, SD, SM), Chief of the SAAF
Lieutenant Colonel Dolf Prinsloo, Mirage F1AZ Pilot
Commandant Johan Rankin, Mirage F1AZ Pilot
Comandant Major Dup, 3 Squadron
Comandant Major de Beer, 3 Squadron
Major Mossie Basson
Major Ed Every, Mirage F1AZ Pilot (flying No. 245 first squadron
    KIA on 20 February 1988 by FAPLA SA-13 missile)
Major Frans Coetzee, Mirage F1AZ Pilot
Captain Trompie Nel, Mirage F1AZ Pilot
Captain Carlo Gagiano Mirage F1AZ Pilot (now general and SAAF Chief)
Captain Arthur Piercy, Mirage F1AZ (flying No. 206 was damaged by SAM
    strike and crash-landed on 27 September 1987)
Captain Anton van Rensburg, Mirage F1AZ Pilot
Captain Reg van Eeden, Mirage F1AZ Pilot
Captain Willie van Coppenhagen, Mirage F1AZ (flying No. 223 Pilot was
    KIA 19 March 1988)
Captain A. A. Stapa, Impala Mk 2 Pilot (KIA 14th November 1987 vicinity
    Cuvelai, Angola by antiaircraft fire)
Lieutenant Richard Glynn Atlas, AM3C Bosbok Pilot (KIA 3 September
    1987 by SA-8 missile

APPENDIX C

U.S.S.R. FORCES

General Mikhail Petrov
Lieutenant General Leonid Kuzmenko
Lieutenant General Pavel Gusev
Colonel Vyacheslav Alexandrovich Mityaev
Colonel Sagachko
Colonel Gorb, Interpreter 21st Brigade (KIA November 1987)
Lieutenant Colonel A. A. Mikhailovich, Chief Advisor 21st Brigade
Lieutenant Colonel S. Y. Pavlovich, Chief Artillery Advisor 21st Brigade
Major D. C. Rashidovich, 21st Brigade
Captain V. Vyacheslav, SA-8 Antiaircraft Missile Specialist
Senior Lieutenant Anatoly Alekseevsky
Lieutenant Oleg Snitko, Interpreter 21st Brigade (KIA 1 October 1987)
Second Lieutenant Z. I. Anatolyevich, Interpreter 21st Brigade
Warrant Officer Valentine Matveichuk
Sergeant Major F. A. Mikhailovich, Technical Specialist 21st Brigade
Igor Zhdarkin, advisor/translator 21st FAPLA brigade
P. Bondarenko, technician 21st FAPLA brigade
A. Moskvin, translator 21st FAPLA brigade
Sergey Mishchenko, 21st FAPLA Brigade

FAPLA FORCES

General Pedro Maria Tonha (Pedalé), Minister of Defense 1980–95 (died 22 July 1995 in London)

General Antonio Dos Santos Franca (N'Dalu), Army Chief of Staff, Minister of Defence, First Angolan Ambassador to the United States in 1995, Nonexecutive Chairman De Beers Angola 2005

General Roberto Leal Monteiro (Ngongo), Angolan Ambassador to Russian Federation 2000–2006, Angolan Minister of Internal Affairs 2006

Admiral Feliciano dos Santos

General Geraldo Sachipengo (Nunda), defected from UNITA 1992, Deputy Commander in Chief 1994

General Nunda, FAPLA Advisor Savimbi Elimination Team 2002, Commander in Chief 2010

General Pedro Benga Lima (Foguetão/Rocket), Chief of Operations Division, Commander Lomba Front, now President Simportex company

General Eugénio

General Matias Lima Coelho (Nzumbi)

General Mateus Miguel Angelo (Vietnam)

General Antonio Faceira

General Antonio José Maria

General Implacavel

Brigadier General Helder Cruz, FAPLA engineer Cuito Cuanavale 1987

Brigadier Raul Antonio (Recordacao) (KIA 8 April 2001)

Brigadier Passe Ukuki

Brigadier Eugenio Figueiredo

Lieutenant General Marques Correia
Lieutenant General António Valeriano
Lieutenant General Simione Mikuni (KIA 23 October 1999)
Colonel Manuel Correia de Barros, Commander MGPA Kuando Kubango,
    Chief of FAPLA Central Headquarters/Operative Direction Center,
    now Deputy Director Angolan Strategic Studies Center
Colonel Domingos Hungo
Colonel Da Silva Neto
Colonel Alexandre Lemos de Lucas (Bota Militar)
Colonel Mele Francisco Camacho
Lieutenant Colonel Agostinho Nelumba (Sanjar), Chief Advanced
    HQ Cuito Cuanavale, now General Agostinho Nelumba
Lieutenant Colonel Antas, Commander Logistics Supply Menongue to
    Cuito Cuanavale, now a general
Lieutenant Colonel Mario Placido Cirilo de Sa (Ita), Intelligence Chief,
    now a general and Director Angolan Strategic Studies Center
Lieutenant Colonel Armando da Cruz Neto, Commander 4th Military
    Region-Huambo, now a general
Lieutenant Colonel Joao de Matos, major regional commandant 1987, Chief
    of Staff 1994–2001
Lieutenant Cololonel Luis Pereira Faceira
Brigade Commander N'Geleka
Commander Silva 47th Brigade
Commander George Chikoti, defected from UNITA 1989, Deputy Foreign
    Minister 2002
Major Joao Domingos Baptista Cordeiro (Ngueto), Forward Commander
    Cuito Cuanavale, Commander 6th Region (CC), later general, died in
    helicopter crash 2002
Major Tobias, 47th Brigade Commander
Major Elieus Guilermo Correia (Kuxixima)
Major Armindo Moreira
Major Batista
Major Mateus Timoteo
Major Roberto Fernando de Matos
Major Joao Carlos Carvalho
Major Armindo Moreira
Captain Nguleica, Commander 21st Brigade
Captain Colarinho
Sergeant Antonio Francisco da Silva, Antiaircraft unit Xangongo

APPENDIX E

UNITA FORCES

Jonas Savimbi Commander in Chief, killed 22 February 2002

Brigadier Demosthenes Amos Chilingutila, Chief of Staff 1987, Deputy Minister of Defence 1996-2008

General Arlindo Chenda Pena (Ben Ben), Deputy Chief of Staff 1987, Chief of Staff 1989, FAA Joint Chief of Staff 1996, died October 1998

General Antonio Sebastiao Dembo, Northern Front Chief of Staff, Commander Special Commandos (Tupamaros), died March 2002

Jeremias Chitunga Vice President, UNITA Peace Negotiator 1992, killed November 1992 in Luanda

Pedro Chingunji (Tito), Foreign Affairs Secretary 1980–1991, executed 1991

Brigadier Samuel Martinho Epalanga, Chief Liaison Officer SADF

General Samuel Epalanga, Head of Security Service, captured January 2002

Brigadier Geraldo Sachipengo Nunda, Senior Political Commissar, Northern Front Commander 1984, defected to FAPLA 1992, FAA Commander in Chief 2010

General Paulo Armindo Lukamba (Gato), Secretary General 2002

General Abreu Muhengu Ukwachitembo (Kamorteiro), Military Chief of Staff 2002

General Esteves Pena (Kamy)

General Pedro Apolo Yakuvela

General Eugenio Manuvakola, defected to FAPLA 1997, President UNITA Renovada 2002

General Altino Sapalalo (Bock), executed 13 April 1999

General Samuel Chiwale
General Jacinto Bandua, Commander Strategic Procurement, defected 2000
General Abìlio Kamalata (Numa), Commander Lucusse Front 1987–88,
    Political Affairs Secretary 2003, Secretary General 2007
General Abel Chivukuvuku, arrested 1992–1997, Angola Unity Parliament
    UNITA member 1998, SADF Liason 1987
General Miguel N'zau Puna, defected 1992
General Miguel Mario Vasco (Kanhali Vatuva), died November 2007
General Alcides Sakala Simoes
General Felino (Apolo), Operational Command
General Chata (Smart), Foreign Affairs Secretary 1991–2002
General Lutoki Wiyo, defected 1996
General Ukama Regresso, defected 1996
General Vaso Chimuco
General Antero Vieira Menze, executed 13 April 1999
General Julio Armindo (Tarzan), executed 13 April 1999
General Fernando Elias Bandua, executed 13 April 1999
General Assobio de Bala, executed 13 April 1999
General Daniel Fuma, executed 13 April 1999
General Galiano da Sivo e Sousa (Bula Matadi), KIA 18 February 2002
General Rodrigues, captured 2002
General Elizeu Catumbela, captured 2002
General Elain Malungo Pedro (Kalias)
General Joao Batista Tchindandi (Black Power)
General Almeida Ezequiel Chissende (Buffalo Bill),Commander Clandestine
    Intelligence, KIA 19 February 2002
General Artur Vinama, SADF liaison, General FAA
General Andrade, Communications Chief, General FAA
General Diogenes Malaquias (Implacavel), defected 2000
General Teodoro Edmundo Torres Capindal, captured 2001
Genertal Antero Cufuna, captured 2001
General Rodrigues, captured 2002
General Lucas Paulo (Kananay)
General Marques Correia Banza
General Arlindo Samuel (Samy)
General Jose Baptista Ngueto
Lieutenant General Matias Lima (Zumbi), defected September 2001
Brigadier George Njolela Diamantino (Big Joe), Action/Rapid Intervention
    Brigade (Bate Brigade), killed 22 February 2002

Brigadier Sabino Jamba Machado, Chief of Military Intelligence
    Division 2002
Brigadier General N'Gele, defected 1996
Brigadier General Tchipa, defected 1996
Brigadier Peres Jonas (Grito), executed 13 April 1999
Brigadier Domingo Sopite, Communications Chief, captured January 2002
Brigadier Ilidio Paulo Sachiambo, captured 2002
Brigadier Joao Cristiano Sussula, Commander East Moxico Province
Brigadier General Renato Mateus, Commander Lucusse Front 1986–87,
    Operations Chief, defected 1992
Brigadier General Wambu Kasito, Chief Intelligence Officer,
    Attorney-at-Law, Luanda
Brigadier David Wenda
Brigadier Mbula, KIA 22 February 2002
Brigadier Arlindo Catuta, captured 2002
Brigadier Faustino Pelembe, captured 2002
Brigadier George
Brigadier General N'Gele, defected 1996
Brigadier General Tchipa, defected 1996
Brigadier Peres Jonas (Grito), executed 13 April 1999
Brigadier D. Katata (Veneno), defected 2000
Brigadier Cerqueira, killed 2001 Umpulo
Brigadier Basilio Sapalanga
Brigadier Augusto Domingos Lutock Liahuka
Brigadier Luis Ndimba, captured 2001
Brigadier Eurico Sandongo (Lulu), captured 2001
Brigadier Alfonso Prata
Brigadier Isais Tchitombe
Brigadier Abel Augusto
Brigadier Cerqueira (KIA October 2001)
Brigadier Jose Liahuka David
Commander George Chikoti, defected 1989
Commander Adriano Makevela Mackenzie, defected 1992
Commander Nola
Commander Jorge Sangumba, executed 1991
Colonel Bernard Sombongo, executed 13 April 1999
Colonel Altino Rafael Cassange, defected May 1997
Colonel Arlindo (Mindo)
Colonel Batista, 15th Battalion

Colonel Aleluia Bikingui
Colonel Benguela
Colonel Setti, 3rd Regular Battalion, SADF liaison
Colonel Sekera, SADF liaison
Colonel Antonio Vakulakuta
Colonel Nato
Colonel Gatow, SADF liaison
Colonel Shangonja, SADF liaison
Colonel Tiago Bernado Chingui, captured 2002
Colonel Jose Antonio Gille, defected 2000
Colonel Lucas Kangunga (Kalia), defected 2000
Colonel Aristides Kangunga, defected 2000
Colonel Antonino Filipe
Colonel Jorge Muachilunda
Colonel Lucas Moises Kanjimi
Colonel Aurelio Alves Chipako (Vida de Deus)
Colonel Andrade Chassungo Santos
Colonel Joao Vicente Viemba, UNITA MP 1999
Colonel Isaias Samakuva
Colonel Candido Mucho, captured June 2001
Colonel Estevao Virgilio Simao Satchipa, captured 2001
Colonel Paulo Calado, captured 2001
Lieutenant Colonel Felisberto Mortalha, died in helicopter crash 2002 with
    FAPLA Ngueto above
Lieutenant Colonel Americo Gato, Training Commander, later brigadier
    general and chief of FAA military training academy.
Lieutenant Colonel Armindo Moises Kassessa
Lieutenant Colonel Sabino Comigo
Lieutenant Colonel Amilcar Marcolino Ngongo, defected 1999
Lieutenant Colonel Octavio
Lieutenant Colonel Vituzi
Lieutenant Colonel Aurelio Joao Jura (Kalhas)
Lieutenant Colonel Anastacio Sicato
Lieutenant Colonel Joao Chiwisi
Lieutenant Colonel Eduardo Moreira, captured 2000
Lieutenant Colonel Pedro Nunda (Caxindindi), captured November 2001
Major Nicolai Kafundanga, SADF liaison
Major Mickey, SADF liaison
Major Calipe, SADF liaison, UNITA Chief of Reconnaisance

Major Ernesto
Major Quile, Press Liaison Officer
Major Cano Americano, surrendered 2002
Major Anacleto Eduardo Chingufo (Quito), defected 1999
Major Jaka Jamba
Major Zola Luzolo Daniel
Major Henrique Afonso Raimundo
Major Martires Correa Victor
Major Anacleto de Oliveira, defected 1999
Major Kamalata Vixe Silvano, captured 2001
Captain Walther, SADF liaison
Captain Paulo, SADF liaison
Captain Bemba Kaliato, surrendered 2001
Captain Geraldo Jaime, Press Liaison Officer
Captain Lucas, Press Liaison Officer
Captain Dias, Press Liaison Officer
Captain Rui M'bala
Captain Mario Jacinto, Secret Services, surrendered 2000
Captain Pepe
Captain Luis Antonio Mango, FAPLA defector
Captain Daniel Muliata
Captain Lourenco Makanga
Captain Tito Xavier Namelelu, captured 2001
Lieutenant Paulo Tumo, captured 1997
Lieutenant Sousa Chipeio
Lieutenant Jorge, SADF liaison
Lieutenant Alvaro Aranha, SADF liaison
Lieutenant Tiago Delfim, defected 1999
Lopes Antonio (Escuirinho), defected January 1997
Private Manuel Tito, defected 1999
Eugene Kayumba, Artillery Reconnaissance Scout, captured 11 November
    1987 Chambinga River

NOTES

1. Kahn, *Disengagement from Southwest Africa*, 32.
2. <http://www.scotsman.com/news/world/the-man-who-finally-toppled-savimbi-1-501796>.
3. Fidel Castro, 19th April 1976: "Angola constituye para los imperialistas yanqui un giron africano." (Angola constitutes for the American Yankee an African Giron). Latin American Network Information Center, Castro Speech Database; Saney, *Latin American Perspectives, Issue 150 Vol.33 No.5*. Turton, *My Family History, 1975–2011*.
4. Shubin, *Wars: The Memoirs Of Veterans Of The War In Angola*.
5. George, *The Cuban Intervention in Angola*, 200.
6. Voice of America, Radio Marti Program, Office of Research and Policy, United States Information Agency, *Cuba Annual Report 1987*; Zhdarkin, *We Did Not See It Even in Afghanistan: Memoirs of a Participant of the Angolan War*; Kahn, *Disengagement from Southwest Africa*, 76.
7. There is some confusion whether the FAPLA attack on Mavinga included the 25th Infantry Brigade. Most of these "brigades" were actually in the form of lightly armed militia and had the strength of a reinforced battalion. The 25th was considered one of the best so-called "Maneuver Brigades" equipped with a company each of T-55 tanks and up to three mechanized infantry battalions with BMP-60s or BMP-1s, supported by artillery battalion that included a mix of heavy mortars, howitzers (usually 122mm D-30s), as well as some multiple-rocket launchers (122mm BM-14s and BM-21s), and capable of mounting mobile operations of significant size. In the article "Angola and South West Africa: A Forgotten War (1975–89)" in *Raids* magazine (No. 44, July 1995), Yves Debay stated, "In early August, the communists attacked with five brigades, driving back UNITA forces from their positions until the South Africans launched Operation 'Modular' to

support their allies." The five brigades would have been the 16th, 21st, 25th, 47th, and 59th. There is some evidence that the 16th Mechanized and 47th Armored were virtually destroyed by the SADF near the Lomba River at Mavinga and never returned to full strength thereafter. The Battle of Cuito Cuanavale material suggests that only three brigades returned to fight at Cuito: the 21st, 25th, and 59th.

8. *The Independent* (UK) newspaper, 1 August 1995.

9. At Freedom Park, Pretoria, South Africa on 30 August 2006 at a ceremony hosted by the Freedom Park Trust, Cuban Ambassador to South Africa, Ms Esther Armenteros, handed over a journal containing the names of 2,106 Cuban soldiers.

10. John Hoyt Williams, "Cuba: Havana's Military Machine," *The Atlantic*, August 1988; Latin American Network Information Center, Castro Speech Database *Press Conference on Grenada 26 October 1983*; Cambio 16 Spain May 1986 interview General Rafael Del Pino.

11. George, *The Cuban Intervention in Angola*, 201.

12. James, *Historical Dictionary of Angola*, 43; George, *The Cuban Intervention in Angola*, 326–8, notes 25, 55; Cambio, 16 Spain May 1986 interview General Rafael Del Pino.

13. Latin American Network Information Center, Castro Speech Database: "26 July Anniversary Rally 1978" (erroneously listed under June 1978).

14. Brittain, *Death of Dignity*, 7–8; James, *Historical Dictionary of Angola*, 43; George, *The Cuban Intervention in Angola*, 326–8, notes 25, 55.

15. Shubin, *The Hot 'Cold War': The USSR in Southern Africa*, 97.

16. "History is not Neutral," <domza.blogspot.com/2006_12_01_archive.html>.

17. Kahn, *Disengagement from Southwest Africa*, 78.

18. Waters, *Making History Interviews with four generals of Cuba's Revolutionary Armed Forces*, 126.

19. Kahn, *Disengagement from Southwest Africa*, 109.

20. Robert Scheina, *Latin America's Wars: The Age of the Professional Soldier Volume 2*, 333.

21. Sarria, *Angola: Relatos Desde Las Alturas*; MiG-23 pilot Lt. Col. Eduardo Gonzalez Sarria, author of *Angola: Relatos Desde Las Alturas*, email interviews June 2010.

22. Ibid.

23. Colonel Paul Fouche, email November 2010; Colonel Fred Oelschig, retired SADF UNITA liaison officer, email interviews.

24. Ibid; Colonel Paul Fouche, email November 2010.

25. Piet Nortje, 3 December 2009, on Harris change by Ferrreira.

26. Nortje, *32 Battalion*, 233–249.

27. Colonel Gerhard Louw, email October 2010.

28. George, *The Cuban Intervention in Angola*, 334, note 13; Lewis, Jack (director), *Brothers in Arms*, South Africa, 2007.

29. Walter Volker, email 14 March 2011.

30. U.S. Department of Commerce, "Sub-Saharan Report," 25 November 1986; Nortje, *32 Battalion*, 233–49.

31. Lord, *Vlamgat: The Story of the Mirage F1 in the South African Air Force*, 267–270.

32. Ibid, 274; *The Northern Daily Leader* (Australia), 16 January 2003, <www.northerndailyleader.com.au/story/1096639/pilot-facing-drugs-charge/>.

33. Lord, *Vlamgat The Story of the Mirage F1 in the South African Air Force*, 168.

34. S. A. Greeff, "South Africa'a Modern Long Tom," *Military History Society Journal*, Vol. 9, No. 1.

35. Colonel Gerhard Louw, email, October 2010; Christopher Crossley email December 2010.

36. Richard Wiles, email, February 2011.

37. Christopher Crossley, email, December 2010.

38. Missing Voices Project, Colonel Paul Fouche, 82nd Citizen Force Brigade, interviewed by Mike Cadman, 15 April 2008, Historical Papers, The Library, University of the Witwatersrand; Heitman, *War in Angola: The Final South African Phase*; Colonel Gerhard Louw, email, October 2010.

39. Russell Jones, *An Immigrants War* (unpublished) and email, 30 October 2009; Government of Cuba, <www.cubagob.cu/otras_info/minfar/defensa_ingles/ifar/iservicio_militar.htm.>.

40. Russell Jones, *An Immigrants War* (unpublished) and email, 30 October 2009.

41. Missing Voices Project, Dr. M, 82nd Citizen Force Brigade interviewed by Mike Cadman, 15 April 2008, Historical Papers, The Library, University of the Witwatersrand.

42. Russell Jones, "An Immigrants War" (unpublished) and email, 30 October 2009.

43. Richard Wiles, email, February 2011.

44. Heitman, *War in Angola: The Final South African Phase*; Christopher Crossley, email, December 2010; Wiles, Richard, email, February 2011.

45. Zhdarkin, *We Did Not See It Even in Afghanistan: Memoirs of a Participant of the Angolan War*.

46. Kahn, *Disengagement from Southwest Africa*.

47. Paiva Domingos da Silva was a senior MPLA commander of the Luanda independence conflict who died in July 1987 just before the Battle of Cuito Cuanavale.

48. Defected from UNITA 1992.

49. Died June 2002.

50. Defected from UNITA 1989.

51. Associated Press, 13 February 2013 <bigstory.ap.org/article/book-tying-angola-generals-diamonds-protected>; *The Independent* (UK) newspaper, 1 August 1995.

52. Panapress, 6 June 2002, <www.panapress.com/Remains-of-Angolan-army-general-Ngueto-buried—13-460674-18-lang2-index.html>.

53. South Africa Parliamentary Millenium Project, "Brigadier-General Espirito Santo, FAPLA Soldier in Battle," <www.pmpsa.gov.za/FILES/pdfs/angola.pdf>.

54. United Kingdom Home Office Report, Sept. 1999; Hodges, *Angola: Anatomy of an Oil State*, 85.

55. Missing Voices Project, Colonel Paul Fouche, 82nd Citizen Force Brigade, inter-

viewed by Mike Cadman, 15 April 2008, Historical Papers, The Library, University of the Witwatersrand; Helmoed-Romer Heitman, *War in Angola: The Final South African Phase*; MiG-23 pilot Lt. Col. Eduardo Gonzalez Sarria, author of *Angola: Relatos Desde Las Alturas*, email interviews June 2010.

56. ANC Document collection, "Stuart Commission Report," 14 March 1984.

57. Nortje, *32 Battalion*, 233–249.

58. Manuvakola defected to FAPLA in 1997; Chivukuvuku was arrested and held from 1992 to1997; Sapalalo was executed on 13 April 1999; Bandua defected in 1999; Wiyo and Regresso defected in 1996; Vieira and Armindo were executed on 13 April 1999.

59. *Human Rights Watch*, "Violations of Media Freedom in the 2008 Election," 23 February 2009; Kukkuk, *Letters to Gabriella: Angola's Last War for Peace*.

60. Colonel Fred Oelschig, retired SADF UNITA liaison officer, email interviews.

61. Ibid.

62. Videotape interviews of three UNITA officers shown to U.N. Security Council by Canadian Ambassador Robert Fowler on 18 January 2000, <http://www.un.org/News/dh/latest/fowlangola.htm>.

63. Colonel Fred Oelschig, retired SADF UNITA liaison officer, email interviews.

64. Ibid.

65. Ibid.

66. The Nordic Documentation on the Liberation Struggle in Southern Africa Project <http://www.liberationafrica.se/intervstories/interviews/nzau_puna/Nzau_puna.pdf>.

67. Judah, Tim, "Time to come home," *The Guardian*, 11 October 2003.

68. Colonel Fred Oelschig, retired SADF UNITA liaison officer, email interviews.

69. Heitman, *War in Angola: The Final South African*.

70. Antonio Duarte, *Lisbon O Jornal*, 26 September 1986, 4–8; U.S. Department of Commerce, "Sub-Saharan Report, 25 November 1986.

71. Major Robert R. Burke, USMC, "UNITA—A Case Study in Modern Insurgency," (Thesis, Marine Corps Command and Staff College, 2 April 1984).

72. Kukkuk, Leon *Letters to Gabriella: Angola's Last War for Peace*.

73. Brittain, *Death of Dignity*, 65.

74. *Angola Peace Monitor*, Issue No. 1, Vol. V, 7 October 1998.

75. Antonio Duarte, *Lisbon O Jornal*, 26 September 1986, 4–8; U.S. Department of Commerce, "Sub-Saharan Report," 25 November 1986; *The Independent* (U.K.), obituary, 20 October 1998; UNHCR Report, 1 May 1997; *Southern Africa Report*, Volume 11, No.2, January 1996; Victoria Brittain, *Angola: It's Not Over*. Brittain, *Death of Dignity*.

76. Colonel Fred Oelschig, retired SADF UNITA liaison officer, email interviews.

77. Heitman, *War in Angola: The Final South African Phase*; Nortje, *32 Battalion*, 233–249; George, *The Cuban Intervention in Angola*; Colonel Fred Oelschig, retired SADF UNITA liaison officer, email interviews.

78. South African Military History Society, Cape Town Branch, Newsletter No. 357, August 2008.

79. Turton, "My Family History, 1975–2011"; Nortje, *32 Battalion*, 233–249.

80. Heitman, *War in Angola: The Final South African Phase*; Colonel Fred Oelschig, retired SADF UNITA liaison officer, email interviews.

81. *Die Burger*, 19 January 2009.

82. Colonel Fred Oelschig, retired SADF UNITA liaison officer, email interviews.

83. Nortje, *32 Battalion*, 233–249. Piet Nortje, email, 10 November 2009.

84. Colonel Fred Oelschig, retired SADF UNITA liaison officer, email interviews.

85. <uk.geocities.com/sadf_history1/dfrench>.

86. Colonel Fred Oelschig, retired SADF UNITA liaison officer, email interviews.

87. Heitman, *War in Angola: The Final South African Phase*.

88. Ibid.

89. Alan Eyre and Ouida Lewis, "The Remarkable Life of Isaac Edmestone Barnes of Jamaica 1857–1930," *Jamaica Journal*, Vol. 30 Nos. 1–2, Institute of Jamaica 130th Anniversary Issue.

90. Heitman, *War in Angola: The Final South African Phase*; Bridgland, *The War for Africa*.

91. South African Press Association, <dispatch.co.za/1999/03/15/southafrica>.

92. SANDF Motivation Sheet, Colonel R. Hartslief.

93; Colonel Fred Oelschig, retired SADF UNITA liaison officer, email interviews.

94. Zhdarkin, *We Did Not See It Even in Afghanistan*.

95. Brad Saunders, email interview, 17 August 2009.

96; Colonel Fred Oelschig, retired SADF UNITA liaison officer, email interviews.

97. Brad Saunders, email interview, 14 August 2009.

98. <uk.geocities.com/sadf_history3/wbrider>.

99. Heitman, *War in Angola: The Final South African Phase*; BBC News, 2 June 2002; Angola Press, 6 June 2002.

100. Contrary to some published sources during the skirmishes at the Lomba River the SADF battle group did not use tanks. Olifant tanks were added to the battle group thereafter; Heitman, *War in Angola: The Final South African Phase*.

101. Missing Voices Project, Roelof Voster, Tank Commander, interviewed by Mike Cadman 14 January 2008, Historical Papers, The Library, University of the Witwatersrand.

102. Richard Wiles, email, February 2011.

103. Heitman, *War in Angola: The Final South African Phase*.

104. Ibid.

105. Ibid; Lord, *Vlamgat The Story of the Mirage F1 in the South African Air Force*.

106. Ibid. John Battersby, *The New York Times*, 20 April 1988.

107. Richard Wiles, email, February 2011.

108. Heitman, *War in Angola: The Final South African Phase*.

109. <www.ejection-history.org.uk>, SADF claim shot down 17 November 1987 by

Ystervark 20mm AAA; MiG-23 pilot Lt. Col. Eduardo Gonzalez Sarria, author of *Angola: Relatos Desde Las Alturas* email interviews June 2010.

110. Heitman, *War in Angola: The Final South African Phase.*
111. James Brooke, *The New York Times*, 16 December 1987; Voice of America, Radio Marti Program, Office of Research and Policy, United States Information Agency, *Cuba Annual Report 1987*; Heitman, *War in Angola: The Final South African Phase.*
112. Paul Fauvet and Marcelo Mosse, *Carlos Cardoso: telling the truth in Mozambique*, p.194.
113; Colonel Fred Oelschig, retired SADF UNITA liaison officer, email interviews.
114; Crocker, *High Noon In Southern Africa.*
115. Zhdarkin, *We Did Not See It Even in Afghanistan.*
116. Ibid.
117. Lord, *Vlamgat The Story of the Mirage F1 in the South African Air Force.*
118; Colonel Fred Oelschig, retired SADF UNITA liaison officer, email interviews.
119. *Washington Post*, 2 November 1987, A17.
120. Richard Wiles, email, February 2011.
121. George, *The Cuban Intervention in Angola.*
122. Missing Voices Project, Colonel Paul Fouche, 82nd Citizen Force Brigade interviewed by Mike Cadman, 15 April 2008, Historical Papers, The Library, University of the Witwatersrand; Heitman, *War in Angola: The Final South African Phase.*
123. Zhdarkin, Igor. *We Did Not See It Even in Afghanistan.*
124. Missing Voices Project, Colonel Paul Fouche, 82nd Citizen Force Brigade interviewed by Mike Cadman, 15 April 2008, Historical Papers, The Library, University of the Witwatersrand; Heitman, *War in Angola: The Final South African Phase.*
125. Missing Voices Project, Colonel Paul Fouche, 82nd Citizen Force Brigade, interviewed by Mike Cadman 15 April 2008, Historical Papers, The Library, University of the Witwatersrand; Russell Jones, "An Immigrants War" (unpublished) and email, 30 October 2009.
126. George, *The Cuban Intervention in Angola.*
127. Heitman, *War in Angola: The Final South African Phase.*
128. Ibid.
129. Colonel Fred Oelschig, retired SADF UNITA liaison officer, email interviews; Nortje, *32 Battalion*, 233–249; Heitman, *War in Angola: The Final South African Phase.*
130. Julian Hocken, Halo Trust, email, November 2010.
131. Jim Pansegrouw, email, November 2010.
132. Colonel Roland de Vries, email, November 2010.
133. <http://www.timesonline.co.uk/tol/comment/obituaries/article3752665.ece>.
134. James Brooke, *The New York Times*, 18 May 1988.
135. South African Military History Society, Cape Town Branch Newsletter, No. 360, November 2008, No.337, September 2006.
136. James Brooke *The New York Times* 9 January 1989.

137. *The National Security Archive*, 5 May 2006.
138. *Washington Post*, 2 November 1987, A17; Institute for Science and International Security report, 11 February 2009.
139. John Carlin, Th*e Independent* (U.K.) 30 March 1993.
140. Jeff Gerth, *The New York Times*, 16 November 1989.
141. *Pretoria News*, 9 November 2007.
142. This incident has been reported in a variety of ways: <Ejection-history.org.uk> describes this as an SA-7 tail hit on 27 September 1987; *Angola: Claims & Reality about SAAF Losses* by Tom Cooper and Jonathan Kyzer confirms an air-to-air R-23 or R-60 missile hit during engagement with a MiG-23ML. There is some anecdotal evidence from these two sources of MiG-23ML No.C477 being shot down. In his book *Vlamgat* Brig. Gen. Dick Lord, former Commander of the SAAF, confirmed a MiG-23 missile strike on the Mirage; MiG-23 pilot Lt. Col. Eduardo Gonzalez Sarria, author of *Angola: Relatos Desde Las Alturas*, email interviews June 2010.
143. The United States Air Force (USAF) counted World War II aerial victory credits if destruction involved shooting an enemy aircraft down, causing the pilot to bail out, intentionally ramming the airplane to make it crash, or maneuvering it into the ground or water. If the enemy airplane landed, despite its degree of damage, it was not counted as destroyed. This was the case with Capt. Arthur Piercey, pilot of SAAF Mirage F1AZ damaged 27 September 1987 near River Lomba by MiG-23ML piloted by Maj. Alberto Ley Rivas; Cuban researcher Ruben Urribarres claims damage by Mig-23MF using an R-60 missile.
144. *Granma* newspaper, 27 November 1987.
145. MiG-23 pilot Lt. Col. Eduardo Gonzalez Sarria, author of *Angola: Relatos Desde Las Alturas*, email interviews, June 2010.
146. *Flight International*, 28 November 1987.
147. Lord, *Vlamgat The Story of the Mirage F1 in the South African Air Force.*
148. Ibid; Maier, *Angola: Promises and Lies,* 28.
149. Lord, *Vlamgat The Story of the Mirage F1 in the South African Air Force.*
150. Ibid; "The SADF announced that the body of an SAAF Mirage pilot and the remains of his plane have been found in the operational area. Maj Willie van Coppenhagen disappeared a few days previously while returning from a mission in Angola. SAAF Mirage F1AZ No.223 written off on 19/03/88. Aircraft crashed during low-level night operation in Angola" <newsite.ipmssa.za.org>. Killed in action, in eastern Ovamboland returning to Rundu from a night strike on Baixa Longa in Angola, in Dassault Mirage F1AZ #223. Due to the long 1500 meter forced landing damage trail one theory developed was an engine flameout as opposed to a missile strike with small impact site.
151. MiG-23 pilot Lt. Col. Eduardo Gonzalez Sarria, author of *Angola: Relatos Desde Las Alturas*, email interviews, June 2010.
152. Tom Cooper, email, 8 December 2009.

153. MiG-23 pilot Lt. Col. Eduardo Gonzalez Sarria, author of *Angola: Relatos Desde Las Alturas*, email interviews, June 2010.
154. Lord, *Vlamgat The Story of the Mirage F1 in the South African Air Force*.
155. Ibid.
156. Colonel Manuel Correia de Barros, Vice-Presidente do Conselho Executivo (Deputy CEO) Centro de Estudos Estratégicos de Angola-Strategic Studies Centre of Angola, *Resultados de uma Revolta de Peões*; Kahn, *Disengagement from Southwest Africa*. George, *The Cuban Intervention in Angola*.
157. <aviation-safety.net>.
158. Waters, *Making History Interviews*, 43.
159. Richard Dovey, SADF Roll of Honour, <justdone.co.za>.
160. Lord, *Vlamgat The Story of the Mirage F1 in the South African Air Force*; Tyrone Heyl, email, 21 February 2011.
161. Russell Jones, *An Immigrants War* (unpublished) and email, 30 October 2009.
162. Gerhard Gerber, emails, August 2009.
163. At Freedom Park, Pretoria, South Africa, on 30 August 2006, at a ceremony hosted by the Freedom Park Trust, Cuban Ambassador to South Africa, Ms Esther Armenteros, handed over a journal containing the names of 2,106 Cuban soldiers; George, *The Cuban Intervention in Angola*.
164. Sarria, *Angola: Relatos Desde Las Alturas*. There is widespread discrepancy between the dates claimed for MiG shootdowns and the official Cuban information, sometimes by several weeks. This may be due to the promptness of UNITA/SADF announcements and the Cuban delay in official information or family notification. Lord, *Vlamgat The Story of the Mirage F1 in the South African Air*.
165. Jacklyn Cock and Laurie Nathan, *War and society: the militarisation of South Africa*, 118; <SADF.info>.
166. Richard Dovey, SADF Roll of Honour, <justdone.co.za>; South Africa War Graves Project.
167. K.Grundy, *The Militarisation of South African Politics* (Oxford University Press, 1988).
168. <http://en.wikipedia.org/wiki/List_of_private_contractor_deaths_in_Iraq>.
169. Jonathan Clayton, *The Times*, 13 October 2007.
170. Colonel Fred Oelschig, retired SADF UNITA liaison officer, email interviews.
171. Russell Jones, *An Immigrants War* (unpublished) and email, 30 October 2009.
172. Colonel Fred Oelschig, retired SADF UNITA liaison officer, email interviews; *Escambray*, Sancti Spíritus, Cuba, <http://en.escambray.cu/>; General Raul Menendez Tomassevich died on 17 August 2001; Kukkuk, *Letters to Gabriella: Angola's Last War for Peace*.
173. Ibid.
174. Hodges, *Angola: Anatomy of an Oil State*; Kukkuk, *Letters to Gabriella: Angola's Last War for Peace*.
175. Ibid; Hodges, *Angola: Anatomy of an Oil State*.

176. Ibid.
177. Tako Koning, email interviews, April 2010.
178. Galvez,William. *Camilo Senor de la Vanguardia;* Havana: Editorial de Ciencias Sociales (1979).
179. Commander Cintra Frias was recalled from Angola in mid 1989 for the Ochoa investigation and by one account gave crucial information in an interview with investigators that led to Ochoa's arrest, trial, and eventual execution.
180. *Jamaica Observer*, 11 September 2009.
181. Missing Voices Project, Howard Fletcher, pilot interviewed by Mike Cadman, 15 January 2008, Historical papers, The Library, University of the Witwatersrand.
182. Zhdarkin, *We Did Not See It Even in Afghanistan*; Heitman, *War in Angola: The Final South African Phase.*
183. Zhdarkin, *We Did Not See It Even in Afghanistan.*
184. Hilton Hamann, *Johannesburg Frontline*, November 1986 p.14–16; U.S. Department of Commerce, "Sub-Saharan Report," 11 February 1987.
185. *Jamaica Observer*, 11 September 2009.
186. First Lieutenant Patrus Christoffel Snyman, acting Company Commander, B Company, 101 Battalion.
187. Zhdarkin, *We Did Not See It Even in Afghanistan.*
188. John Battersby, *The New York Times*, 20 April 1988.
189. Voice of America, Radio Marti Program, Office of Research and Policy, United States Information Agency, *Cuba Annual Report 1988*; Colonel Fred Oelschig, retired SADF UNITA liaison officer, email interviews.
190. Ibid.
191. <panafricannews.blogspot.com/2007/06/cuba-in-africa-internationalists-tell.html>.
192. Anthony Lobaido, *WorldNetDaily*, 17 July 2004.
193. U.N. Angola Peacekeeping Mission Report 1996.
194. Kukkuk, *Letters to Gabriella: Angola's Last War for Peace.*
195. Julian Hocken, Halo Trust, email, November 2010; Jim Pansegrouw, email, November 2010.
196. Roland De Vries email, November 2010.

BIBLIOGRAPHY

Brittain, Victoria. *Death of Dignity*. Trenton, New Jersey: Red Sea Press, 1998.

Craig, William. *Enemy at the Gates The Battle for Stalingrad*. New York: Penguin, 2001.

Crocker, Chester. *High Noon In Southern Africa: Making Peace in a Rough Neighborhood*. New York: W.W. Norton, 1993.

Fernandez Marrero, Jorge and Jose Garciga Blanco. *Angola: Saeta al Norte*. Havana: Ediciones Verde Olivio, 2003.

Fred Bridgland. *The War for Africa: Twelve Months That Transformed a Continent*. Gibraltar: Ashanti Publishers Ltd., 1990.

George, Edward. *The Cuban Intervention in Angola, 1965–1991: From Che Guevara to Cuito Cuanavale*. London: Frank Cass, 2005.

Gillespie, Richard. *Cuba After Thirty Years: Rectification and the Revolution*. Florence, Kentucky: Routledge, 1990.

Grundy, K. *The Militarisation of South African Politics*. Oxford: Oxford University Press, 1988.

Heitman, Helmoed-Romer. *War in Angola The Final South African Phase*. Gibraltar: Ashanti Publishing, 1990.

Hodges, Tony. *Angola: Anatomy of an Oil State*. Lysaker, Norway: Fridtjof Nansen Institute, 2001.

Human Rights Watch. *Angola: Arms Trade and Violations of the Laws of War Since the 1992 Elections*. New Haven: Yale University Press, 1995.

James, Martin. *Historical Dictionary of Angola*. Lanham, Maryland: Scarecrow Press, 2004.

Kahn, Owen Ellison, *Disengagement from Southwest Africa: Prospects for Peace in*

Angola & Namibia. Piscataway, New Jersey: Transaction Publishers, 1991.

Kukkuk, Leon. *Letters to Gabriella: Angola's Last War for Peace: What the UN Did and Why*. Sarasota, Florida: FLF Press, 2005.

Labuschagne, Bernice. "South Africa's Intervention in Angola: Before Cuito Cuanavale and Thereafter." Thesis, Stellenbosch University, 2009.

Lord, Dick. *Vlamgat: The Story of the Mirage F1 in the South African Air Force*. Weltevredenpark, South Africa: Covos Day, 2000.

Lord, Dick. *From Fledging to Eagle: The South African Air Force During The Border War*. Johannesburg: 30 Degrees South, 2008.

Maier, Karl. *Angola: Promises and Lies*. London: Serif, 1996.

Morris, Michael F. "Flying Columns in Small Wars: An OMFTS Model." Thesis, Marine Corps University, 2000.

Nortje, Piet. *32 Battalion: The Inside Story of South Africa's Elite Fighting Unit*. Cape Town: Zebra Press, 2003.

<panafricannews.blogspot.com/2007/06/cuba-in-africa-internationalists-tell.html>.

Saney, Isaac. *Latin American Perspectives*, Issue 150, Vol. 33, No. 5, September 2006.

Sarria, Eduardo Gonzalez. *Angola: Relatos Desde Las Alturas*. Havana: Editorial De Ciencias Sociales, 2003.

Scheina, Robert. *Latin America's Wars: The Age of the Professional Soldier, Volume 2*. Dulles, Virginia: Potomac, 2003.

Shubin, Gennady. *Wars: The Memoirs of Veterans of The War In Angola*. Moscow: Memories Publishers, 2007.

Shubin, Vladimir. *The Hot 'Cold War': The USSR in Southern Africa*. London: Pluto Press, 2008.

Turton, Anthony. "My Family History, 1975–2011," <www.anthonyturton.com>.

Vivo, Raul. *Angola: Fin Del Mito De Los Mercenarios*. Havana: Federico Engels de la Empresa de Medios de Popaganda, 1976.

Voice of America, Radio Marti Program, Office of Research and Policy, United States Information Agency, *Cuba Annual Report 1987*. New Brunswick, New Jersey: Transaction Publishers, 1989.

———. *Cuba Annual Report 1988*. New Brunswick, New Jersey: Transaction Publishers, 1991.

Waters, Mary-Alice. *Making History Interviews with four generals of Cuba's Revolutionary Armed Forces*. Atlanta: Pathfinder Press, 1999.

Zhdarkin, Igor (Tamara Reilly trans.). *We Did Not See It Even in Afghanistan: Memoirs of a Participant of the Angolan War (1986–1988)*. Moscow: Memories Publishers, 2008.

INDEX

1 Military Hospital (SADF), 77
1 Parachute Battalion (SADF), 91, 96, 107, 165, 169
1 Recce Regiment (SADF), 108, 168, 171
1 South African Infantry (SADF), 112, 165, 168
12th Fighter Squadron (Cu), 152
13th Fighter Squadron (Cu), 152
16th Mechanized Brigade (FAPLA), 26, 68, 90, 109, 119, 123, 131, 141
101 Light Infantry Battalion (SADF), 44, 98, 107, 142, 148–149, 170, 178

2 Field Engineer Regiment (SADF), 146
2 South African Infantry Battalion (SADF), 112
20 Artillery Regiment (SADF), 44, 89–90, 99
20 Brigade (SADF), 42–44, 47, 50, 89–90, 106, 109, 112
21st Infantry Brigade (FAPLA), 26, 63, 68, 88, 90, 97–99, 101, 103, 106–107, 109, 115, 123–124, 126–127, 131, 138–142, 165
22nd Helicopter Transport–Attack Regiment (FAPA), 70
25th Air Combat Fighter Regiment (Cu), 38, 127, 152–153
25th Infantry Brigade (FAPLA), 26, 38, 83, 90, 123, 133, 139, 141
201 Battalion (SADF), 178, 180

3 Squadron (SAAF), 152
3rd Regular Batalion (UNITA), 75, 108, 139
30 Aniversario, 31
32 Infantry Battalion (Buffalo) (SADF), 17, 44, 46–47, 89–90, 92–93, 98, 107, 124, 126, 144, 149, 169

4 Artillery (SADF), 169
4 Recce Regiment (SADF), 88
4 South African Infantry Battalion (SADF), 44, 105, 121–122, 124–126, 139, 142, 164, 168–170
4th Helicopter Squadron (FAPA), 70
4th Regular Battalion (UNITA), 75, 176
40th Anti–Tank Brigade (FAPLA), 177–178
43 Mechanised Brigade (SANDF), 113
44 Parabat Regiment (SADF), 146, 170
47th Armored Brigade (FAPLA), 26, 67–68, 88, 90, 101, 103, 107–108, 115, 118, 123, 131–132, 141, 153, 181

5 Recce Regiment (SADF), 89

5 Signals Electronic Intelligence
Collection Unit (SADF), 160, 169

5th Regular Battalion (UNITA), 75

50th Division (Cu), 136

51 Battalion (SADF), 179

59th Mechanized Brigade (FAPLA), 26,
68, 90, 95, 103, 107–109, 119, 125,
131, 139, 141–143

61 Mechanised Battalion (SADF),
43–44, 50, 103, 108–109, 118, 121,
123, 132, 139, 142–144, 160, 164,
168–169, 172

62 Mechanised Battalion Group
(SADF), 44

7 South African Infantry Battalion
(SADF), 170, 178

Acquired Immune Deficiency Syndrome
(AIDS), 18, 130

Action Brigade for Explosive
Techniques (BATE) (UNITA), 79

Afghanistan, 25, 71, 87, 129–131, 143, 150

African National Congress (ANC), 25,
49, 72, 113, 150, 182

Aguilar, Hector, Colonel (Cu), 38

Aircraft
Antonov-26, cargo transport, 163, 166
Atlas AM-3C Bosbok, 90
Atlas Impala, light jet, 52, 155–156, 168
Buccaneer, 89, 131, 151, 158
C-130 Hercules, cargo transport,
138–139, 162
C-160 Transall, 138
Hind, helicopter, 69–70
MI-17, helicopter, 166
MiG, fighter, 38–40, 42, 47–48, 50–
51, 59, 64, 69, 101, 116–119, 127,
129, 136–137, 139–140, 144–145,
147, 150, 152–157, 159–163, 166–

167, 176
Mirage, fighter, 51–52, 68, 131, 144,
152–153, 158–162, 168
Puma, helicopter, 42, 125, 157, 162–
163, 180

Alfonso Doval, Juan Francisco, 1st
Lieutenant (Cu), 39

Algeria, 41, 131

Allegations of poison gas use, 117, 131

Alejandro (code–name), See Castro, Fidel

Alonso Reina, Luis, Colonel (Cu), 39

Alves, J.R., 2nd Lieutenant (SADF), 43,
105, 169

Anatolyevich, Z.I., 2nd Lieutenant
(USSR), 64

Andulo, Angola, 81, 174

Angelo, Mateus Miguel, Colonel
(FAPLA), 66, 68

Angola, 7, 17–19, 21–22, 25, 27–28, 30–
40, 42–46, 49, 52, 56, 58–63, 65,
67–71, 74–75, 77, 80–89, 105, 108,
113, 118–119, 121, 125, 128–131, 133,
135, 138, 142, 146, 148–149, 152–156,
159, 161–163, 165–168, 170–171,
173–175, 177, 182, 184–187

Angola News Agency, 155

Angolan Air Force and Antiaircraft
(FAPA/DAA), 65

Angolan National Army (FAA), 21, 67,
75–76, 85, 119, 174

Angolan National Liberation Front
(FNLA), 17, 30, 32, 46

Angolan People's Air Force (FAPA), 38–
40, 42, 50, 69–71, 76, 103, 115, 118,
127, 135, 137–138, 140, 143–144,
147, 152–164, 176

Anstee, Margaret, U.N. special
representative to Angola, 86

Antas, Lieutenant Colonel (FAPLA),
66, 70

Antiaircraft Defense and Revolutionary
Air Force in Angola (DAAFAR)

(Cu), 28, 38–39, 152
Armed Forces for the Liberation of Angola (FALA)—military wing of UNITA, 74–75
Armindo, Julio, General (UNITA), 74
Armscor, 150–151
Army Browns—SADF uniforms, 172
Australia, 52
Avila Guerrero, Venancio (Steel), Colonel (Cu), 38, 137, 145, 149–150
Avila, Eladio, 1st Lieutenant (Cu), 39

Badenhorst, Rudolf J. (SADF), 108, 170
Baghdad, Iraq, 171
Bakongo tribe, 17
Bandua, Jacinto Ricardo, General (UNITA), 74, 76
Baptista, Arsenio, Sergeant (SADF), 126
Barbados, 18
Barnard, Johannes P., Rifleman (SADF), 165, 168
Basson, Mossie, Major (SAAF), 157
Basson, Staff Sergeant (SADF), 60
Batista, Major (FAPLA), 67, 136
Battalion 017 (UNITA), 83
Battersby, John, 182
Battle of Cuito Cuanavale, 18–19, 21–22, 36, 39, 42, 52, 56, 64, 67, 69, 71, 75, 82, 89–91, 93, 95–96, 105–107, 112, 121, 125–127, 148, 150–154, 157, 160–164, 166–168, 170–171, 174–177, 185–186
Battle of Dead Road, 46
Ben, Ben. See Pena, Arlindo Chenda
Benecke, Melvin A., Lance Corporal (SADF), 94, 96, 168
Benguela, Angola, 34, 83
Bennett, Les, Captain (SADF), 52
Beukman, Antonie, Sergeant (SADF), 88
Beukman, William G., Rifleman (SADF), 108, 164, 168
Big Joe. See Diamantino, George Njolela

Bloemfontein, South Africa, 171
Boa Esperanza—UNITA safe area, 77
Bock. See Sapalalo, Altino
Botha, P.W., President, 183
Bratislavia, Slovakia, 113
Brazzaville, Congo, 31, 184
Breitenbach, T.C., 96
Breytenbach, Jan, Colonel (SADF), 46
British Aerospace, 52
Bulgaria, 182
Bulgin, Sam, Attorney General, 8
Bull, Gerald, 53
Burke, Robert R., Major (USMC), 83
Burt, Richard Brent, Sergeant (SADF), 88

Cabinda, Angola, 32–33, 68, 86
Cahama, Namibia, 163
Calipe, Major (UNITA), 88
Calueque, Angola, 178, 181
Camacho, Mele Francisco, Colonel (FAPLA), 67
Cameroon, 113
Camp 22, 62
Cangonga, Angola, 83–84
Canjimi, Lucas, 79
Cape Town, South Africa, 48, 58, 110–111, 121, 148, 159
Cape Verde Islands, 18
Carbo Galvez, Orlando, Captain (Cu), 39, 160
Cardoso, Carlos, 129
Caricoque, Angola, 81
Carnation Revolution, 17
Castro, Fidel, 27, 30–31, 34–38, 135–136, 149
Castro, Raul, 30, 38, 131, 135
Caxito, Angola, 85
Cayman Islands, 8
Chambers, David, 84–85
Chambers, Eleonore, 84–85
Chambinga River, 119, 123, 139, 176, 181
Chambinga, Angola, 119, 122, 127, 141

Chastanet, Michael, 174, 177
Chavez Godoy, Juan Carlos, Lieutenant
(Cu), 39, 153
Chavez Marrero, Ernesto L., Lieutenant
(Cu), 39, 127, 166
Chikoti, George, Commander
(FAPLA), 67
Chile, 47, 157
Chilingutila, Demosthenes Amos,
Brigadier (UNITA), 73, 75, 86–87
Chimuco, Vaso, General (UNITA), 74
China, 17, 79, 82
Chingunji, Pedro (Tito), Foreign Affairs
Secretary (UNITA), 173
Chitunda, Jeremias, Vice–President
(UNITA), 84–85
Chivukuvuku, Abel, General (UNITA),
74, 85
Chiwale, Samuel, General (UNITA), 74,
79
Chiwisi, Joao, Lieutenant Colonel
(UNITA), 186
Christie, Renfrew, 150
Cienfuegos, Camilo, Commandante
(Cu), 174
Cienfuegos, Cuba, 34
Cilliers, Marna, 112
Cintra Frias, Leopoldo (Polo), General
(Cu), 37–38, 44, 135, 137, 150, 174,
184
Cirilo de Sa, Mario Placido, Lieutenant
Colonel (FAPLA), 66
Claasen, P.G., Rifleman (SADF), 121, 169
Coa River, 88
Coelho, Matias Lima, General
(FAPLA), 66
Coetzee, 2nd Lieutenant (SADF), 180
Coetzee, Frans, Major (SADF), 51–52
Coetzee, Renier, Colonel (SADF), 43
Coetzee, W.D., Lance Corporal
(SADF), 94
Combat Group Alpha, 20 Brigade

(SADF), 44, 47, 101
Combat Group Bravo, 20 Brigade
(SADF), 43–44, 47, 97–104, 112
Combat Group Charlie, 20 Brigade
(SADF), 44, 47, 101, 105, 124
Congo, 31, 34, 78, 184
Cordeiro, Joao Domingos Baptista,
Major (FAPLA), 67–68, 118–119
Coronation (code-name). See UNITA
Coutada Publica do Longa-Mavinga
Nature Reserve, 93
Crocker, Chester, 129–130
Crooks, Mark, Captain (SADF), 52
Cruz Bourzac, Francisco, Brigadier
General (Cu), 38, 163, 165–166
Cruz, Helder, Brigadier General
(FAPLA), 89
Cuanavale River, 21, 88
Cuando Cubango, Angola. See Menongue
Cuatir River, 138–139
Cuba, 7, 17–18, 28, 30, 34–37, 39–40, 133,
163, 166, 174, 177, 181–182, 185–186
Cuban Military Mission Angola
(MMCA), 136–137, 149, 166, 167
Cubango River, 138
Cuito Cuanavale, Angola, 7, 18–19, 21–
23, 25–26, 28, 36–42, 44, 47, 50–51,
53, 59, 63, 66–68, 70–71, 76, 82–83,
87– 89, 92, 97–98, 105, 119, 126–128,
130–132, 135–141, 144–146, 149–
150, 152, 155–162, 166–168, 171,
185–187
Cuito River, 21, 88, 137
Cuito River Bridge, 88, 137
Cunzumbia River, 23, 88, 93
Cuvelai, Angola, 155
Cuzumbia River, 92
Dala River, 140–142

de Barros, Manuel Correia, Colonel
(FAPLA), 66
de Beer, Jaco, Captain (SADF), 52

de Beer, Rikus, Captain (SADF), 51
De Beers Angola, 67
De Bruin, F., Rifleman (SADF), 103, 108, 168
de Carvalho, António José Condessa, Rear Admiral, Vice Minister of Defense and Commander (MGPA), 65
De Jager, Frikki, Trooper (SADF), 118, 169
De Klerk, M.M., Lance Corporal (SADF), 43, 105–106, 169
De Lange, Jacques, Signalman (SADF), 160, 169
de Lucas, Alexandre Lemos, Colonel (FAPLA), 66
de Matos, Joao Baptista, Chief of Staff (FAA), 66–67, 174
de Matos, Roberto Fernando, Major (FAPLA), 67
de Trinidade, Mac, Sergeant (SADF), 92
De Villiers, A.W., Gunner (SADF), 165, 169
De Vries, Roland, Colonel (SADF), 42
del Pino, Rafael, Brigadier General (Cu), 28, 35
Dembo, Antonio Sebastiao, General (UNITA), 73, 173
deWet, Jacobus, Sergeant (SADF), 88
Diamantino, George Njolela, Brigadier (UNITA), 79–80
Diaz, Guillermo, Colonel (Cu), 136
Dicinkulene, Angola, 77
Diederichs, J.H., 2nd Lieutenant (SADF), 149
Digue, Andre, (SADF), 121
Digue, Pierre, Sergeant (SADF), 121
Directorate of People's Defense and Territorial Troops (ODP) (FAPLA), 65
Directorate of Special Tasks (DST) (SADF), 91
Dirico, Angola, 88
Djekele, Rifleman (SADF), 94

Domingos da Silva, Paiva, 65
Donguena, Angola, 177–178
Dos Santos Franca, Antonio, General, Vice Minister of Defense and Chief of General Staff (FAPLA), 65, 67, 82, 128, 129, 150
Dos Santos, Jose Eduardo, President, 36–37, 175, 185
Doval, Alfonso, 1st Lieutenant (Cu), 160–161, 167
du Plessis, Pierre, Captain (SADF), 52
Du Preez, Corporal (SADF), 180
Du Preez, Naas, civilian contractor, 171
Du Randt, Johan, Commandant (SADF), 43, 90
Du Toit, Wynand, Major (SADF), 97, 176
Duarte, 83
Duran, Eliecer (Cu), 177
Durban, South Africa, 118
Duvenhage, 2nd Lieutenant (SADF), 181
Duvenhage, T.A., Corporal (SADF), 122, 169
Dyncorp International, 171

Earp, Dennis, General (SADF), 51
East Germany, 182
Els, F.C. (SADF), 99
Epalanga, Samuel Martinho, Brigadier General (UNITA), 73, 173
Ernesto C. (Cu), 28– 35
Escalona Reguera, Juan, Brigadier General (Cu), 38
Espinosa Martin, Ramon, General (Cu), 33
Ethiopia, 135, 154
Every, Ed, Major (SAAF), 51, 144, 158, 167

Fernández, Geomar, Lieutenant (Cu), 38, 177
Ferreira, Deon, Colonel (SAAF), 43–45, 47, 89–90, 99, 157

Foguetão or Rocket. *See* Lima, Pedro

Fouche, Paul, Colonel (SADF), 43, 141

Fourie, Hein, Lieutenant (SADF), 119

Fourie, Piet, Sergeant (SADF), 90

Fowler, Ambassador (Can), 76

France, 78

Franken, Pierre, Major (SADF), 89, 92, 95, 104

Fred Oelschig, Colonel (SADF), 23, 46, 75, 77, 87, 89, 92, 132

Free Angola, 77–78

French, Damian, Trooper (SADF), 106

Front for the Liberation of the Enclave of Cabinda (FLEC), 32–33

Gagiano, Carlo, Commandant (SAAF), 52, 153

Garcia Ensmorado, Miguel, 177

Gato, Americo, Lieutenant Colonel (UNITA), 76, 88

Geldenhuys, Jannie, General (SADF), 43, 110, 124, 167–168, 184

Geneva Convention, 177

Geneva, Switzerland, 177, 184

Genius Mineira, 67

George, Edward, 25, 89, 166

Germany, 78

Glynn, Richard, Lieutenant (SAAF), 52, 90, 167

Gómez Betancourt, Ciro, Lieutenant Colonel (Cu), 142

Gonzalez Sarria, Eduardo, Lieutenant (Cu), 39, 162

González, Armando (El Guajiro), Lieutenant Colonel (Cu), 39, 160

Gorb, Andrei, Colonel (USSR), 64, 139, 171

Gouws, J.P., Major (SADF), 51

Gray Security, 113

Grenada, 27, 37

Groenewald, Andre S., Rifleman (SADF), 143, 168

Groenewald, Pieter H., Rifleman (SADF), 143, 169

Grootfontein, Namibia, 39, 51

Group 4 Securicor, 113

Guevara, Ernesto (Che), 35, 166

Gulf Oil Company, 36

Gusev, Pavel, Lieutenant General (USSR), 25, 63, 87

Haifiku, L., Rifleman (SADF), 181

Haimbodi, H., Rifleman (SADF), 181

Halloween Massacre, 84

Halo Trust, 146

Hamutanya, Isaac (SADF), 179

Harris, Jock, Colonel (SADF), 43–44

Hartslief, Lothar, 111

Hartslief, Perrin, 111

Hartslief, Robert (Robbie), Commandant (SADF), 43–44, 47, 83, 90, 92, 97–101, 103–104, 110–114, 144

Hartslief, Werner, 111

Hattingh, Dewald, Captain (SADF), 178, 180

Havana, Cuba, 27, 29, 31, 33, 36–37, 84, 135–136, 150, 174, 177

Heitman, Helmoed–Romer, 167–168

Henda, General (UNITA), 86

Hendricks, Clinton, Bombadier (SADF), 144, 169

Herboldt, Ronald, 48–49

Herbst, Phillipus, Sergeant (SADF), 88

Heredia Perez, Bernardo (Shogun) (Cu), 38, 177

Hernandez, Juan Oscar, Colonel (Cu), 39

Heydenrych, Gerhardus, Sergeant (SADF), 88

Heyl, Tyrone, Gunner (SADF), 164

Hind, Adriaan, 2nd Lieutenant (SADF), 115, 169

Holdsworth, Digby, Captain (SADF), 51

Howes, John M., Rifleman (SADF),

123–124, 169
Hube River, 125
Human Rights Watch, 84
Hungo, Domingos, Colonel (FAPLA), 66
Hutchinson, Lieutenant Colonel
    (SADF), 43

International Atomic Energy Agency, 151
International Committee of the Red
    Cross, 177
Iran, 55, 150–151
Iraq, 23, 55, 133, 143, 171–172
Ita. *See* Cirilo de Sa, Mario Placido
Ivory Coast, 78, 176

Jack, Stuart, Governor, 8
Jamaica, 7
Jamba, Angola, 22–23, 25, 75, 77, 182
Jamba, Sousa, 86
Johannesburg, South Africa, 86, 110,
    130, 153
Joint Military Monitoring Commission,
    49, 75, 184
Jones, Russell, Medic (SADF), 60, 165
Jordan, 149
Joubert, Pierre, Captain (SADF), 52

Kamalata. *See* Numa, Abilio Camalata
Kamorteiro. *See* Ukwachitembo, Abreu
    Mehengu
Kamy. *See* Pena, Esteves
Kapakalenga, Rifleman (SADF), 94
Kapepura, Ernest, Rifleman (SADF), 124
Kasrils, Ronnie (MK), 25, 49, 150
Katanga, Congo, 34
Kavango River, 77, 88
Kavango, Angola, 77, 79
Kayumba, Eugene (UNITA), 176, 181
Kibi, mortar instructor (UNITA), 93
Kiev, Ukraine, 115
Kleynhans, Jan Hendrik, Corporal
    (SADF), 143, 169

Kleynhans, Dawid, Captain (SADF), 51
Kock, Piet (SADF), 145
Kolomnin, Sergey, Colonel (USSR), 171
Konstantin, General (USSR), 36
Kooij, Lieutenant (SADF), 105
Kosovo, 113
Kroonstad, South Africa, 110
Kuito, Angola, 174
Kukkuk, Leon, 173
Kulunga, Francisco, 79
Kuwait, 133, 187
Kuyler, M.J., Trooper (SADF), 106, 169
Kuzmenko, Leonid, Lieutenant General
    (USSR), 25, 63
Kwando River, 77

Lamas Rodríguez, Carlos, Colonel (Cu),
    39
Lambrechts, Leon, Commandant
    (SADF), 179
Landala, Angola, 32
Las Coloradas, 39
Lecuona, Marius J., Lance Corporal
    (SADF), 160, 169
Lehman, Johan, Major (SAAF), 133
Lelong, Steven E., Sapper (SADF), 165,
    169
Ley Rivas, Alberto, Major (Cu), 39, 153
Licua, Angola, 78
Liebenberg, Henk, Sergeant (SADF), 88
Liebenberg, Lieutenant (SADF), 107,
    141
Lima, Pedro Benga, General (FAPLA),
    66, 115
Lisbon, Portugal, 17, 78, 177
Lobito, Angola, 34
Lomba River, 19, 23, 25, 41, 43, 50, 55,
    63, 69, 73, 75, 82, 87–90, 92–93, 96–
    98, 101, 103, 106–107, 109, 113, 115,
    117–118, 122–123, 127–128, 130–
    131, 133, 139, 148, 152–153,
    164–165, 185–186

London, England, 26, 67, 184
Longa, Angola, 50, 82, 159–161
Lopez Cuba, Nestor, General (Cu), 163, 187
Lopez Miera, Alvaro, Colonel (Cu), 136
Lord, Dick, Brigadier General (SAAF), 53, 124, 159, 161, 164, 168
Lorente, Miguel, General (Cu), 37, 149
Lotter, Dawid, Major (SADF), 44, 101, 105
Louw, Gerhard, Commandant (SADF), 146–148
Luanda, Angola, 22, 32–33, 46, 48, 64, 68, 74, 79–80, 84–86, 136, 146, 150, 161, 171–173, 182, 187
Lubbe, Johan, Captain (SADF), 52
Lucusse, Angola, 82
Luus, Lance Corporal (SADF), 96
Lyon, Evan, Rifleman (SADF), 124
Lyttelton Engineering Works, 53

M'banza, Congo, 187
Maceo, Antonio, 28
Malan (SADF), 141
Malanje, Angola, 82, 182
Mananza, J.R., Sergeant (SADF), 105
Mandela, Nelson, 110
Mansfield, P., Lance Bombadier (SADF), 169
Manuel, Adriano, Sergeant (SADF), 88
Manuvakola, Betinho, Colonel (UNITA), 74
Manuvakola, Eugenio, General (UNITA), 73–74
Marais, Leon, Commandant (SADF), 44
Maria, Antonio Jose, Colonel (FAPLA), 184
Mariel, Cuba, 31, 34
Maritz, D.H., Corporal (SADF), 148
Maritz, G.M., Sergeant (SADF), 160
Maritz, Koos, Captain (SADF), 104
Marques, Rafael, 67

Martínez Puente, Rubén, Brigadier General (Cu), 38
Mateus, Renato, General (UNITA), 84
Mauricio, Fernando, Rifleman (SADF), 124
Mavinga River, 23
Mavinga, Angola, 19, 22–23, 25–26, 41, 43–44, 62, 76–78, 82, 87–90, 97, 106, 117, 128, 130, 138–139, 153, 162, 164–165, 182, 186
Mbundu Tribe, 173
McCallum, Alfred D., Captain (SADF), 43, 105–106
McCann, M.S., 2nd Lieutenant (SADF), 142, 170
McLachlan, George (Pat), Colonel (SADF), 43
Meinhardt, Captain (SADF), 180
Menéndez Tomassevich, Raúl, General (Cu), 172–173
Menongue, Angola, 21, 38–39, 50, 66, 70, 83, 119, 127–128, 138–139, 144, 152, 158, 161
Mes, Rudi, Captain (SADF), 52
Meyer, Willie, Major General (SADF), 184
Mianei River, 83
Mickey, Major (UNITA), 73, 99–100
Mikhailovich, A.A., Lieutenant Colonel (USSR), 64
Mikhailovich, F.A., Sergeant Major (USSR), 64
Minne, Norman, Major (SADF), 51
Miramar, Cuba, 34, 84, 135
Mitton, Marius J., Rifleman (SADF), 123–124, 169
Mityaev, Vyacheslav Alexandrovich, Colonel (USSR), 64
MK (Umkhonto we Sizwe)— armed wing of the African National Congress, 25, 49, 72, 113, 182
Mkona, Michael (ANC), 182

Mnguni, Mthunzi (ANC), 182
Monteiro, Roberto Leal, General (FAPLA), 66–67, 171
Morales Ramos, Lorenzo, Captain (Cu), 39, 166
Moreira, Armindo, Major (FAPLA), 67
Morejon, Colonel (Cu), 185
Morocco, 73, 82
Mortalha, Felisberto, Lieutenant Colonel (UNITA), 68, 119
Mozambique, 170
Mucusso, Angola, 77
Muehlenbeck, F.A., Rifleman (SADF), 105, 121, 169
Muller, Mike, Commandant (SADF), 142, 144–145
Muller, Piet, Colonel (SADF), 89
Mynhardt, Tobie, Captain (SADF), 179

N'Dalu. See Dos Santon Franca, Antonio
N'Geleka, Brigade Commander (FAPLA), 67
Namibia, 22, 25, 28, 37, 39, 42, 46, 48, 51, 79, 87, 126, 152–153, 161, 170
Nanjing, China, 79
National Union for the Total Independence of Angola (UNITA), 17, 19, 21–23, 25–27, 36, 42–48, 51, 56, 59, 67–69, 71, 73–94, 97–101, 103, 106–108, 117, 119, 123, 125–128, 130–132, 137–145, 147, 149, 153, 157, 160–161, 166, 171–177, 181–182, 185–186
NATO, 36, 59
Ndalatando, Angola, 68
Nel, Trompie, Captain (SADF), 52
Nelumba, Agostinho, Lieutenant Colonel (FAPLA), 66
Neto, Agostinho, 17, 30
Neto, Alberto Correia, General, Vice Minister of Defense and Commander (FAPA/DAA), 65

Neto, Armando da Cruz, Lieutenant Colonel (FAPLA), 66
Neto, Da Silva, Colonel (FAPLA), 66
New York, New York, 184
Ngele, General (UNITA), 86
Ngongo. See Monteiro, Robert Leal
Ngueto. See Cordeiro, Joao Domingos Baptista
Ngueto, Lieutenant General (FAPLA), 67, 68
Nieuwenhuizen, Vincent, Rifleman (SADF), 143
Nigeria, 113
No. 1 Squadron (SADF), 51–52
No. 3 Squadron (SADF), 51–52
Nordic Africa Institute for Nordic Documentation on the Liberation Struggle in Southern Africa Project, 79
Northrop Corporation, 151
Nortmann, Hannes, Major (SADF), 98–100, 104
Numa, Abìlio Camalata, General (UNITA), 74, 85
Nunda, Geraldo Sachipengo, General (FAPLA, formerly UNITA), 21, 66, 73, 173
Nunda, Pedro, Lieutenant Colonel (UNITA), 172
Nyumba, F., Rifleman (SADF), 94
Nzumbi. See Coelho, Matias Lima

Ochoa Sanchez, Arnaldo, General (Cu), 37–38, 44, 114, 135, 166, 174, 184
Oelschig, Colonel (FAPLA), 185
Oettle, Johannes, Sergeant (SADF), 88
Ondangwa, Namibia, 90, 155, 168
Oosthuizen, H.A., Lance Corporal (SADF), 108
Operation Alpha Centauri, 158
Operation Boleas, 113
Operation Carlotta, 28, 30, 33–35

Operation Displace, 146
Operation Hooper, 56
Operation Modular, 56, 87, 89
Operation Packer, 56
Ovimbundu tribe, 17, 81, 173

P Battery, 20 Artillery Regiment
    (SADF), 45, 89–90
Paihama, Kundi, General and Defense
    Minister (UNITA), 172
Panama City, Panama, 28
Panama, 35
Panda, Angola, 78
Papenfus, Johan (SADF), 177, 180–181
Paulo, Captain (SADF), 91
Pavlovich, S.Y., Lieutenant Colonel
    (USSR), 64
Pedalé. *See* Tonha, Pedro Maria
Pedro, Joaquim, Rifleman (SADF), 126
Pelindaba Nuclear Facility, 151
Pena, Arlindo Chenda, Division General
    (UNITA), 22, 73, 75, 81–86, 88, 114,
    125, 150, 175
Pena, Demarte Dachala, 86
Pena, Elias Salupeto, UNITA official, 84,
    85
Pena, Esteves (Kamy), General
    (UNITA), 73, 173
Pena, Felisberto Isaac, 86
People's Armed Forces for the
    Liberation of Angola (FAPLA), 19,
    22–23, 25–26, 37, 41–42, 44–51, 53–
    54, 56, 58, 61, 63, 65–72, 75–79,
    82–85, 87–109, 115–119, 122–133,
    136–150, 153–160, 162, 164–168,
    171–177, 181, 184–186
People's Movement for the Libertion of
    Angola (MPLA), 17, 30–34, 36, 41,
    77, 83–84, 172, 185
People's Navy of Angola (MGPA), 65–
    66, 70–71
Perez Rodriguez, Juan (Capri), Captain

(Cu), 39, 161, 166
Perez Rospide, Luis, General (Cu), 187
Petrov, Mikhail, General (USSR), 25, 63
Petrus, F., Lance Corporal (SADF), 181
Petrus, J., Rifleman (SADF), 181
Pienaar, M.G., Sergeant (SADF), 165,
    170
Piercey, Arthur, Captain (SAAF), 52,
    153, 160, 167
Playa Giron, 31
Pointe Noir, Congo, 31
Pollsmoor Prison, 58, 148
Poltgieter, Johannes, civilian contractor,
    171
Pomfret, South Africa, 47
Pongolola, General (UNITA), 86
Port Elizabeth, South Africa, 96
Portugal, 17, 78
Portuguese West Africa, 21
Pretoria Regiment (SADF), 170
Pretoria, South Africa, 27, 43, 53, 56, 77,
    111, 146, 150, 165–166
Price, W.A.F., Lance Corporal (SADF),
    172
Primer Congreso, 31
Project African Warrior, 145
Puna, Miguel N´Zau, Secretary General
    (UNITA), 79

Q Battery, 20 Artillery Regiment
    (SADF), 45
Quesada Aguilar, Ramon, Captain (Cu),
    39, 153–154, 166, 176
Quiala Castaneda, Barbaro Raul,
    Warrant Officer (Cu), 39
Quifangondo, Angola, 46

Rankin, Johan, Commandant (SAAF),
    51, 159–160
Rashidovich, D.C., Major (USSR), 64
Rautenbach, Staff Sergeant (SADF), 94
Raymond, Mark, Captain (SADF), 52

Redelinghuys, J., Lance Corporal (SADF), 125–126, 169

Regresso, Ukama, General (UNITA), 74, 86

Revolutionary Armed Forces (FAR), 37, 135–136

Rhodesia, 155

Rhodesian/Zimbabwe Air Force, 156

Risquet, Jorge, 177, 185

River Kwanza, 72

Robert, W., Rifleman (SADF), 181

Roberto, Holden, 17, 46

Roberts, Clinton (SADF), 99

Roberts, K.A., Gunner (SADF), 164

Rodriguez Perez, Carlos (El Gordo), Captain (Cu), 39, 161, 166

Rogers, Geoff (SAAF), 90

Rojas Garcia, Manuel, Lieutenant Colonel (Cu), 39, 153–154, 166, 176

Rosales del Toro, Ulises, General (Cu), 163, 184

Rossouw, Wayne (SADF), 99

Ruacana, Namibia, 177, 181, 184

Rudman, Les, Commandant (SADF), 90–92, 94–96

Rundu, Namibia, 25, 43, 46, 51, 62, 76, 78, 87, 89–90, 126, 138, 144, 152–153, 159, 161–162

Rundu, Namibia, 42

Rupping, Riaan, Sergeant (SADF), 104

Russian Union of the Veterans of Angola, 171

S Battery, 20 Artillery Regiment (SADF), 45, 90, 164

Sabastiao, Captain (FAPLA), 72

Sachse, Bert, Commandant (SADF), 92, 106, 185

Sadler, A. T. N., Private (SADF), 165, 170

Sal Island, Cape Verde Islands, 184

Saldanha Bay, South Africa, 111

San Antonio de los Baños, Cuba, 29–30

San José de las Lajas, Cuba, 165

Sanjar. See Nelumba, Agostinho

Sapalalo, Altino, General (UNITA), 74

Sarria, Eduardo (Cu), 154

Saunders, Brad, Rifleman (SADF), 115–116

Savate, Angola, 45

Savimbi, Ana, 172

Savimbi, Jonas, Leader (UNITA), 17, 21, 43, 73–74, 77, 79, 80–82, 85, 132, 172–174, 176–177, 182, 185

Schoeman, Andre, Captain (SADF), 52

Schutte, Pieter M., Rifleman (SADF), 123–124, 170

Sellstrom, Tor, 79

Senen Viamonte, Jose, Lieutenant Colonel (Cu), 136

Serfontein, Brigadier General (SADF), 181

Serpa Pinto Air Base, 127, 152

Serpa Pinto, Angola. See Menongue

Shangonja, Colonel (UNITA), 88

Shedd, John Augustus, 162

Sierra Leone, 113, 185

Silva, Commander (FAPLA), 66–67, 107, 181

Simoes, Alcides Sakala, General (UNITA), 74

Sinclair, John, Captain (SADF), 52

Skinner, Chris, Captain (SADF), 52

Smit, Francois du P., Private (SADF), 108, 168, 171

Smit, H.B., Trooper (SADF), 148

Smit, Kobus (Bok), Commandant (SADF), 44, 101

Snitko, Oleg, Lieutenant (USSR), 64, 115, 171

Sopite, Domingo, Brigadier General (UNITA), 173

South Africa, 8, 17–18, 22, 25, 27, 37, 41, 46–47, 49, 53, 57, 79, 84, 86, 90, 100, 105, 110–111, 113, 130, 133, 149–151,

165, 170–171, 174, 177, 182
South Africa Army College, 111
South Africa Military Academy, 110–111
South African Air Force (SAAF), 22–
  33, 39, 42, 47–48, 51–53, 68–90, 92,
  101, 118–119, 124–125, 132–133,
  138–139, 143–144, 151–153, 155–
  163, 167–168, 175
South African Airways, 151
South African Defense Force (SADF),
  18–19, 22–23, 25, 28, 40–50, 52–53,
  55–62, 68–69, 71, 73, 75–78, 82, 87–
  96, 98–103, 105–113, 115–133,
  136–151, 153, 156–158, 160–161,
  164–168, 170–172, 176–178, 181–
  182, 184–186
South African Medical Service, 125, 169
South African Military College. See
  South Africa Army College
South African National Defense Force
  (SANDF), 45, 57, 111–113, 145, 171
South West Africa People's
  Organization (SWAPO), 25, 77, 79
Soviet Union (USSR), 17–18, 31, 34,
  68–69, 130, 186
Stapa, Andre A., Captain (SAAF), 52,
  124, 155–156, 167–168
Stayanoff, Russ, 28
Stellenbosch, South Africa, 111, 151
Sterzel, S., Sergeant (SADF), 94
Steward, A., Private (SADF), 122, 170
Stewart, Greg M., Corporal (SADF),
  146, 170
Stompie (SADF), 116
Subiaurre Carmenate, Pedro Ernesto
  (Coco), Parachutist (Cu), 166
Summer, S.A., Lance Corporal (SADF),
  94
Sunguete, General (UNITA), 86
Suter, Michael C., Sapper (SADF), 142

Tablai, Miguel, civilian contractor, 171

Tarzan. See Armindo, Julio
Tchipango, Waite, Lance Corporal
  (SADF), 106
Techamutete, Angola, 163, 167
Thaba Tswane, South Africa, 111
Thackwray, General (SADF), 91
Theron, Tai, Captain (SADF), 145
Thom, Adriaan M., Rifleman (SADF),
  121, 169
Tito, Manuel, Private (UNITA), 74
Tobias, Major (FAPLA), 67
Toka. See de Carvalho, Antonio Jose
  Condessa
Toms, Ivan, 58
Tonha, Pedro Maria, General and
  Minister of Defense (FAPLA), 26,
  65, 67–68, 175
Tonkin, Frank, Captain (SADF), 52
Tortolo Comas, Pedro, Private (formerly
  Colonel) (Cu), 27, 37
Trujillo Hernandez, Humberto, Colonel
  (Cu), 39, 140
Truter, Paulus, Major (SADF), 51
Tumpo River, 22, 25, 82, 127, 137, 139,
  141, 146, 172
Tumpo, Angola, 22, 25, 82, 98, 127, 137,
  139, 143–144, 146, 148
Turner, Clive, Captain (SADF), 52

Uitenhage, South Africa, 96
Ukraine, 115
Ukwachitembo, Abreu Muhengu,
  General (UNITA), 73
Umpulo, Angola, 86
Union Steel Corporation, 53
UNITA Renovada, 74
United Kingdom (UK), 171
United States of America (USA), 17–18,
  27–28, 36, 132, 171, 186
University of Havana, 29
University of Pretoria, 111
University of Stellenbosch, 110–111

University of the Western Cape, 150
University of the Witwatersrand, 153
Urribarres, Ruben, 162

van Coppenhagen, Willie, Captain
    (SAAF), 52, 159, 167–168
van der Merwe, Johannes, Sergeant
    (SADF), 88
van der Merwe, Petro, 111
van Eeden, Reg, Captain (SADF), 52
Van Heerden, J., Corporal (SADF), 126,
    170
van Heerden, Neil, Director General of
    Foreign Affairs for South Africa, 184
van Heerden, Seun, Captain (SADF), 52
Van Niekerk, Pieter, Corporal (SADF), 89
van Rensburg, Anton, Captain (SADF),
    52, 152–153
Van Wyk, Leon F., Lance Corporal
    (SADF), 144
van Zyl, Captain (SADF), 143
Van Zyl, Coenie, Corporal (SADF),
    179–181
Van Zyl, D. W., Rifleman (SADF), 124
Venter, H.J., Lance Corporal (SADF),
    96, 170, 179–180
Venter, V.Z., Lance Corporal (SADF),
    170
Vermeulen, Nicolas J., Rifleman
    (SADF), 148
Vieira, Antero, General (UNITA), 74,
    107
Vietnam. See Angelo, Mateus Miguel
Vimpulo River, 124
Visagie, Pieter A., Rifleman (SADF),
    109, 164
Voice of the Resistance of the Black
    Cockerel—UNITA radio station, 75
Voortrekker Heights, South Africa, 111
Voster, Roelof (SADF), 119
Vyacheslav, V., Captain (USSR), 64

Wala, Simao Carlitos, Brigadier General
    (FAPLA), 173
Walther, Captain (SADF), 73
Warsaw Pact, 29
Washington, DC, 78

Weapons/Weapons Systems
    7.62mm machine gun, 55, 92, 102
    14.5mm heavy machine gun, 98
    20mm cannon, 55
    20mm Ystervark vehicles, 44
    23mm machine gun, 76
    60mm mortar, 76
    81mm mortar, 44, 55, 75, 83, 91, 138,
        180
    90mm cannon, 55
    107mm multiple rocket launcher, 76
    120mm mortar, 45, 76, 139, 157
    122mm mortar, 76
    AA-8 Aphid, air-to-air missile, 39, 153
    AK-47, assault rifle, 75, 83, 92, 165
    AKM, assault rifle, 154
    B10, antitank gun, 95
    BM-21, truck–mounted multiple
        launch missile system, 68, 125–
        126, 136, 145
    BMP (Troyka), infantry combat
        vehicle, 31, 69
    BP, armored personnel carrier, 69
    Browning .50 cal. machine gun, 92,
        94–95, 124, 160
    BTR, armored personnel carrier, 48,
        64, 68–69, 90, 98, 102, 108, 125,
        132, 148, 152, 157
    Buffel, wheeled armored vehicle, 44,
        53, 180–181
    Cactus, antiaircraft missile, 157
    Casspir, wheeled armored vehicle, 44,
        46, 48, 53, 92, 94–96, 98, 104, 106,
        138, 144, 177–181
    Cluster bomb, 500 or 1,00 pound,
        156–157

Eland, armored car, 55
G5, howitzer, 42, 45, 53–55, 59, 71, 92, 95–97, 101–103, 107–119, 124, 131, 137–139, 145, 156–157, 164–165, 168
G6, howitzer, 53–54
Gecko, SA-8 missile system, 90
Gemsbok, recovery vehicle, 92
Jericho, surface-to-surface missile delivery system, 151
Kukri, air-to-air missile, 160
Kwevoel, logistical vehicle, 92, 138
Matra 550, air-to-air missile, 153
Milan, missile launcher, 134
Olifant, tank, 42, 44, 105–106, 119–120, 123–124, 137, 142, 144, 148–149, 165
Panhard, armored car, 55
PB, amphibious armored personnel carrier, 68
PKM, machine gun, 75, 92
Plofadder, experimental minefield clearing device, 147
Predator, unmanned aerial vehicle, 158
PT-76, amphibious tank, 108
R-60, air-to-air missile, 163
Raptor, stand-off bomb, 158
Ratel, wheeled armored vehicle, 42–44, 50, 55–59, 98–100, 102, 104–106, 109, 113, 115–116, 118, 121–125, 127, 133–134, 142–143, 157, 160
RPD5, machine gun, 29
RPG-7, rocket propelled grenade, 29, 75–76
RPK, light machine gun, 29
SA-7, surface-to-air missile, 144, 158–159, 163
SA-8, surface-to-air missile, 133
Stinger MANPAD, man-portable-air-Defense, shoulder-launched

surface-to-air missile, 45, 132, 139, 153
Strela, man–portable air defense missile, 68, 159
T-54, tank, 68
T-55, tank, 38, 68–69, 88, 100–102, 104–106, 108–109, 113, 115, 119, 121–122, 124, 129, 133–134, 137, 142, 144–145, 149
TOW, man-portable-air-Defense missile, 132
Valkiri, multiple launch rocket system, 45, 139, 158
ZRK, mobile SA-8 missile system, 68
ZSU, antiaircraft gun, 143, 145, 155
ZT3, antitank guided missile, 100
Wehmeyer, Dries, Commandant (SADF), 52
Well, Well, General (UNITA), 86
Wessels, Carel, Captain (SADF), 52
Wessels, Leslie, Sergeant (SADF), 88
White, Pierman (SADF), 118
Wiles, Richard (SADF), 133
Wilke, Fred, Major (SADF), 88
Wiyo, Lutoki, General (UNITA), 74, 86
Woodhouse, Glen (SADF), 115–116
Wortel (SADF), 141–142

Xangongo, Namibia, 163

Yakuvela, Pedro Apolo, General (UNITA), 73
Yara, Cuba, 37

Zaire, 30, 32–33, 83
Zapata Tamayo, Orlando, 177
Zhdarkin, Igor Anatolevich, Lieutenant Colonel (USSR), 63–64, 131
Zimbabwe, 156